D1389674

FORSAKEN WARRIORS

FORSAKEN WARRIORS

The Story of an American Advisor
with the South Vietnamese
Rangers and Airborne,
1970–71

ROBERT L. TONSETIC

CASEMATE
Philadelphia & Newbury

Published in the United States of America and Great Britain in 2009 by
CASEMATE
908 Darby Road, Havertown, PA 19083
and
17 Cheap Street, Newbury, Berkshire, RG20 5DD

ISBN 978-1-935149-03-3

Cataloging-in-publication data is available from the Library of Congress
and the British Library.

10 9 8 7 6 5 4 3 2 1

Printed and bound in the United States of America.

For a complete list of Casemate titles please contact:

CASEMATE PUBLISHERS (US)
Telephone (610) 853-9131, Fax (610) 853-9146
E-mail: casemate@casematepublishing.com

CASEMATE PUBLISHERS (UK)
Telephone (01635) 231091, Fax (01635) 41619
E-mail: casemate-uk@casematepublishing.co.uk

CONTENTS

*For the brave U.S. and South Vietnamese soldiers
who wore the Maroon and Red Berets of the
ARVN Rangers and Airborne.*

INTRODUCTION

This book is about the author's experiences as a Senior Advisor to South Vietnamese Ranger and Airborne battalions during the latter years of the Vietnam War. During the years 1970–1971, the withdrawal of U.S. forces proceeded at a rapid pace, and the Republic of Vietnam Armed Forces (RVNAF) were assuming the major role in combat operations throughout the country. The story is written as a personal memoir of that period, but it is in no way representative of the total advisory effort in Vietnam. Thousands of U.S. officers, warrant officers, and non-commissioned officers from all branches of the armed services served in advisory capacities during the Vietnam War, along with numerous civilians representing various government agencies.

Surprisingly, few have written about their experiences, leaving a gap in the literature that needs to be filled lest the lessons learned be forgotten. While it is doubtful that future counter-insurgency operations will involve the numbers of U.S. combat forces that were deployed in Vietnam, it is likely that such conflicts will require the deployment of U.S. advisors to train and assist indigenous forces. Hopefully, future advisory efforts will benefit from the experiences of the MACV advisors.

The advisory effort in South Vietnam began in the mid-1950s, organized under the Military Assistance and Advisory Group (MAAG). In the early years, the emphasis was on training and equipping South Vietnamese forces, and U.S. advisors were forbidden from participating in a direct combat role, although they could accompany

1

ground forces as observers and offer advice. The newly organized
ARVN Ranger units were among the first to benefit from this U.S.
advisory support. By 1961, the Communist insurgency had gained sufficient strength to seriously threaten the Diem regime, and the
Kennedy administration increased the number of advisors to 3,200. A
year later, U.S. military assistance to South Vietnam was reorganized
with the establishment of the U.S. Military Assistance Command
Vietnam (USMACV). Initially, priority was given to assigning advisors
at the province and regimental levels. Beginning in 1964, the program
was expanded and field advisors were assigned to selected districts and
combat battalions.

The ramp-up in advisors continued in the ensuing years until all
districts and combat battalions had U.S. advisors. The program was
further expanded in 1968, when advisory teams were deployed to
assist territorial Regional Forces (RF) and Popular Forces (PF). By
1970, the number of MACV field advisors peaked at around 14,000,
of which some 3,000 were serving with combat units at the regimental and battalion levels.

The phase-down of the advisory program began in 1971. By 1 July
of that year, all Battalion Combat Advisory Teams (BCATs), with the
exception of Airborne and Marine teams, were phased out. Over the
next two years, the drawdown continued and the U.S. MACV headquarters was disestablished in March of 1973, formally ending the
advisory effort in South Vietnam. This book provides just one snap-
shot, among many thousands, of the overall advisory effort during the
Vietnam War.

Regardless of when and where U.S. field advisors served in
Vietnam, they faced daunting challenges. Immersed in an alien culture
with little or no familiarity with the language, they provided much
needed assistance to their South Vietnamese counterparts, often in
extremely dangerous and hostile circumstances. With little external
support, most served with distinction, receiving little recognition for
their efforts.

The origins of this book can be traced to a manuscript that I wrote
in 1971, at the conclusion of my advisory tour. The manuscript was
never completed and was put aside until 2008, when I decided to
expand upon it by doing further research on events that were such an

important part of my overall Vietnam experience, bringing a sense of closure to that period of my life.

Research for the book was a daunting challenge, since surviving records are few in comparison to records pertaining to U.S. units and their operations during the Vietnam War. Mr. Richard Boylan, Senior Archivist at the National Archives and Records Administration, was extremely helpful in locating those records that do exist at the archives. Organization and cataloguing of the records is still a work in progress. Other sources used in my research were found at the U.S. Army Center for Military History, the Vietnam Center and Archive, Texas Tech University, and the Moise Vietnam War Bibliography. Other sources can be found in notes and bibliography sections of this book.

PROLOGUE

The Caribou's twin Pratt Whitney engines roared to full power and the assault airlift aircraft sped down the Ton Son Nhut runway. Gaining altitude over the sweltering city, the aircraft banked south toward the Mekong Delta. The early morning sunlight glistened off the lush, green rice paddies below. Minutes after takeoff, the Caribou flew over the village of Binh Tri Dong.

In the rice paddies just north of the village, I spotted what remained of the dirt berm of an abandoned military outpost. I recognized it at once as the site of Fire Support Base Stephanie, occupied by the 199th Infantry Brigade's 4th Battalion, 12th Infantry during the May Offensive of 1968. Two years earlier, the rifle company that I commanded defended the firebase and fought off determined North Vietnamese army assaults in the surrounding rice paddies.

My mind wandered back to May 1968. The now placid, emerald-green rice paddies bore no trace of the many brave men who died here two years earlier. I'll never forget that hallowed ground. Too many young Americans died there, some under my command. I wondered if the families of the young NVA who died there ever learned of their fate. There were the two young teenage NVA soldiers that I captured after they ambushed one of my squads. Were they still languishing in an ARVN POW camp? Some of the despair I had felt two years earlier surged back into my head. Put all that aside for now and focus on the present, I thought. You're going to war again.

5

Our destination was Can Tho, some 100 miles south of Saigon. My orders read, Captain Tonsetic: assigned to Military Region 4, Advisory Team 96 for duty as Senior Advisor, Cai Cai Ranger Camp. My second combat tour in Vietnam was underway.

CHAPTER 1

A FORTUNATE SON

Fort Benning, Georgia, 1969
Nine months earlier, I was living my dream. I'd had my fill of war in 1968 and never intended to return to Vietnam. The Army did not press the issue in my case. I was sent to Fort Benning near Columbus, Georgia, for the Infantry Officers Advanced Course in 1969. My course began in January of that year. That same month, American and North Vietnamese delegates squared off in Paris, arguing over the shape of the table to be used for their negotiations. It was also the month that Richard Nixon was inaugurated for his first term in office. I sat transfixed in front of my TV on 20 January, watching as 300–400 demonstrators hurled rocks and bottles at our new commander in chief's limousine as it drove down Pennsylvania Avenue. We led a life sheltered from politics in Columbus. It was a typical southern army town that supported the military, and was proud to be "the home of the U.S. Army Infantry."

On the same day that our course began, I submitted my application for a Regular Army commission. At the time, the Army had two main categories of professional officers: Regular Army and Reserve officers on indefinite active duty. West Point graduates were commissioned directly into the Regular Army, while most ROTC and OCS graduates were commissioned as Reserve officers. I was commissioned through the ROTC program at the University of Pittsburgh, and entered the Army with a Reserve commission. There were advantages and disadvantages to serving as a Regular. Regular Army officers usually received more consideration for career enhancing assignments and

7

selection for attendance at Army schools, such as the Command and General Staff College and the Army War College.

Regular Army officers could also serve for 30 years before retirement, while Reserve officers usually served for 20 years. It was almost impossible for an officer to be promoted to full colonel or general officer in less than 20 years. However, Regular officers had to compete for promotion in two systems in order to remain on active duty. First, there was the Army of the United States (AUS) promotion system. All officers on active duty competed for promotion in this system. It was an "up or out" system, but each officer had two opportunities to compete for advancement to the next higher grade. Regular Army officers also had to compete for promotion before Regular Army promotion boards. Consideration came along only once for each rank. If a Regular officer was not selected for advancement to the next higher rank, the officer was forced to leave the Army. The only exception came at the rank of Regular Army major. Once an officer was promoted to this rank, he was tenured until retirement. Thus, it was sort of a double jeopardy system for Regulars. Since I planned to make the Army my career, I wanted to be a Regular Army officer. Why not "go for the gold," I thought. As it turned out, I made the right decision. Ten thousand captains who held Reserve commissions were forced to leave the Army in the early 1970s as part of a Reduction in Force (RIF).

Along with 150 other captains, I sat through countless lectures on tactics, logistics, intelligence, and other military subjects that were meant to prepare us for future command and staff assignments. Surprisingly, the Army remained focused on a possible war with the Soviets in Europe throughout the Vietnam War. Most of the tactics instruction and map exercises were built around a European scenario, such as a defense of the Fulda Gap, with armor and mechanized infantry formations. Counter-insurgency warfare had a lower priority in the Infantry School's Program of Instruction (POI) at that time. It was as if the Army had already written off the war in Vietnam, and was ready to take on the Red Army on the plains of Central Europe. Given the Soviet invasion of Czechoslovakia in August 1968, this line of thinking was not entirely out of touch with reality.

Every officer in the class had at least one tour in Vietnam under their belts, and that nine-month course was a breather. I lived in a nicely furnished, off-post apartment with all the amenities, including a swimming pool and clubhouse. Most of us frequented the Custer Terrance Officer's Club at the end of each day's instruction for happy hour. Friday night happy hours often lasted past midnight, and after that there was always a party at a classmate's off-post apartment. As a 27-year-old bachelor, I was an eager participant in the social activities.

Weather permitting, I spent my weekends playing golf, lounging at the pool, and water skiing with a couple of buddies on the muddy Chattahoochee River. Other than a plethora of liquor stores, pawnshops, bars, and strip clubs that catered to drunken GIs, Columbus had little else to offer. For me, it was just a temporary stop leading to my next assignment.

* * *

When we submitted our assignment preferences—"dream sheets"—midway during the course, and I selected Germany as my first choice. I'd had my fill of Asia after a tour in Thailand and Vietnam, and I'd become ambivalent about the war. U.S. casualties continued to mount as the Paris peace talks dragged on. Moreover, I'd always dreamt of seeing Europe. Most of my buddies scoffed at me, believing that we were all headed back to Vietnam; they were about 98 percent correct.

A few days before we received our reassignment orders, we learned that Lieutenant William Calley was to be prosecuted for war crimes committed at My Lai. It was the worst stain on the Army's reputation since the massacre of Native Americans at Wounded Knee. My Lai did irreparable harm to both the Army and the war effort.

I had absolutely no empathy for Calley, and was disgusted and abhorred by what happened there. Most of my classmates were of the same mind, with one possible exception: Captain Ernie Medina, Lieutenant Calley's company commander. When Calley was charged, Medina dropped out of the course and retained F. Lee Bailey as his attorney.

I knew Ernie pretty well. In fact, we often sat next to each other during classes in Infantry Hall, and I was invited to Thanksgiving dinner at his family quarters. It was hard to believe that Ernie was involved in the massacre at My Lai, but he was in fact the company commander and senior officer on the ground. Captain Medina was eventually court-martialed, but not convicted. Nonetheless, realizing his career was over, he resigned his commission and left the Army. He later took a job at an aviation company owned by his lawyer, F. Lee Bailey.

The My Lai affair had badly tarnished the image of the Army, especially the officer corps, and I thought that was unfair, as did almost all of my contemporaries. During my tour with the 199th Infantry Brigade, we operated in the heavily populated III Corps area and came in contact with civilians on an almost daily basis. To my knowledge, there were no atrocities ever committed by members our brigade, and I'm sure that held true for the vast majority of U.S. units.

It was July, the same month that Neil Armstrong and "Buzz" Aldrin landed on the moon, when we received our orders for our follow-on tours. I was one of three officers in our class who received orders to Germany. Most everyone else was assigned to second, or in some cases third, tours in Vietnam. Needless to say, most of my buddies assumed I had friends in high places in the Army. They were wrong.

Actually, I received orders for Germany because I'd served back-to-back 12- month tours in Thailand and Vietnam, and apparently the Army thought that I needed a break. My Special Forces assignment in Thailand was not considered a combat tour, but the Army did consider it a hardship tour. In many ways it was a prequel to my Vietnam assignment, since it provided me with valuable experience in counter-insurgency warfare and training.

I deployed with Company D of the 1st Special Forces Group from Fort Bragg in October of 1966. The company was redesignated as the 46th Special Forces Company during my tour. In partnership with the Thai Special Forces, our detachments spread throughout the large country to quell a growing threat from Communist insurgents in the northeastern and southern regions of the country.

My "A" Detachment was part of Detachment B-430, commanded by Lieutenant Colonel Zoltan Kollat. In November of 1966, Detachment B-430 and its A Detachments made a parachute jump into southern Thailand to establish a counter-insurgency training camp about 12 miles from Trang. The camp that was built with the assistance of an Army engineer construction platoon was located about 60 air miles from the Malaysian border.

At the time, there was an on-going Communist Terrorist (CT) insurgency on both sides of the border. Along with our Thai Special Forces counterparts, we trained regular Thai Army units before they were sent after the elusive CT units that roamed the mountainous border area. Heavy emphasis was placed on live-fire training, so we built several quick-reaction type jungle ranges to support this training.

The U.S. ambassador at the time decreed that we could not carry our weapons, and we were ordered not to participate in combat operations. A Thai security platoon was assigned to protect the camp, but we had little confidence in them, so we worked out our own emergency defense plan. It is noteworthy that every Thai company we trained was later successful in tracking down Communist insurgents in the region. With the exception of one rather young CIA type and a few missionaries, we were the only Americans in southern Thailand.

Our B Detachment Camp was later named after one of our own, Sergeant First Class Billy Carrow, who died in an accidental shooting incident. Billy jumped with the 503d Parachute Regiment on Corregidor, "The Rock," in 1945, during the liberation of the Philippines, and he was an irreverent character who looked like he just stepped out of a World War II Bill Mauldin cartoon. We all loved him.

We had more than one member of our Detachment who wore gold stars on their parachutist wings for WWII combat jumps. It was a very professional team. In early 1967, Lieutenant Colonel Kollat was assigned to lead a Task Force that would train the first Thai unit to deploy to Vietnam, the "Queen's Cobras" Regiment. LTC Kollat, the Task Force Slick Commander, selected me to become a member of the Task Force Infantry Training Committee. The Regiment received its initial training at Chon Buri, south of Bangkok, and completed predeployment training at Kanchanaburi, the site of the famous Bridge over the River Kwai.

I did not accompany the Queen's Cobras to Vietnam, opting instead for an assignment with the U.S. 199th Light Infantry Brigade in Vietnam. At that time, Special Forces was not a separate branch for officers, and in order to remain competitive for promotion, you had to have command assignments in regular infantry units.

Prior to my Vietnam assignment, I was provided an opportunity to complete a six-week course in jungle warfare at the British Jungle Warfare School in Malaysia. I had to get a civilian passport because the Malaysian government did not want it known that U.S. military personnel were being trained in their country, especially those who were headed for Vietnam.

I flew to Singapore and spent the night at the hotel Singapura, since the Raffles Hotel was out of my price range. The following day I took a taxi to the Malaysian border and entered the country. From the border, I took a bus to the school that was just outside Jahore Bahru. In order to keep a low profile, Americans attending the school were issued British field uniforms. That took some getting used to since the Brits wore woolen uniform shirts and heavy trousers, despite the fact that the school was only three degrees of latitude from the equator.

Cadre assigned to the school were from elite British regiments, such as the Parachute Regiment, the Special Air Services (SAS) Regiment, or one of the Gurka battalions. The officers and their sergeants had all seen action during the Malaysian insurgency, or in Borneo, where the Brits and Australians fought a bloody little war with Indonesian forces who were trying to seize control of the whole island.

The jungle warfare course was the best training experience I had as a junior officer, bar none. The only thing I didn't like about the school was the dress code in the officers' mess. The prescribed dress was dark civilian trousers, long-sleeve white shirt, and a necktie; a dinner jacket was optional. Tradition is important in the British Army, even in the tropics. On our free weekends, I played poker and made the rounds of the bars in Jahore Bahru with the British officers. It was an interesting experience, and I've been an anglophile ever since.

Frankfurt Germany, 1970

My assignment orders to Germany specified that I was to report to V Corps headquarters in Frankfurt on 10 January 1970. The orders also indicated that I was to attend the Army's five-week Pathfinder Course at Fort Benning before heading for Europe. The Army's Pathfinders parachuted in to mark drop zones for airborne drops by larger units on major airborne operations. They also organized helicopter landing zones, and served as air traffic controllers at forward Army airstrips. There was one catch: the highest rank in a Pathfinder Detachment at that time was a lieutenant. Perhaps the Army just wanted to keep me busy until my January reporting date in Germany. Nonetheless it was good training, and I learned a few things that came in handy later on. It also gave me the chance to make a few more parachute jumps.

After graduating from Pathfinder School, I spent two weeks in Pittsburgh with my family over Christmas before flying to Europe, where I spent the remainder of my leave in Paris and London. During those two weeks, I lived it up. I booked myself into the Paris Hilton near the base of the Eiffel Tower. The Hilton Hotel chain offered a 50 percent discount to military personnel. Quite a nice gesture I thought. During the day I toured the city, and at night I sampled the Paris nightlife, hitting the dives on Pigalle before taking in the late show at the Moulin Rouge.

The following week, I hopped a train that took me to Cherbourg, where I caught a ferry to Dover. It was January and the Channel was rough, but nevertheless I enjoyed the crossing. I arrived in London by train and took a taxi to the Hilton Hotel that overlooked Hyde Park. It was freezing cold and foggy during my week in London, but I had a blast blowing most of the money I'd saved while I was in Vietnam.

My assignment within V Corps was a disappointment because I thought that they would further assign me to one of its divisions, the 3d Infantry or the 8th Infantry—that's where most infantry captains were assigned. Instead, the corps adjutant general assigned me to the G-3 Staff section of the V Corps headquarters. It was housed in Frankfurt's I.G. Farbin building that served as General Eisenhower's headquarters right after World War II. Later it became the headquarters of the U.S. V Corps.

The I.G. Farbin building is located in Frankfurt's Westend Nord district, and it is one of the few buildings in the city that survived the intense Allied bombing raids during WWII. There were several other U.S. facilities located nearby, including a family housing area, PX, and bachelor officer quarters. As far as Frankfurt is concerned, the district surrounding the V Corps was one of the better areas of an otherwise drab city that reminded me more of New York than Germany.

Colonel Jack Gaustad, a crusty old Armor officer and World War II veteran, was the G-3. During my arrival interview with the colonel, he picked up immediately on the fact that I was a bachelor, and made a point of telling me that his daughter, who was attending college in the States, was going to spend the summer in Frankfurt. Nice, I thought, she must be a real loser if her father has to set her up with one of his bachelor officers. Well, as I found out later, I was dead wrong. The colonel's daughter was a real knockout, but by that time I was in the process of leaving Germany.

Most of my abbreviated tour in Germany was spent shuffling papers in the I.G Farbin building. Since all the other officers in the G-3 section were majors or lieutenant colonels, I caught all the projects and duties no one else wanted. I worked force structure issues; prepared the FORSTAT readiness-briefing report; signed for all the G-3 vehicles and tents; and wrote the corps annual historical report. Instead of patrolling the Fulda Gap and training with the troops in the snow at Hohenfeld and Grafoenwoehr, I was stuck in Frankfurt, completely bored with the tedium of staff work.

Fortunately, I had an able assistant, Specialist Peter Flood, who could have done both our jobs standing on his head. Peter had a master's degree from Columbia and had started his own movie company prior to being drafted. He actually sold a couple of his films to a major company. I was a bit surprised, however, when he walked into the office one day and said he needed a day off, as he was picking up his new Porsche that he'd purchased. When I queried him how he could afford it on a Specialist Fourth Class pay, he said he was paying cash for it. I was still making payments on a '69 Pontiac at the time. That's what I liked about draftee army, it was an amazing mix of characters and talent from all walks of life.

The V Corps headquarters went to the "woods" a couple of times during alerts while I was there. My immediate boss, Major Jim Gallagher, and I were responsible for setting up the corps alternative command post during alerts and field training exercises. The alternate command post would take over only if the main command post was knocked out by a Soviet artillery or air strike, or was overrun.

On one alert, we moved by military convoy to the exercise area north of Frankfurt and set up in a snow-covered pine forest. It wasn't what I'd call roughing it. We had expandable vans mounted on five-ton trucks and once we got our generators running, we had lights and heat. All we had to do was monitor the radios, message traffic, and keep our situation maps up-to-date. On the third day, the three-star corps commander dropped by and told us what a great job we were doing. To tell the truth, I was bored to death, but I knew there were thousands of GIs out there sleeping in the snow who would have changed places with me in a heartbeat.

By spring I began to get restless. Living in bachelor officers' quarters never appealed to me, but German apartments were expensive, especially in Frankfurt's desirable Westend district. There were a few single American women that taught at the DODs high school, and I had a couple of dates, but they were few and far between. Since I didn't speak the language it was practically impossible to meet, let alone date, any German girls. In fact, most of the eligible girls in the Westend district were university students who were as anti-war as their U.S. counterparts.

Several anti-war demonstrations were held near the U.S. facilities that spring. I watched one of the demonstrations from my BOQ window. There were about 1,000 demonstrators. A few managed to climb onto the roof of the building that housed the PX and began waving the Viet Cong flag before the German Poletzi arrested them. Those demonstrations bothered me; not that I was completely sold on the war in Vietnam, but we were in Germany to keep Ivan off the backs of the Germans. Make no mistake about it: the 400,000 Soviet troops stationed in East Germany weren't window dressing. They posed a real threat to Western Europe during the Cold War.

The following Monday I walked into my office, sat down at a typewriter, and typed out a request for reassignment to Vietnam. I'd agonized over my decision all weekend over a bottle of Johnnie Walker Red. I figured it was my only chance of leaving Germany before my three-year tour was complete.

When I hand carried my paperwork to Colonel Gaustad's office, he looked at it and said, "Captain Tonsetic, this will never be approved and I'm going to recommend disapproval."

I replied, "Yes sir, but you know by regulation that you've got to send it forward."

"That's true, but the General will disapprove it too," the gruff colonel answered.

Actually, the colonel wasn't that bad a guy, and before I left his office he made me a counteroffer.

"Captain Tonsetic, I can understand that as a young officer you might be a bit bored with staff work, but you're going to do quite a bit of it in your career. What is it that you want? I can get you to an infantry battalion in one of our divisions, if you want that. Just give your current job another six months."

I still think he wanted me to hang around until his daughter came over for the summer. The colonel's offer was tempting, but I didn't take the bait. Besides, I knew full well what was going on in the troop units throughout Germany. Most were filled with draftees who somehow escaped the levees for Vietnam. Morale was low, and there were serious discipline problems in most battalions centered on racial tensions and drug abuse. Inevitably, some of these problems spilled over on the Germans. The crime rates in areas near U.S. bases skyrocketed. Rapes, murders, and robberies—allegedly perpetrated by American GIs—were splashed all over the German newspapers.

"Sir, I've thought about this for weeks, and I think that when the Army is at war, an infantry officer should be in the theater of war," I replied. Since I'd already played the Vietnam card, I wasn't about to back down.

"Your point is well taken captain, but the Army will do the right thing, and I think you'll be staying with us," the colonel concluded.

At the end of April, President Nixon shocked the nation when he announced that he'd authorized U.S. troops to invade Cambodia. Probably too little too late I thought. If we'd have gone into Cambodia right after the Tet Offensive of 1968, when we had Charlie on the ropes, we might have won the war. I still hadn't heard anything on my request to return to Vietnam.

Four days later there was a student demonstration at Kent State, and the Ohio National Guard shot and killed four students and wounded nine others. This was disturbing to me for many reasons, some personal. I had two sisters who were students at Penn State

University, and hoped that they had enough good sense to stay clear of any demonstration.

I began to think that my transfer request was "dead in the water," so I gritted my teeth and went back to work. Two weeks later, I was at the corps motor pool inventorying all the vehicles and equipment I signed for when the warrant officer in charge of the motor pool walked up to me and said that I was to report to the corps commander in his office "pronto." Shoot, I thought, what have I done so wrong that the commanding general wants to see me personally.

Lieutenant General Hutchin was the V Corps Commander at the time. I'd met the general a couple of times while going through receiving lines at social events, and he did swear me in when my Regular Army commission was approved after I arrived in January, but as a lowly captain, our paths rarely crossed. Before I reported to the general, I had to report to his chief of staff, a brigadier general.

"Tonsetic, what does the old man want to see you about anyway?" the brigadier queried.

"I have no idea Sir," I replied.

"Neither do I," he said, pointing to the door of the commanding general's office."

Taking a deep breath I knocked on the door and was summoned by the general to enter his rather small, inauspicious office. After saluting and reporting in the prescribed manner, General Hutchin, a courtly gray-haired man, pointed to a leather easy chair beside his desk.

"Have a seat captain," he said.

This is going to be some bad news, I thought, wondering if there had been a death in my family or something.

"I've got your request here for reassignment to Vietnam, what's this all about?"

I used the same logic I used with the colonel.

"Sir, as an infantry officer, I want to go to the sound of guns." It came across as kind of corny to me, but the general's ears perked up.

"Well, I was in the same situation as you when I was a captain. I served in World War II as a young infantry officer, and when the Korean War broke out, I was stuck in a staff officer's job in the States. I volunteered for Korea for the same reasons. I'm going to approve your request and send it on to Washington," he said as he signed my paperwork. "Good luck captain," he intoned.

"Yes Sir, thank you Sir," I replied. I stood up and assumed the position of attention and saluted, knowing the short interview was over.

I found out later that the general was twice awarded the Distinguished Service Cross in Korea. It was good to know that at least one lieutenant general still had some mud on his boots.

It took two more months for my paperwork to get through the Army officer personnel system, but by the end of June, I had my orders for Vietnam in hand. In the interim, I bought my parents a plane ticket to Germany so that we could tour Europe together. My father was a hardworking steelworker who went into the mills right out of high school. He and my mother somehow managed to raise five children, sending four to college, all on his rather meager salary. With the assistance of a partial scholarship, I was the first to graduate. My parent's expectations were that I would fulfill my two-year commitment to the Army, and then settle down to raise a family and pursue a civilian career. They didn't question my decision to remain in the Army, but I felt that I had somehow let them down. Their visit was my attempt to assuage some of my self-imposed guilt. I took a two-week leave to drive them to Switzerland, Rome, Italy, and Paris, France. My father was a devout Catholic, and attending Mass at St. Peters Basilica in the Vatican was the dream of a lifetime. I figured my parents earned it after worrying about me while I was in Vietnam the first time. Now I was about to put them through it all over again. They never questioned my decision.

I took a 30-day leave in the States before leaving for Vietnam. During my leave, I almost became engaged to a high-school classmate, but I backed out at the last moment. I promised to meet her in Hawaii on rest-and-recreation (R&R) leave, but as it turned out, that never happened either. Jackie drove me to the Greater Pittsburgh Airport for my flight to San Francisco, where I was scheduled to catch a flight from Travis Air Force Base to Vietnam.

As we pulled into the airport parking lot, the car radio was playing John Denver's tune, "I'm leaving on a jet plane, don't know when I'll be back again." We both had tears in our eyes as we unloaded my baggage. We shared a loving embrace at the gate, promising that we would remain faithful, and reassuring each other that better days were ahead for us. As the airliner took off I stared out the window, wondering if I'd ever see my hometown again.

Saigon, September 1970 •

After reporting in at Travis Air Force Base in San Francisco, I learned that my flight to Vietnam would depart the next day. It was an Airlift International charter flight that had all the amenities of a commercial airline flight, except for the booze. After checking into a transient BOQ, I walked to the Travis officer's club for a drink and dinner. I met two other officers at the bar who were also on their way to Vietnam for the second time. All three of us were all booked on the same flight.

The next morning we made our way to the terminal a couple of hours before our flight was scheduled to depart. It took that long for the Army and Air Force personnel to check our baggage, make sure we were on the manifest, and call the roll a half dozen times before giving us permission to board the flight. My traveling companions and I took our time boarding, since it was customary for officers to board last. We were fortunate to get a row of seats at the very front of the aircraft. The airline stewardesses (that's what they were called in those days) sat on fold-down jump seats across from us. They weren't bad looking I thought, trying not to stare. As it turned out, the stewardesses were very friendly, and we enjoyed their company throughout the flight when they weren't busy serving meals. Our innocent flirtations were no doubt mild compared to what their co-workers were putting up with in the aft section of the aircraft, where most of the lower-ranking troops were seated. After refueling stops in Alaska and Japan, we landed without incident at Bien Hoa airbase on the evening of 2 September 1970.

* * *

Unlike the bleary-eyed troops, who were beginning their first tour, I was fairly relaxed. As Yogi Berra said, it was "déjà vu all over again" for me. Our khaki uniforms were already soaked with sweat by the time we boarded the olive-drab, 40-passenger Army busses that would transport us to the 90th Replacement Detachment at Long Binh.

An MP Jeep with a mounted M-60 machine gun pulled in front of our convoy to lead the way. Darkness descended as the convoy began to roll. The busses followed almost the same route that my infantry company followed on the first night of the Tet Offensive of 1968, but I noted that the landscape had changed. Part of the route took us through a portion of a rubber plantation, but it was hardly recognizable since most of the rubber trees had disappeared. Rome plows had pushed the tree line back several hundred meters on both sides of the road. The ARVN POW camp, where my first platoon fought off a determined enemy attack during the first day of Tet '68, was still there.

When we reached Highway 13, our transport turned south and headed in the direction of Saigon. We passed the main gate of Camp Frenzell-Jones, the main base camp of my old outfit, the 199th Light Infantry Brigade, and the gate of the II Field Force headquarters. Both installations came under artillery fire and ground assaults during the early morning hours of 31 January 1968. At the same time, Charlie Company, 4-12 Infantry, the unit that I commanded, was fighting a desperate battle with a battalion of the 275th VC Regiment just a few kilometers to the north. A floodtide of memories, some not so good, rolled through my mind as we sped down the highway.

Moments later our convoy rolled through the gate of the 90th Replacement Battalion. Nothing much had changed in the past two years. It was a curious place where the old mixed with the new. Troops departing Vietnam were easily distinguishable from those that had just arrived. First, while most were still in their early twenties, the departees had all the youth and vigor drained from their bodies. With sunken eyes and far-off stares, the combat vets looked three times their age. Twelve months in Vietnam had made them old in body and spirit before their time. On the other hand, their replacements looked like adolescents starting their first day in high school, wide eyed, half scared to death, and full of false bravado.

We stopped at a building where we presented our assignment orders and were instructed to fill out personnel data cards, the usual stuff—name, rank, service number, and who to notify in case we were KIA. Then we converted our "greenbacks" for military payment certificates (MPC). U.S. greenbacks were highly sought after by the Vietnamese, and were worth more than their face value on the black market. After exchanging our money, we were issued bedding and pointed to our temporary lodgings, the officers going in one direction, the enlisted soldiers in another. I ended up in the same temporary barracks that I stayed in before my departure in 1968. Once more, the bunk number assigned to me was the same one I had slept in before. It was as if my life was running in reverse.

The next morning we finished our processing, and the officers who were assigned to U.S. units departed to join their units, while those of us who had orders to MACV advisory detachments awaited transport to the MACV replacement center in Saigon. When I volunteered for my second tour, I requested assignment as an advisor. I'd already concluded that this war was no longer our fight, and I did not want to see another young American soldier killed or maimed for life in a war that our nation no longer supported.

Our group of about 30 officers went to lunch at the 90th Replacement Battalion's officers club, where we spent a couple of hours waiting for a representative from our new command, MACV, to show up with our transportation. Finally, an unkempt looking soldier walked into the club looking for his passengers. He announced that his bus had broken down in route, and had to wait for a replacement vehicle. I figured he'd probably stopped at one of the Vietnamese car washes that lined the busy highway between Saigon and Long Binh. At one of these car washes, a GI could get his truck, Jeep, or bus washed while he downed a beer, bought one of the "hostesses" a Saigon tea, and negotiated with the proprietor for 20 minutes of private female companionship.

We boarded our transport and sped down the highway toward the capital. Not much had changed in the landscape. Rice paddies stretched as far as the eye could see on both sides of the road. Farmers wearing the traditional, loose-fitting black pajamas and conical straw hats worked their fields behind their water buffalos, and women attired in shapeless black trousers and white tunics walked along the dikes with baskets suspended from long poles across their shoulders. There were tin-roof shanties scattered along the highway, with a moped or two-parked outside. Barefooted children played among the few scrawny chickens that pecked away in the dirt outside their dwellings.

The traffic along the highway was heavier than I remembered with an assortment of army vehicles, dilapidated civilian trucks carrying baskets of rice, vegetables, and firewood, along with an occasional old Renault or Citroen, and an untold number of motor scooters. All of these conveyances were driven "pedal to the metal" on the long, straight-open stretches of the highway.

As we neared the city, we drove past areas where thousands of refugees were living in squalor. Many lived in large cardboard boxes and cartons scattered among piles of garbage beside the highway. Those more fortunate lived in shanties, made from flattened aluminum beer and soda cans nailed to scraps of plywood. A putrid odor of rotting garbage, mildew, and excrement permeated the atmosphere around the camps.

We crossed the Y Bridge and entered the city that was once known as "the Paris of the East," or "the Pearl of the Orient." Almost immediately we were caught up in Saigon's snarled traffic, and our bus slowed to a crawl. Saigon's traffic jams are best described as a free for all melees. Vietnamese drivers observed no rules or courtesies once they got behind the wheel, and the horn was the outlet for their frustrations. Any pedestrians who crossed a street put themselves into an immediate life-or-death situation. I've driven in Paris, Rome, New York, and Los Angeles, and Saigon topped them all.

Moreover, the pollution hanging over the city was ten times worse than I remembered, and the heavy pall of carbon monoxide fumes made it difficult to breathe.

The architecture of the city was unchanged—French colonial buildings, multi-story buildings, store fronts with steel shutters that were pulled down during the heat of the day, open-air markets, barber shops, and restaurants and cafes, some with sidewalk tables, lined the streets. There were also the massage parlors and garish neon-lit bars with hostesses, some in western-style miniskirts, and others in traditional silk *ao dais*, beckoning passersby from the open doorways. The tree shaded residential streets were more appealing. We drove past once opulent white and yellow stucco French villas, some with court-yards and lush gardens hidden behind flowering bougainvillea-covered walls. In 1970, Saigon still retained traces of the old French colonial period.

None of us were smiling when our driver made a wrong turn and got us lost. We ended up in the Gia Dinh section of the city. Fortunately, there was an Army major on the bus who was stationed in Saigon on a previous tour, and he gave the proper directions to our driver. Camp Alpha was located in the western part of the city near Ton Son Nhut Airport and MACV headquarters. It was not my first visit. In addition to functioning as the MACV troop replacement center, Camp Alpha was a processing center for troops going on rest and recreation (R&R) leave. I'd processed through the facility when I took my R&R to Bangkok in July of 1968. Some improvements had been added since my last visit.

At the gate there was a sign that read, "Through these gates pass the world's best soldiers." We passed a swimming pool, a movie theater, and an enlisted club. Recent arrivals, some stripped to their skivvies, lounged around the pool. We've been in this country far too long I thought.

When we arrived at the processing center, a clerk from the Adjutant General's section had us fill out another series of forms and documents before handing out a schedule of daily briefings that we were expected to attend over the next three days. Since we had a number of field grade officers in our group, I thought the paper pushers could have at least spared a second lieutenant to welcome us. Apparently, our specific advisor assignments were still not finalized. The possibilities ranged from the Mekong Delta to the DMZ.

For the next three days, we sat through too many boring briefings on every subject from the current Viet Cong infrastructure to the common venereal diseases in Vietnam. The counterintelligence-briefing officer cautioned us not to become intimate with any Vietnamese civilian, male or female, as they might be covert Communist agents. That one drew a chuckle from the audience. To break the monotony, we were permitted to visit Saigon in the evenings as long as we were back in camp by the curfew. I'd heard they served good steaks at the Massachusetts's Officers billets not far from Ton Son Nhut, so I caught a bus to that facility one evening. As it turned out, they also had a bar with live entertainment.

After finishing my steak, I headed into the bar where I ran into Major Jim Ingram, a Special Forces acquaintance of mine. As the Filipino band was downright awful, Jim and I and a couple of others decided to visit the Vietnamese Air Force Officer's Club (VNAF) on Ton Son Nhut airbase. We piled into Jim's Jeep to check out the club's licentious reputation. Rumor had it that Vice President and former Air Force General Ky's wife received a share of the club's profits. The club lived up to its reputation, and I barely made curfew at Camp Alpha. I was beginning to enjoy Saigon, and I asked Jim if there were any job openings in the J3 section of MACV where he worked. Unfortunately, they weren't hiring any infantry captains at the time.

The following day our assignments were finalized and we drew our field gear and weapons. As it turned out, I never used much of the gear. Most of it, including the flak jacket, shelter half, Army-issue jungle hammock, protective mask, entrenching tool, and steel helmet, stayed in my duffle bag back in Can Tho during most of my tour. Rangers always travel light and fast, and the ARVN Rangers were no exception.

Some items that I considered essential weren't issued to us. These items included a waterproof map case, a compass, a strobe light, and a survival kit. When I asked the supply sergeant about these items, he looked at me like I was nuts. All the items were in the Army inventory, but MACV apparently never requisitioned them for their field advisors. Fortunately, I was able to procure all of the aforementioned items during my tour.

We were also issued an M-16 rifle, but no .45-caliber pistol. I would have preferred the CAR-15 to the M-16, but it wasn't standard issue in MACV either. The CAR-15 is basically an M-16 with a shortened barrel, and it was easier to carry and use when you're trying to do two or more things at once, like talking on the radio or reading a map. In addition, I always liked to carry a pistol as a backup weapon of last resort. It could also be concealed in your waistband, or in a shoulder holster during visits to Vietnamese bars and restaurants where you'd look foolish carrying a rifle.

I requested an airborne advisory assignment with the Vietnamese Airborne Division that was based in Saigon, but that was not in my immediate future. Instead, I was assigned as Senior Advisor with the

ARVN border Rangers at the Cai Cai Camp near the Cambodian border in the Mekong Delta.

The Delta is a huge area of some 26,000 square miles in the southernmost portion of Vietnam. It was formed by the five branches of the Mekong River, which total about 300 miles in length. For the most part, it is a low-level fertile plain ideally suited for growing rice. As a result, it is also one of the most heavily populated areas in Vietnam. Even under wartime circumstances, there were more than 9,000 square miles of Delta land under rice cultivation.

The southernmost tip of the Delta, known as the Ca Mau Peninsula, is covered with jungle and mangrove swamps and is sparsely populated. Although most of the Delta is less than ten feet above sea level, there are two mountainous areas with elevations in excess of 247 meters. *Ba Nui*, Seven Mountains, is a scenic range of seven mountains near the Cambodian border in the western portion of the Delta. The Chung Son mountain complex stretches along the Gulf of Siam in Ha Tien Province. The mountains nearest the coast are actually large cavernous limestone formations, with numerous large caves and underground streams.

The typical terrain of the Mekong Delta offered advantages and challenges for U.S. and South Vietnamese forces. While cross-country movement was impeded by numerous rivers, streams, and canals—as well as inundated rice paddies during the rainy season—the Delta was well suited for airmobile operations. The wide-open rice paddies made ideal landing and pick-up zones, and facilitated resupply and medical evacuation. The relatively open terrain also made it difficult for the enemy to move about during daylight hours, but using the numerous waterways, the enemy forces were able to move considerable distances during the hours of darkness.

The Delta region also offered an abundance of food sources for the government troops, as well as the enemy. There was no shortage of fish, prawns, rice, pineapple, and bananas to supplement the troops rations, and the Viet Cong guerillas were quite capable of living entirely off the land. The swampy nature of the terrain in large portions of the region presented certain medical and health risks, particularly for non-indigenous troops, and jungle rot, malaria, and other tropical fevers were constant hazards for most of the year. For the most part, I was aware of the challenges I would face, since I'd operated in similar terrain during the final months of my first tour in Vietnam.

* * *

I met a couple of other captains who also received orders to Ranger assignments in the Mekong Delta. One was George Crocker, a West Pointer from the state of Arkansas. George was also beginning his second tour in Vietnam. With a positive outlook and a charismatic personality, he was great company. On his first tour, George served with 9th Division's Mobile Riverine Force in the Delta, and like me he'd completed the infantry officers Advanced Course at Fort Benning. George was headed for the border camp at To Chau in the Seven Mountains region not far from the Cambodian border.

None of us knew much about the ARVN Rangers, but I did have some experience with the 5th Ranger Group during the first months of my tour with the 199th Light Infantry Brigade. At that time, the 5th Ranger Group was preparing to assume the Brigade's mission of responding quickly and decisively to counter enemy threats directed against Saigon. During the fall of 1967, I was part of a team from the 199th Light Infantry Brigade that was in charge of certifying that the Rangers were ready to assume that mission.

The ARVN Rangers, or *Biet-Dong-Quan* (BDQ) in Vietnamese, were formed in 1960, by order of South Vietnamese President Ngo Dinh Diem. The primary mission of these highly kinetic and lightly-equipped forces was to carry the fight to the insurgents, striking them in their remote sanctuaries and base areas. They were also charged with reinforcing ARVN units defending remote outposts and districts throughout the country. Initially, the ARVN Rangers were organized as separate companies. By the summer of 1963, there were a total of 86 Ranger companies spread across four corps areas.

Early in the war, U.S. Ranger advisors were deployed as mobile training teams (MTTs) to the Ranger training centers, and later U.S. advisors were assigned directly to the South Vietnamese Ranger units. In 1962, the Vietnamese Ranger companies were organized into battalions, and later into five groups with multiple battalions. The Ranger Groups were typically assigned to one of the four corps headquarters, but could be deployed anywhere else in the country where they were needed.

The ARVN Rangers were not without their critics during their early years. In July 1966, Deputy Ambassador Porter headed a study group on the "Roles and Missions" of the Republic of Vietnam Armed Forces (RVNAF). In the group's report, it was recommended that the Rangers be disbanded, "...because of their frequently intolerable conduct toward the populace." MACV headquarters opposed the recommendation on the grounds that it would seriously reduce ARVN combat strength, and it was never implemented. However, the Rangers got the message, and they began to improve their relations with the civilian population.

There was never any doubt that the Rangers proved their worth in battle. The battalions distinguished themselves time after time on battlefields throughout the country. In all, 11 U.S. Presidential Unit Citations (PUC) were awarded to Vietnamese Ranger units. During the Tet Offensive of 1968, the 5th Ranger Group distinguished itself in the battle for Saigon, while other ARVN Ranger units fought in the battle for Hue, and at Khe Sanh. The Rangers again distinguished themselves during the May 1970 invasion of Cambodia.

The role and mission of the Ranger forces was greatly expanded during Vietnamization. By the summer of 1970, the U.S. 5th Special Forces Group was phasing out of Vietnam, and all of its border camps along the Laotian and Cambodian borders, manned by the Vietnamese CIDG (Civilian Irregular Defense Group) troops, were to be absorbed into the regular Vietnamese army as border Ranger battalions. The 5th Special Forces Group had performed the border surveillance mission since its arrival in 1964, building camps along the Cambodian and Laotian borders, and recruiting CIDG troops to man the camps and conduct border surveillance operations.

The regular Vietnamese army never really liked or trusted the CIDG troops, and the feeling was mutual. The CIDG troops were mainly recruited from ethnic minorities such as the various Montagnard tribes, the Hoa Hoa sect, and ethnic Cambodians and Chinese living within the borders of South Vietnam. The U.S. Special Forces paid and trained the irregulars, most of whom were excellent fighters who didn't mind killing Vietnamese of any political persuasion.

In IV Corps there were eight CIDG border camps under the control of Company D, the 5th U.S. Special Forces Group headquartered in Can Tho. The border camps stretched from the Plain of Reeds in the east to the Gulf of Thailand in the west. All eight camps were in the process of converting to border Ranger battalion camps during the fall of 1970. Four border Ranger battalions were assigned to each of the two newly organized border Ranger Group headquarters.

There were also four maneuver ARVN Ranger battalions operating in the Mekong Delta at that time. The maneuver battalions were assigned to the 4th Ranger Group headquartered in Can Tho. With the addition of two new Ranger Groups in IV Corps, it was deemed necessary to create a Regional Ranger Command to command and control all Ranger forces operating in the Delta. The new headquarters, commanded by an ARVN Ranger full colonel, was designated as the Military Region 4 (MR-4) Ranger Command.

At the time of my arrival in September 1970, the reorganization was still a work in progress. The U.S. Senior Advisor to the 4th Ranger Group, Lieutenant Colonel Witek, was responsible for the organization and supervision of the newly authorized Border Ranger Combat Advisory Teams, this in addition to overseeing the 4th Ranger Group Battalion Combat Assistance teams.

CHAPTER 2

ASSIGNMENT: DELTA RANGERS

It was my first flight into the heart of the Mekong Delta. The Caribou aircraft generally followed the narrow ribbon of Highway 4 as it stretched southward toward Can Tho. The seemingly endless panorama below was spectacular. The monsoons had turned the dry and cracked rice paddies into shimmering, emerald-green rice fields. The narrow dikes that trapped the rainwater for the rice plants created a checkerboard pattern that was crisscrossed by long, straight canals that were used for transport and irrigation. Nipa palms, stands of bamboo, and other species of tropical foliage grew along the canal banks. Hamlets and villages stretched along the banks of some of the larger canals, along with groves of banana and papaya trees. The Mekong River and its tributaries fed water into the canals and provided another important food source, as the waterways were teeming with fish, shrimp, prawns, and eels.

As we flew over Vinh Long, we could see that the northern branch of the Mekong splits into four smaller branches after it flows past the town on its way to the sea. The southern branch flows directly toward the sea after flowing through Can Tho. From 2,000 feet, the Delta looked deceptively beautiful and peaceful—"a land of milk and honey"— the rice basket of Vietnam.

We circled Can Tho, catching a bird's eye view of the Delta's largest city before landing. The city was bustling with all sorts of vehicular traffic and river commerce. Large floating markets stretched along the central portion of the waterfront, and I was surprised by the size, sprawl, and vitality of the city.

* * *

The Caribou's landing gear slammed into the PSP runway at Can Tho airfield and the pilot taxied the aircraft toward a small terminal. I was amazed that the pilot used less than 1,000 feet of runway for the landing. There were dozens of fixed and rotary wing aircraft parked along the tarmac—everything from WWII vintage C-46s to the much smaller Army Otters and Beavers, to CH-47 Chinook heavy-lift helicopters, as well as UH-1Ds (Hueys) and Cobra attack helicopters. There were also several Air America aircraft parked on the tarmac. Air America was a civilian passenger and cargo airline operated by the Central Intelligence Agency (CIA) in Southeast Asia during the war. We were transported in a dilapidated Air Force bus to our temporary billets at the Delta Hotel in Can Tho City. It is sited at the confluence of the Can Tho and Hau Giang rivers and is the Delta's largest city. Some 170 kilometers south of Saigon, the city is an important agricultural market center for the entire Delta. The city saw heavy fighting during the Tet Offensive of 1968, and the scars of that attack were still clearly visible two years later. Can Tho was also the headquarters of IV Corps that controlled military operations in Military Region 4, and was the last major South Vietnamese city to fall to the Communists during their final offensive in 1975.

The Delta Hotel, an aging relic from French colonial days, was leased by MACV to house incoming personnel. It wasn't a four-star or even a one-star hotel, but it had showers and toilets, so I could overlook the damp reek of mold that covered its pale walls, and the fetid odor of garbage that drifted in from the street. No one from the IV Corps headquarters showed up to brief us, so we spent the afternoon sitting in the lobby, playing Hearts and watching a Vietnamese boy carry case after case of Budweiser beer up the alley in front of the hotel and around the corner. Evidently, there was some serious black marketeering going on within the PX system in Can Tho.

By 5:00 p.m., ominous black clouds that heralded the daily monsoon downpour gathered in the sky above Can Tho. We waited until the rains subsided before venturing out to a Vietnamese restaurant. The rainy season would last another month before subsiding.

We ended up spending three days at the hotel while we completed our processing at the Eakin Compound, the home of the Delta Regional Assistance Command. There were two U.S. generals, a two-star and a one-star, and around 22,000 U.S. servicemen assigned to this command. That was far fewer troops than were stationed in the I, II, or III Corps areas. Most of the 22,000 troops were assigned to aviations units, signal units, and combat support units. The U.S. 9th Infantry Division, the only U.S. Army Division ever stationed in the IV Corps area, began its withdrawal during the summer of 1969. The division's last combat brigade departed in October of 1970. Thereafter, all ground combat forces in the IV Corps area of operations were South Vietnamese. At the time of my arrival there were three ARVN infantry divisions—the 7th, 9th, and 21st—stationed in the Delta along with the 4th Ranger Group. In addition, there were Regional and Popular Force units stationed at numerous locations throughout the Delta.

Eakin Compound was a far cry from MACV headquarters in Saigon, but it did have a swimming pool and an air-conditioned NCO club. It was quite livable during the dry season, but was often flooded during the rainy season. The other major U.S. compound in Can Tho was the Civil Operations and Revolutionary Development Support (CORDS) compound. That facility was nicknamed "Palm Springs," because of the plush living quarters assigned to the senior staff. Personnel assigned to a CORDS headquarters lived a lifestyle that was the envy of all others who served in Vietnam.

The Senior Advisor to the 4th Ranger Group had moved his headquarters element into the Special Forces (SF) Compound at Can Tho Airfield. The Rangers were in the process of absorbing the Special Forces border surveillance mission, and Delta Company 5th Special Forces Group was in the process of standing down. The compound wasn't a bad set up. Special Forces in Vietnam fought hard and generally lived pretty well, particularly at the C Detachment level. In this case, they had a superb mess hall, a nice little club, *the Alamo Lounge*, and a combination bar/recreation room for a place to unwind. Since the Delta Company headquarters was not closing down until December 1970, the Ranger advisors were allocated a building that was once part of the dispensary. We promptly dubbed it the "cell-block" due to the size of the rooms. There was one small office area, about eight feet by four feet, and eight tiny sleeping rooms with two or three cots squeezed into each room. During my first overnight stay, a large rat jumped on my cot and scurried across my chest; it was not an uncommon occurrence in the cellblock.

The Rangers cellblock was supervised by Staff Sergeant "Ranger Eddy" Moreno. Ranger Eddy looked after everything, including us. He performed all the duties of a first sergeant, and he had no clerks to help him out when we arrived. It was just he and our boss, a lieutenant colonel. Ranger Eddy handled all the paperwork, supply, and logistics. He even made the mail run every day to Eakin Compound. I volunteered to ride shotgun with him during my first week. We'd drive into Can Tho in the colonel's Jeep, pick up the mail and other paperwork at the Compound, and stop for a beer or two at the NCO Club. He knew every NCO at Eakin on a first name basis, and he was an excellent scrounger.

He'd also been on one of the Ranger Battalion advisory teams earlier in his tour and received a Silver Star and Soldier's Medal for bravery. I hope the Army retired Ranger Eddy as a Sergeant Major—he deserved it. Oh yeah, he literally did save my life on one occasion, but I'll get to that later in the story.

One evening after having a few beers at the SF's Alamo Club, I was walking back to the Ranger billets when I saw a figure approaching in the darkness. At first I thought it was one of the SF soldiers, since the person was clad in camouflage fatigues and wore a green beret. It was obvious the person was a little tipsy, as he was having difficulty walking in a straight line. When I got up close, I noticed that the person was a female.

She asked, "Can you help me find my room captain?"

Only then did I recognize her. It was Martha Raye, one of Special Forces' biggest supporters. I knew she was visiting the compound, but hadn't met her.

"Yes Ma'am," I said, as I turned her around and led her back to the SF visiting officers quarters.

Martha Raye had been entertaining the troops since 1942, and was especially fond of the Green Berets, so much so that they made her an honorary "colonel." She was later awarded the Presidential Medal of Freedom and when she passed away in 1994, she was buried in the military cemetery at Fort Bragg, North Carolina, where she would be close to her beloved Green Berets.

Our senior Ranger Advisor was Lieutenant Colonel James E. Witek. The colonel was an infantry officer, master parachutist, Ranger, and former 4th Ranger Group Senior Advisor. I can't say he was the best officer I ever served under, but like most of us he gave it his best. Lieutenant Colonel Witek was charged with organizing a new MR-4 Ranger command advisory team that would oversee all Ranger Group and Battalion Advisors in the Delta. In my entrance interview with him, Witek would not confirm my assignment to the Cai Cai border Ranger camp, but told me to "hang loose" for a few days. This didn't bother me a bit. I had about 350 days left to serve on my tour, and I was in no hurry to get shot at again.

The colonel had to put together a staff in a hurry. I knew he urgently needed an Adjutant, an Intelligence Officer (S-2), Operations Officer (S-3), and a Supply Officer (S-4). Since I had S-3 experience with the 199th Brigade, I hoped he was considering me for the S-3 slot. The S-3 was a major's billet, but as yet there was no major on board. I had four years in grade as a captain, but promotions had slowed down to a trickle now that the war was winding down.

A couple of days later, Colonel Witek called me into his office and said,

"I'm changing your assignment. You're not going to the Cai Cai border camp. I need to do something about the 44th Ranger Battalion. Their senior advisor is a lieutenant, and I've been told it's the worst battalion in the 4th Group. There's some talk that the battalion commander is about to be relieved, and I'm assigning you as the senior advisor. The battalions on stand down now at their base camp in Cai Rang, about five miles south of Can Tho, but their going on an operation upcountry in a couple of weeks. I want you to join that team and find out what the hell's going on in that battalion. Any questions?" he concluded.

I knew that the 44th was one of the maneuver Ranger Battalions, and I'd run into the lieutenant on a couple of occasions when he dropped by a few times to pick up his mail.

Since it was obvious that the colonel was not in the mood for negotiating, I simply said, "Roger Sir."

Before driving down to Cai Rang, I did a little homework on the 44th Ranger Battalion. The unit had received a wide range of awards from both the Republic of Vietnam, as well as the United States. The 44th Battalion had received Vietnam's National Order Fourragere, and the Vietnamese Gallantry Cross with Palm unit award. The latter was awarded seven times. I was even more impressed when I learned that the battalion had received the U.S. Presidential Citation. Relatively few U.S. infantry battalions received that unit award during the Vietnam War.

The 44th Ranger Battalion also claimed the legendary "Tiger Lady" as one of its own. Madame Ho Thi Qui was the wife of Major Le Van Dan, a commander of the 44th Rangers in the early 60s. Like her husband, the Tiger Lady served in the French colonial army and rose to the rank of master sergeant. After her marriage, she stayed in the army and fought side by side with the Ranger battalion that her husband commanded. Known as "Big Sister" by the Rangers, she accompanied the unit into many battles. Legend has it that she wore the camouflage uniform of the Rangers, along with the steel helmet painted black-and-yellow stripes with the trademark black tiger head. With a pearl-handled Colt .45 strapped to her waist, she was always in the thick of the action, moving forward under fire to aid wounded men. She received many of her country's awards for bravery. The story, however, had a sad ending. She was shot and killed by her husband after she found him with his young mistress. Tiger Lady was a national figure and heroine among the Vietnamese populace, and her mystique and legend continued long after her death.

After reviewing the 44th's history, it was time to introduce myself to the battalion and the advisory team. The home base of the battalion was in Cai Rang, a village some three miles south of Can Tho.

First Lieutenant Pete Morris (not his real name), and Staff Sergeant Roberts, the two senior members of the 44th Ranger Battalion's Combat Assistance Team (BCAT), picked me up for the short drive to Cai Rang. We followed Highway 4 south for a couple of miles, and crossed the single-lane concrete bridge spanning the Hau Giang River before turning off the highway into the village. The battalion's compound was located on the river about a quarter of a mile from the bridge.

The headquarters was set up in a French colonial government building. The buff-colored stucco was peeling off the exterior of the two-story structure. A sentry clad in tight-fitting camouflage fatigues and a red beret popped to attention when he recognized the Jeep, and waved us through the gate. We drove past a field where the troops were living in a collection of dilapidated barracks and army GP large and medium tents. They were erected so close together that each guide rope crossed another.

We stopped at the front entrance of the headquarters and entered the building. The battalion commander's office and his staff officers occupied the first floor of the building. Several clerks were pecking away at their typewriters, while others were busy pouring over stacks of documents and ledgers. Two unmanned machine guns rested at the ready on the floor beneath an open window.

After determining that he was not in his office, we headed to the stairway that led to the second floor. The advisory team was housed in a large room on the second story of the building. The Ranger battalion commander and his family occupied most of the second floor and shared a wide balcony with the advisors.. There was a sandbag bunker on the balcony right outside the door to the team room, and beside it sat a generator that powered a U.S. refrigerator. The balcony overlooked the river where sampans, laden with cargos of vegetables, glided lazily past the Ranger camp and headed for the village marketplace.

The team room had a high ceiling, and the shuttered windows had neither screens nor glass. Four canvas cots with mosquito netting hung across them were shoved next to the wall. A couple of folding tables were set up in the center of the room, and an M-60 machine gun and an assortment of metal ammo boxes littered the floor. Sergeant David Dolby, the other member of the team, met us there.

Sergeant Dolby informed us that Major Thi, the battalion commander, had left with his family for leave in Saigon and wouldn't return until the battalion departed for its next operation. I spent the rest of the morning getting to know the team members and sharing some of my own military background and experience with them. I also learned a little bit about my lieutenant and two sergeants.

Lieutenant Morris was the only one of us who wasn't on a second

combat tour in Vietnam. He was an Officer School Candidate graduate with a Reserve Officer commission. I saw neither a set of "jump"
(paratrooper) wings nor a Ranger tab on his fatigues. Morris looked
like he'd be more at home working a staff job in some headquarters,
and had little to say except when it came to criticizing the battalion
commander. My impression was that he was not happy to have a captain assigned to the team; it was a step down for him.

Twenty-six-year-old Staff Sergeant Roberts was a lanky, blond-
haired Texan with a harsh western drawl. I always pictured him
punching cattle in west Texas when he spoke. His first tour was with
the "Wolfhounds" of the 25th U.S. Infantry Division, where he'd been
awarded the Silver Star and Purple Heart. His war stories always started when he took a long draw on his pipe and began, "I'll tell you
whott Sir!"

I noticed that Sergeant Roberts maintained a slightly distant air
when he was around me. It was apparent that Roberts and Lieutenant
Morris were pretty tight, and it took the sergeant some time to shift
his loyalties to me. Perhaps he wanted to see how I reacted under fire.
He didn't have long to wait.

The other member of the team was Sergeant David Dolby. The
twenty-four-year-old Pennsylvanian was a Congressional Medal of
Honor recipient. He won the Medal in 1966 while serving in the 1st
Cavalry Division. His citation reads that he single-handedly knocked
out three NVA machine gun nests when his platoon was taken under
fire.

Dolby was a bit of a loner, and spent hours field stripping and
cleaning the team's M-60 machine guns. Sergeant Roberts told me
later that Dolby would walk point for the entire 400-man Ranger battalion armed with the M-60, and that concerned me a bit. Sergeant
Dolby only stayed with us for about a week after I arrived. A general
in MACV headquarters found out that a Medal of Honor winner was
in the field with the Rangers, and he was reassigned, much to his dis-
pleasure, to the MACV Recondo School. The Army considers its
Medal of Honor winners national heroes and role models for the
troops. As such, they try to keep them out of harm's way as much as
possible. I agree, but I sure could have used Sergeant Dolby on my first
combat operation with the Ranger battalion.

Both Lieutenant Morris and Staff Sergeant Roberts had low personal and professional opinions of the battalion commander, *Thieu Ta* (Major) Thi. On the other hand, they "sang the praises" of the battalion executive officer, *Dai Uy* (Captain) Yen. It soon became clear to me that Morris thought that Yen should be the commander, and wanted to see Thi relieved of his command. Some of the animosity that Morris bore toward the battalion commander stemmed from the fact that the latter never considered the lieutenant his equal in terms of rank or experience, and therefore refused to accept his advice.

Lieutenant Morris had recommended that the battalion commander be relieved on several monthly MACV SEER reports. The SEER report was part of a MACV system for Evaluating the Effectiveness of Republic of Vietnam Armed Forces. It was submitted each month by all advisors to ARVN units down to the battalion level. The SEER reports included mostly quantitative data on each battalion, but the reporting advisor could submit narrative comments as well. As a result of the poor evaluations, Major Thi was under close scrutiny from his chain of command. However, the senior Vietnamese Ranger commanders were not about to relieve one of their battalion commanders based on the evaluation and recommendation of a U.S. lieutenant.. Nonetheless, the SEER reports were reviewed by a U.S. two-star general at Military Region 4 headquarters, and he was putting some pressure on his Vietnamese counterpart to address the situation.

I wanted to meet Major Thi and observe how he performed under fire before I passed on my own views on the next SEER report. Based on what I'd heard from the team members, I had a gut feeling that the lieutenant was dabbling in the internal politics within the battalion. There was considerable friction between Major Thi and his executive officer, *Dai Uy* Yen. The executive had his own loyal following of junior officers in the battalion, most of who didn't like Thi either. Yen was a bachelor, at least a geographic one, and he and Lieutenant Morris spent considerable time together. I thought that perhaps he was using Morris to get what he wanted—a promotion and command of the battalion. Most of the Vietnamese Ranger officers had been through a "coup" or two, and they knew how to advance their own interests. It was obvious that there was dissension and split loyalty within the officer ranks of the battalion.

* * *

The 44th Ranger battalion typically fielded about 400 men, but the number fluctuated depending on the casualty rate. The battalion was organized with four Ranger companies and a small headquarters staff. Each company was authorized a captain, but most were senior lieutenants. In the 44th, many of the troops were ethnic Cambodians and easy to spot, since they tended to be slightly taller than the Vietnamese with somewhat darker skin. They also tended to have less Mongoloid eyes and wavy hair. Most were fierce fighters, and imbued with beliefs and rituals of their own, usually preferred to serve in the same squad with other Cambodians.

In accordance with their religious beliefs, most had tattoos on their chests meant to protect them in battle. When a Cambodian was wounded, he blamed his tattoo artist for a faulty design. There were also a number of Chinese in the battalion. Most came from the urban centers, such as Saigon's Cholon section or the Chinese section of Can Tho. Even though Chinese families weren't eager to see their sons enter the army, they were in no position to resist—especially the ones who didn't have the money to buy their way out of the draft. As far as I could determine, there was no hostility between the diverse groups represented in the battalion.

* * *

Essentially, the Rangers were light infantry, trained and equipped to fight in the most difficult terrain in the country. Often, such areas were under the control of Communist forces. During my time with the ARVN Rangers, we used aircraft, river craft, and sometimes trucks to reach our forward staging areas. From such areas we typically moved on foot or were inserted by UH-1D helicopters to reach our objectives.

The Rangers had no artillery of their own, relying completely on regular ARVN artillery support, if they were in range. By 1970, the Rangers in IV Corps were armed with modern U.S. weapons, such as the M-16 rifle, M-79 grenade launcher, and M-60 machine guns. Some units had the old U.S. 60 millimeter mortar. The Rangers were also supplied with the M-72 Light Anti-tank Weapon (LAW) and Claymore mines.

The Rangers were easy to distinguish from regular ARVN troops, since they wore tightly-tailored camouflage uniforms. Their shoulder patch was a snarling Black Panther superimposed over a large yellow star, and their headgear was a distinctive maroon beret with a badge containing a winged arrow in a wreath. In battle, they wore steel helmets with the snarling Black Panther painted on the front. U.S. advisors assigned to Vietnamese Ranger units wore the same distinctive uniform as their counterparts.

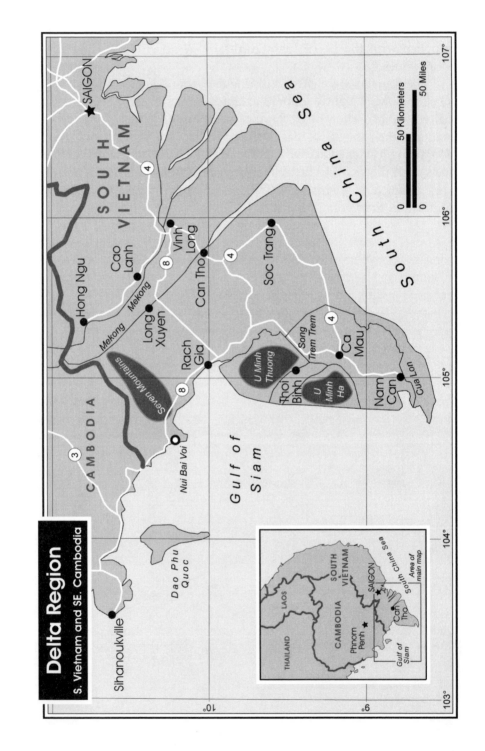

Delta Region
S. Vietnam and SE. Cambodia

SAIGON

SOUTH VIETNAM

Hong Ngu

Cao Lanh

Vinh Long

Mekong

Mekong

Long Xuyen

Can Tho

Soc Trang

Rach Gia

Seven Mountains

Song Trem Trem

U Minh Thuong

Thoi Binh

U Minh Ha

Ca Mau

Nam Can

Cua Lon

Nui Bai Voi

CAMBODIA

Gulf of Siam

Dao Phu Quoc

Sihanoukville

South China Sea

107°

106°

105°

104°

103°

10°

9°

50 Kilometers

50 Miles

THAILAND

LAOS

CAMBODIA

Phnom Penh

SOUTH VIETNAM

SAIGON

Can Tho

South China Sea

Gulf of Siam

Area of main map

CHAPTER 3

"MOUNTAINS WERE BROUGHT FORTH"

On 24 September, I was spending the day at the Can Tho Ranger headquarters attending meetings with the senior advisor, when I received word that the 44th Ranger Battalion was scheduled to move out the next day on a combat operation. For operational security reasons, no one at the headquarters was informed of the battalion's final destination. The commander was simply ordered to move his battalion to a location where he would meet an ARVN liaison officer, who would then provide further orders and instructions.

Movement of the battalion was by truck convoy from the Ranger base camp to the rendezvous point. All this was new to me, but it had its purpose. If there was a "sleeper agent" in the battalion, or if one of the soldiers leaked the information to a family member on where the battalion was bound, the entire operation would be compromised. That line of reasoning made sense, but it had its drawbacks. Since the details of the mission were not known, it was difficult to plan for contingencies. For example, there was no way to know what type of specialized equipment might be needed for the operation.

I was concerned about having the correct map for the area where we were headed, but Lieutenant Morris indicated that the team carried map sheets in the Jeep that covered the entire Delta region. We also had a couple cases of C-rations, several five-gallon cans of gasoline, and other items including radios, batteries, and boxes of ammunition. Since we didn't know our destination, it was impossible to determine what other equipment we might need, and the same was true for the Ranger battalion as a whole. The lack of detailed information required for adequate planning proved costly for the Rangers on this operation.

As it was late in the day, we decided to spend the night at the airfield and hook up with the battalion before they moved out the following morning. That evening we had a steak and lobster dinner in the Special Forces mess, followed by a couple of beers at the Alamo Lounge—it was our last chance in for a good meal and a few beers. Later that evening, I wrote letters to my parents and Jackie. I never revealed to my mother and father the exact nature of my assignment. They'd worried enough about me during my first tour in Vietnam.

In the letter to my parents written on that evening of September 24th, I wrote:

"... I'm getting used to this place. Actually it's not too bad at all. We have hot showers, toilet facilities, and a good mess hall. We even had lobster tonight. The weather is a bit warm, but we normally get some rain each day and this cools it off some."

My parents were still struggling to put two of my younger siblings through Penn State University, with another one right behind them. I tried to help out by sending them a modest check each month, and never gave them the details of my combat experiences with the Rangers while I was in Vietnam. •

* * *

Before sunrise the next morning, we piled into our Jeep and headed for the Ranger camp at Cai Rang. The large courtyard in front of the battalion headquarters was crowded with the ranks of the four Ranger companies, some 390 men in all. The average Vietnamese Ranger was around 19 years old and weighed about 110 pounds. They were much shorter than the average American soldier. All eyes were on the battalion's new senior advisor, or *Co Van,* as we drove up. Over the next 25 days, every fourth soldier standing in that formation would either be dead or seriously wounded.

As we dismounted the Jeep, a young Ranger came out of the headquarter building carrying my rucksack that I'd packed a few days before. The battalion commander had assigned this impish-looking kid as my batboy. Vietnamese officers never carried their own rucksacks, and the battalion commander would lose face if his advisor carried his own gear. The soldier also had instructions to prepare all my meals while we were on operations, and would also serve as my bodyguard. Yon was an ethnic Cambodian who carried a scar from an AK-47 round that passed through his neck. His normal attire consisted of a pair of Ho Chi Minh sandals, black trousers, and a camouflage blouse. His headgear was a floppy, camouflage jungle hat festooned with hand grenade pins. When I spoke to Yon, he always had a mischievous teenage grin on his face.

Major Thi also assigned another young soldier to carry my PRC-25 backpack radio. "Buey" was taller and somewhat thinner than Yon, and he looked more Chinese than Vietnamese. Buey was a shy, brooding young man, and he did not have any friends in the battalion. He was a loner. Nevertheless, he was completely loyal to us. My only problem with Buey was that he was never close at hand when the shooting started. I never knew if he had my safety or his own at heart. Radio operators were prime targets for snipers, and they were easy to pick out because of the radio's antenna. On the other hand, U.S. advisors were also easy to identify because they were, on average, several inches taller than their counterparts. Neither Yon nor Buey spoke more than a dozen words of English. After loading our rucksacks and radios, the pair squeezed into the back of our Jeep.

We had another Vietnamese member of our team, Hai, our interpreter. Hai was a good looking, college-age kid who had an excellent command of the English language, but was more civilian than soldier. On more than one occasion, he overextended his leaves to Saigon and missed movement. As far as I was able to determine, Major Thi never took any punitive actions against Hai for his absences, save for a good dressing down. It was obvious that Hai had some important family connections. Overall, he was an excellent interpreter and provided good insight into what was going on in the battalion.

* * *

The battalion sergeant major called the Rangers to attention as a short, sharp-featured Vietnamese major clad in camouflage fatigues, flak jacket, sunglasses, and a steel helmet with the "Black Panther" emblem exited the headquarters building. Lieutenant Morris told us it was Major Thi, the CO. As yet, I hadn't been introduced to the major, since he had just returned from leave in Saigon.

Major Thi issued a sharp command to the company commanders, and the Rangers broke formation and ran toward a column of 2-1/2-ton trucks that were lined up on the road next to the compound. The major climbed into his highly-polished Jeep with the fearsome Black Panther logo painted on the hood and spare tire cover. Several long radio antennas were mounted on the CO's Jeep. He barked an order to his driver, who laid a six-inch strip of rubber on the pavement as the Jeep lurched forward to take the lead at the head of the column. Sergeant Roberts, who was driving our Jeep, followed suit. We were off to war.

The convoy headed north toward Can Tho on Highway 4, and the trucks strained to keep pace with the major's Jeep. All the drivers were at full throttle. After turning west on Highway 27, the road that paralleled the Song Giang River, the major was finally forced to slow his speed. The road had potholes from the monsoon rains and heavy traffic, and the convoy soon slowed to a crawl. As we bounced along, none of us had any idea where we were going. Lieutenant Morris and Sergeant Roberts said we didn't need a map until we arrived at our destination, but I disagreed. I always liked maps, and didn't feel comfortable without one. A map and a compass are two essential items for any infantry officer. It was soon apparent that my two team members had no more knowledge of the Delta's road network than I did. I prayed silently that our convoy would not be ambushed, because if that were to happen there was no way that I could radio our location to headquarters.

One hour and a half later, the major halted the convoy at the intersection of Highway 27 and Highway 8. The latter highway ran southwest toward Rach Gia on the Gulf of Thailand. The major halted his vehicle next to an ARVN Jeep that was parked off the side of the road. A South Vietnamese captain jumped out, saluted, and handed Major Thi a sealed folder that contained the operation order for the battalion. While the two conversed, I rummaged through our trailer and found a 1 over 250:000 map sheet of the Delta, and quickly pinpointed our location.

The trucks in our convoy pulled off to the side of Highway 8 and the major ordered a one-hour break. We dug into the trailer again for boxes of C-rations. After downing a can of ham slices, I walked over to the major's Jeep to introduce myself. He was sound asleep so I returned to my own vehicle.

It was apparent to me from the beginning that Lieutenant Morris had a short-timer's attitude, but it went beyond that. When I asked him a few questions about the battalion and his officers, I had to pry the information out of him. His attitude was less than professional, and it was obvious that he resented the fact that he was no longer in charge of the team, but that was his problem. I needed him for at least the first few days of this operation.

We reached Rach Gia about noon. The town was a small seaport on the Gulf of Thailand and the homeport of a large fishing fleet—I thought it was rather scenic. The bay was dotted with several sharp limestone karsts that jutted up out of the calm waters. The karsts provided nesting grounds for thousands of sea birds, and the Vietnamese fishing boats glided among them, harvesting the sea.

Rach Gia had a strong Chinese influence with Confucian temples, and most all signs on the shops were in Chinese characters. The marketplace was a large collection of open stalls with thousands of wicker baskets of dried fish, rice, and vegetables. The bleached, pastel-painted buildings reflected the dazzling sunlight which had just broken through the clouds. The war seemed remote in this peaceful town. School children in identical uniforms—boys in blue slacks and white shirts, and girls in blue skirts and white blouses—strolled along the streets during their lunch break.

From Rach Gia, our convoy followed a road north in the direction of the Cambodian border. By mid-afternoon, dark rain clouds appeared again on the horizon. The land became swampy and desolate looking, and the condition of the road that paralleled a wide canal became rougher mile after mile. Small palm-thatched huts lined the canal and naked, brown-skinned children played in the mud-packed yards while their parents stared at us with frightened, forlorn looks from the doorways. Behind each hut was a large bamboo-framed fish trap that could be dipped into the canal, and alongside each hut were one or more beached sampans. It began to rain. Across the canal, the marsh grass stretched inland as far as the eye could see. Lightning streaked across the distant horizon, followed by the rumbling of thunder.

We halted again for a 15-minute break. Rangers jumped from the trucks to relieve themselves along the side of the road, and I did the same. I grabbed a can of fruit cocktail from the C-ration box before we started to roll again. Rain pelted the canvas top of the Jeep and I felt a chill. We crossed several small, single-lane bridges in the next few miles. A small fort guarded each bridge, and the mud walls of each were formed in the shape of a triangle. These outposts were garrisoned by local Popular Forces (PF) platoons. Most of these militiamen wore black pajamas, jungle hats, and sandals. A tattered South Vietnam flag—yellow with red stripes—flew defiantly over each fort.

Most of the PF forts had a few sandbagged bunkers and a crude device known as a "fire arrow." This device was constructed by nailing a number of tin cans, arranged in the shape of a directional arrow, to the top of a rotating circular wooden platform. Gasoline was poured into the sand-filled cans and ignited when an outpost was attacked at night. The arrow was then pointed in the direction of the enemy. Its purpose was to signal orbiting friendly aircraft and point toward the location of the attackers. Fire arrows were a crude but effective device.

The Viet Cong often used the small outposts to train for attacks on larger installations. Sometimes, the soldiers moved their wives and children inside these forts at night for protection. We saw young women, clad in black peasant trousers and blouses with babies on their hips, strolling leisurely up to the barbed-wire barriers around the forts to visit their husbands. In some instances, the Communists cancelled their attacks when they knew that women and children were inside the forts. They were also trying "to the win hearts and minds" of the local populace.

Our convoy reached the district capital of Kien Luong about 4 p.m. The town is located at the neck of a peninsula that juts south into the Gulf of Thailand. There wasn't much to it—mostly private houses, a couple of small stores, and one or two stucco government buildings. The only distinctive feature of the small, unimpressive town was a large cement plant on its outskirts. At that time, the plant was foreign owned. It is still in operation, but was taken over by the Communist government in 1975.

The cement plant was located in Kien Luong, because there are abundant deposits of limestone and sandstone in the area. These minerals are extracted from nearby hills and mountainous rock formations that rise ominously out of the wetlands between the town and the seacoast. These unique terrain features are part of the Mo So mountain system that runs along the coast from the Cambodian border southward into Vietnam. Mo So means limestone mountain in the Khmer language. As I was soon to find out, the mountains were honeycombed with large, complex cave systems that extended deep into the bowels of each mountain. Some say, "what you don't know can't hurt you," but in this case, nothing was farther from the truth.

When the convoy halted in the center of the town, the Rangers dismounted the trucks and quickly melted into the populace as if they planned to take up permanent residence. Small groups of soldiers moved along the streets, selecting private houses where they sought shelter from the rain. There was little doubt that the residents considered the Rangers uninvited guests. After settling in their accommodations, the Rangers began selecting some of the owner's poultry for their evening meal, while others wandered into the local teahouses and bars for some refreshment.

We followed the battalion commander's Jeep to the outskirts of town where the command post for the upcoming operation was located. The controlling headquarters was the 16th Regiment of the 9th ARVN Division, arguably the worst ARVN division in the Delta. The regimental command post (CP) and the U.S. advisors were operating inside GP medium army tents with a few sandbags stacked haphazardly around the perimeter. Nearby was a mixed battery of ARVN 105 and 155mm howitzers in circular, sandbagged firing positions. At least we'll have artillery support, I thought to myself. The barrels of the howitzers pointed menacingly southward toward two cloud-enshrouded mountains that rose defiantly from the wetlands near the coast.

Major Thi and his staff reported to the ARVN command post (CP), and we entered the tent next to it, where the U.S. regimental advisors were housed. Two sergeants and Major Drinkwater, the deputy senior advisor to the regiment, were on duty. Drinkwater, an Armor branch major, greeted us. He seemed somewhat dazed and confused. After a couple of minutes of small talk, he told us that he was in a helicopter crash earlier that day. His command-and-control (C&C) helicopter crash landed after it was hit by enemy ground fire. The major was knocked unconscious and thrown from the aircraft in the accident. He and the helicopter crew were fortunate to be rescued by a sister ship.

The regiment's senior advisor, a middle-aged lieutenant colonel, arrived during our conversation. The colonel, a balding, nervous man, informed us that our Ranger battalion would participate in a regimental-size night attack to seize two freestanding mountains to our south. He further informed us that the ARVN regiment consisted of two infantry battalions and an armored cavalry troop equipped with modified M-113 armored personnel carriers. These tracked vehicles were known as ACAVs, and were common to both U.S. and South Vietnamese armored cavalry units.

The colonel also indicated that Vietnamese Air Force (VNAF), Australian air strikes, U.S. Navy gunships, and ARVN artillery fire support would assist the night attack. Intelligence sources reported that a VC regimental headquarters and two infantry battalions were holed up in a labyrinth of caves and rocks in the two mountains. The attack was scheduled for the following night. A final helicopter reconnaissance of the area was planned for the following morning, and we were invited to fly along on the mission.

Based on enemy strength, the terrain, and the numbers of friendly forces, the chances for a successful attack didn't look favorable to me. U.S. infantry tactical doctrine specifies that the attacker should have at least a 3 to 1 advantage in numbers of troops to ensure success. In this case, we didn't even come close. Given the nature of the terrain, the ratio of attackers to defenders should have been even higher than 3 to 1.

I asked the colonel if ropes, grappling hooks, and other mountain climbing items—as well as flamethrowers to flush the enemy out of the caves—were available for issue to the Rangers. He said that he'd have to ask his ARVN counterparts. That didn't give me a warm and fuzzy feeling.

As a student of military history, I'd read a couple of books on the World War II Pacific campaign. When I thought about mountains and caves, Iwo Jima immediately came to mind. While we weren't making an amphibious assault, and Iwo was a much larger operation, the lessons learned in that campaign still applied. We would be assaulting steep, limestone mountains and trying to dig the VC out of extensive cave systems. The Marines who fought on Iwo Jima were highly trained, motivated, and equipped for the assault. In this case, the poorly equipped ARVN were not trained or prepared for this type of attack.

After the briefings, we hopped into our Jeep and returned to the Ranger battalion command post that was set up in a non-descript house near the center of town. Yon and Buey set up our cots outside under the overhanging roof. We had a supper of C-rations and cooked rice. After supper, one of Major Thi's lieutenants came out and said that Major Thi wanted to see me inside. Finally, I thought. I'd begun to think this guy didn't like Americans, but I soon learned that this was not the case at all.

Thi was seated at a table inside the house, and a couple of Rangers were clearing the empty rice bowls off the table as he addressed me in broken English: "*Dai Uy*, come here, sit down. I see combat patch on shoulder. You fight with Redcatchers, 199th Brigade. Number one! I liaison officer from 5th Ranger Group to 199th Brigade, you know. Very good American unit. Much fighting in Tet battles. You know Cholon two year ago. I like very much your general." The ice was broken at last.

Major Thi's English was limited, but he spoke pretty good French, and I'd studied that language for two years in college. I was far from proficient, but I knew more French than Vietnamese, so we were able to communicate in a mixture of three languages. Like many of his contemporaries, Thi had served in the French colonial army near the end of the first Indo-China War. As far as I could determine, he had about 15 years of service. Like my batboy, Thi bore a scar from an AK round through his neck, and that was the only one I could see. He told me he'd been shot "beaucoup" times by the Viet Minh and Viet Cong. At first I thought he might be a Catholic from the North, but I noticed he was wearing a Buddha suspended from a gold chain around his neck.

The major ordered hot tea and said, "you like?" as he poured a glass and slid it across the wooden tabletop. Our discussion turned to the upcoming attack.

"Attack no good, *Dai Uy*! Many casualties. We need B-52 strike on mountain. I no like this plan. Many Ranger die." I surmised that he was less than optimistic.

I said I'd pass on his request for B-52 support, knowing full well there wasn't a chance in hell of getting an Arc Light strike this late in the game. I'd have bet my next six months pay that the Royal Australian Air Force (RAAF) B-57 Canberra bombers were the heaviest bombing support that we were going to get for the attack.

After a few more minutes of discussion the major said, "I sleep now *Dai Uy*."

I excused myself and headed back outside to lie down on my cot. The rain continued throughout the night.

•

CHAPTER 4

"GO TELL IT ON THE MOUNTAIN"

By the early morning of 24 September, the skies over Kien Luong were still overcast with low-level clouds. We followed Major Thi's Jeep to the ARVN regimental command post. Off to our south, the two mountains were still enshrouded with fog and mist. We had a cup of coffee in the senior advisers tent while we waited for the morning sun to break through the clouds and burn the fog off the mountains. I asked Major Drinkwater, the deputy senior adviser, if his boss had asked the ARVN regimental commander about issuing the Rangers flamethrowers and ropes for the assault.

"Yeah, he did," Drinkwater replied. "The Regimental Commander doesn't think you need flamethrowers. He said they were too heavy for the Vietnamese soldiers to carry, and besides, the regiment didn't have any on hand. They'd have to requisition them through Division, and that would take weeks."

I recalled an incident in 1968, when an NVA flamethrower detachment conducted an attack on a Montagnard village near Dak To. The North Vietnamese had no problem carrying heavy flamethrowers. Now I began to understand why the 9th ARVN Division had such a poor reputation.

"Nice," I said sarcastically. "How about the ropes?"

"The regiment doesn't have any of those either," he answered, and then added, "Tell your battalion commander he might be able to buy or requisition some in town."

"I'll pass it on," I said, thinking we probably could have scrounged the ropes from Special Forces in Can Tho if we had known

51

we were going to engage in mountain fighting.

By 10:00 a.m., the fog lifted and we climbed aboard the UH-1D helicopter that would fly us on the recon mission. We had two ships. Major Thi, his operation officer and executive officer, myself, and Lieutenant Morris flew on one Huey along with Major Drinkwater, who would point out specific objectives for the Ranger battalion. There was also a Vietnamese major from the 16th Regimental head-quarters aboard to explain the plan of attack in Vietnamese to Major Thi. The second was a back up and recovery ship, in case we got shot down. I hoped we wouldn't need it.

The Huey pilots brought their engines to maximum RPM and the aircraft lifted off, gaining several thousand feet of altitude as they approached the mountains. The pilots weren't looking to repeat the previous day's experience. Drinkwater looked a little nervous, inform-ing us through the ship's intercom system that the Communists had at least six 12.75mm anti-aircraft machine guns on the mountains.

We first flew toward the northern cliff face of Nui Ba Voi. It looked to be a couple hundred feet high from the air—straight up that is. My first impression was that the cliff could not be scaled without mountaineering gear, especially under enemy fire. On the other hand, that's what a casual observer might have told the Rangers at Point du Hoc on D-Day. However, the Vietnamese weren't U.S. Army Rangers, and they had not undergone weeks of training and practice scaling near vertical cliff faces.

I noticed some good-size boulders at the base of the cliff, and some holes that looked like cave entrances. Other than the rocks, there was no cover and concealment available. The entire mountain had no veg-etation except for some puny shrubs growing out of the limestone out-crops.

From north to south, Nui Ba Voi was about 1,900 meters in length. Flying down the mountain's eastern side I saw more cliffs, but those cliffs were less steep than the northern face. There was one area, about midway on the eastern slope, where a rockslide had occurred. The slope was strewn with rocks and boulders. At the top of the slide was a small saddle between the highest two points on the mountain. Major Drinkwater said that the saddle was the boundary between the Rangers and the two ARVN infantry battalions that would attack the southern portion of the mountain. I also spotted several cave entrances on the eastern slope of the mountain.

Glancing over at Major Thi, I saw that he was in a heated discussion with the Vietnamese major from regimental headquarters. Thi kept poking his finger at the map and shouting at the Vietnamese major seated next to him. It was obvious that he was angry because he had been assigned the most formidable objective in the attack.

After flying along the eastern face of Nui Ba Voi, our pilot turned north to do a "fly by" of the mountain to the west. We were only a few kilometers from the Gulf of Thailand, and looking out the port side of the aircraft I saw a large, limestone karst jutting out of the muddy, brown sea. Small waves lapped at its base.

Nui Ba Voi and the mountain to its west were separated by 1,000 meters of valley wetlands. There were man-made tracks through the marsh grass between the two mountains. Steamy mists poured out of some of the rock outcroppings on the larger mountain. I later learned it had a cool underground river running beneath it. The cool water produces mists, which give the mountain a mysterious appearance. I also spotted a "punch bowl" area on the top of the same mountain.

Suddenly, the Huey went into a sharp turn to the west and picked up speed. We were being targeted by ground fire. I spotted the green machine gun tracers arching skyward from the mountain below us. Drinkwater told the pilot over the intercom to "haul ass" out of the area. He already was.

Flying back to the command post, I wondered how many recon missions had been flown around the two mountains in the last few days. Nothing like tipping off the enemy that something big was about to happen. Also, I knew that there were bound to be Communist agents wandering around the town and passing information to the VC hiding in the mountains. It was only about a five-kilometer walk from town to the mountains, and I suspected that the VC knew that an attack on their mountain strongholds was imminent. The anti-aircraft fire was just to let us know they were ready and waiting.

When we returned to the 16th Regimental CP, Major Thi, his staff, and myself walked to the briefing tent, where Thi and two other infantry battalion commanders were to receive their final briefing for the attack. The briefing was in Vietnamese, but I was able to discern the plan of attack from the briefer's map overlays.

The 44th Ranger Battalion was to attack the northern face of Nui Ba Voi. After gaining a foothold on the mountain, the soldiers would attack southward down the narrow spine of the mountain to a saddle, where they would link up with the ARVN infantry battalions that had the mission of securing the southern portion of the mountain. The armored cavalry troop would be split, with half the ACAVs providing fire support to the Rangers, and the other half of the troop supporting the infantry battalions. With their .50-caliber machine guns and 106mm recoilless rifles, the armored cavalry would give an added punch to the attack.

The attack was scheduled to begin at 0200 hours the following morning. Preparatory fires included an artillery bombardment of 2,000 rounds, followed by a radar-controlled air strike by the Australian B-57 bombers. Each bomber carried a payload of six 750-pound bombs, four in the bomb bay and two under the wings. The B-57s were based far to the north at Phan Rang. I hoped the "Aussie" pilots were proficient at night bombing. U.S. Navy "Sea Wolf" helicopter gunships, and "Black Pony" fixed-wing gunships would arrive on station after the bombing to provide close, aerial fire support during the attack. I had never worked with Navy gunships before, but I'd heard nothing but good comments from the other Ranger advisers on both these outfits. Since it was still the rainy season, I was concerned about the weather. While heavy rain might help us achieve surprise, it could limit the support provided by gunships.

I would have been impressed with all the support we were promised had I not seen the terrain. Even if everything went off as planned, which it never does in war, the mission was not going to be an easy one. In fact, it just might be a "mission impossible" given the number of troops committed to the operation. As far as I could determine, there were no reserves or reinforcements in the immediate area. Another thing that bothered me about the operation was that it did not refer to any plans for resupply or medical evacuation. As far as I could tell, those areas were not covered during the briefing.

I voiced my concerns about logistic support to Major Drinkwater after the briefing, and he said that ammunition, food, and other supplies would be transported by sampans along a canal to a drop-off point, where they would be loaded on the armored cavalry's ACAVs and moved forward to a location near the base of the mountain. From there, the supplies would have to be carried up the mountain by the Rangers.

Medical evacuations, except for the most serious cases, would be carried out the same way, only in reverse. As far as I could tell from the air, it would be impossible to land a medical evacuation helicopter anywhere on the mountain, as it was far too steep and rocky. Hoists were also out of the question due to the VC's anti-aircraft guns. Any helicopter hovering at low altitude to lower a hoist would be shot out of the sky in two seconds flat. Stretcher-bearers would have to carry the critically wounded down the mountain and out into the wetlands where med-evac helicopters would land. I made a mental note to ensure the Rangers carried plenty of stretchers during the attack.

We drove back to the Ranger command post and repacked our rucksacks, cramming in loose cans of C-rations, extra magazines of ammunition, smoke grenades, and flares. The Jeep and trailer would remain behind at the battalion CP. I ate a can of cold C-rations for dinner and afterwards tried to nap, but my mind raced through a thousand different scenarios of what was about to take place.

* * *

Sheets of rain blew across the darkened landscape as the column of ACAVs turned off the main road and rolled south toward the Ranger assembly area. It was about 10 p.m. when the ACAVs arrived to pick up the companies. Major Thi's plan of attack called for two Ranger companies to move out on foot toward the mountain, while the remaining two companies and the headquarters group would follow mounted on the ACAVs. *Dai Uy* Yen, the battalion XO, would accompany the two dismounted companies, while Major Thi and his staff accompanied the mounted group. I would accompany Major Thi, while Lieutenant Morris and Sergeant Roberts moved with *Dai Uy* Yen and the lead two companies.

They moved out into the darkness soon after the ACAVs arrived. Major Thi planned to give the dismounted companies an hour's head start, since they were moving on foot through the wetlands.

Around 11 p.m., the major gave the word for his men to mount up. The ACAV engines spurted to life as the Rangers began to clamber aboard the carriers, their small bodies bent over with the weight of their oversized rucksacks. They crammed into any empty space they could find on the decks of the vehicles. No one rode in the troop compartments of the vehicles. The troop wells were deathtraps if the vehicles detonated an anti-tank mine. It was better to be blown off the deck than remain trapped inside one of these vehicles—I learned that on my first tour in Vietnam. Accompanied by my batboy and radio operator, I climbed aboard the lead track with the Ranger battalion commander.

The column moved out at a crawl as the tracks churned through the glutinous mud of the swampland toward the final line of departure. The rain that had slowed to a drizzle began to pour down once again, and Bui, my radio operator, offered me a corner of his poncho. The other forms on the deck of the ACAV were also huddled under their rain-soaked ponchos. A voice that spoke from under a poncho beside me turned out to be an American sergeant. He identified himself as an NCO advisor to the armored cavalry troop, and we exchanged a few words over the roar of the engines.

The sergeant advised me in a fatherly manner: "Don't you go into any of them caves capt'n. There's people went in there last year, and never came out." I could tell by the tone of his voice that he was well meaning and dead serious.

"Thanks for the tip Sarge," I replied.

When the column reached a shallow stream, our driver picked up speed and barreled across the muddy bottom, gaining a foothold on the opposite bank with some effort. Two ACAVs behind us were less successful and became mired in the muddy streambed. The cavalrymen quickly attached the steel cables that each vehicle carried to the towing-pintles of the stuck vehicles, and pulled them across to the other side. Having served a tour at Fort Hood as a mechanized infantry platoon leader, I knew the drill all too well. I was wet, cold, and sleepy as the march toward the mountain continued. Every 15 minutes or so, the 16th Regiment's advisors radioed me wanting to know our location and progress. This became annoying after the first few calls. I tried to read my map by flashlight under a poncho, but it was difficult to spot any identifiable terrain features in the flat wet-lands.

Somehow the ACAV column managed to move ahead of the dismounted Ranger companies in the darkness. Night movement by large numbers of troops is difficult to control. U.S. doctrine for a night attack includes provisions for a number of control measures, such as the use of ground guides, phase lines, and check points. The simpler the plan the better, and time permitting, a rehearsal should be conducted. Without these measures, night attacks can easily go awry and this one was no exception.

The mounted column churned to a halt in a swamp laced with meandering streams and canals. The ACAVs formed a circular perimeter, and the Rangers dismounted to secure the final attack position. We waited for the other Ranger companies to arrive. They showed up about an hour later, tired and exhausted after their five-kilometer trek through the muddy wetlands. Lightning flashed across the sky, illuminating the mountains to our south.

The artillery barrage commenced at midnight. Round after round of 105mm and 155mm howitzers shells screamed over our heads and slammed into the limestone mountain. I doubted that the artillery killed many insurgents, knowing full well that except for a few lookouts standing watch on the rocky outcropping, the enemy soldiers were sheltered in the mountain's deep caves. If nothing else, the bombardment ensured that the VC would not get any sleep that night.

The Australian B-57 Canberra bombers arrived on station around 2:00 a.m., their engines barely audible in the cloudy, darkened sky above our heads. The Canberra was designed primarily for bombing from 3,000 feet, but on this night they dropped down below 2,000 feet due to the low cloud cover. The enemy heard their engines and defiantly manned their Chinese .51-caliber machine guns, sending waves of green tracer rounds skyward. It's almost impossible to hit what you can't see, and I thought they were wasting their ammunition. The jet bombers dropped their payloads and roared off into the night as the 750-pound bombs exploded among the rocks atop the mountain. The flashes from the detonating bombs lit the sky like heat lightning on a summer night, and the explosions sounded like thunderbolts. From our location, it was quite a show.

My radio crackled, and the regimental advisor wanted to know our location. I reported that we were in an attack position 1,000 meters from the mountain, but were preparing to move out.

Dai Uy Yen moved out first with his two Ranger companies, once again disappearing into the darkness. After waiting 30 minutes, Major Thi ordered the remainder of the battalion to move out, leaving the ACAVs behind. Once the shooting started, the ACAVs were to move forward and provide fire support with their .50-caliber machine guns. The column moved cautiously through the marsh. I was quickly soaked up to my knees.

After 15 minutes, the major ordered a halt. He huddled beneath a poncho with *Trung Uy* Nghia, his S-3 operations officer, studying a map by flashlight. The battalion's operations officer was a young, slender officer who wore a civilian black raincoat. We were deep in a mangrove swamp and unable to see the mountain that was our objective. It was evident that the major was questioning his S-3 on the direction we were headed. It was a heated discussion, and the major was doing most of the talking. We moved out again, veering off our original course until we reached a small canal. We waded along in the hip-deep canal water. I raised my arms above my head, trying to keep my rifle dry. It was easier going than before. I heard my radio break its silence and looked around for my radio operator, Bui. He was lagging behind two other Rangers who were walking through the canal directly behind me. I didn't want to stop and cause a break in the column, so I ignored the call and trudged on.

As we emerged from the canal and turned south toward our objective, all hell broke loose a few hundred meters ahead of us. I heard the familiar chatter of AK-47 rifle fire, plus RPD machine-gun fire and grenade explosions. The lead two companies had reached the base of the cliff and were being fired on from above.

Major Thi ordered our column to a halt, and I radioed Lieutenant Morris to find out what was going on. Morris reported that he and Sergeant Roberts were pinned down by enemy fire in an area near the base of a cliff with most of *Dai Uy* Yen's two companies. The *Dai Uy* and a group of Rangers were shot off the cliff face shortly after they started their climb. Dragging their dead and wounded, they took cover in a cave at the base of the cliff. Morris wanted to pull back to our location, but I told him to remain where they were and help his counterparts get the situation under control. I then radioed the senior advisor to the regiment to request helicopter gunship support. He indicated a light fire team was on the way.

It was now past daybreak, and suddenly we started taking fire from our rear. It was .50-caliber machine gun fire. The ACAV gunners were trying to put direct fire on the mountain, but some of the rounds were passing a few inches above our heads. I saw one Ranger take a round in his spine before he could flatten himself on the ground. The round severed his spinal column, killing him instantly. I radioed the armored cavalry troop's advisor and told him to cease fire. Major Thi was screaming into his radio at the same time I was, and the tracks soon ceased firing, but the damage was already done. We later learned that one of the troop's .50-caliber machine guns came loose from its mount and was firing erratically.

"You call gunships now *Dai Uy!*" the major requested.

"They're on the way," I replied.

The first gunships to arrive were a pair of U.S. Navy Seawolves, UH-1Bs. The helicopters were armed with two 2.75mm rocket pods, and a machine gun mounted on each side of the aircraft. On the left side was a 7.62 six-barreled Gatling gun mounted on a remote pylon. The left seat pilot controlled this gun while the right door gunner fired a .50-caliber heavy machine gun. The Seawolf lead pilot came up on my radio frequency and asked me to mark the friendly locations and pinpoint the enemy's location.

After "popping" a purple smoke grenade to mark our location, I radioed Lieutenant Morris to do the same.

"Smoke out," I radioed the pilot, "Victor Charlie is on top of the cliffs and on some of the ledges and outcroppings ... there are cave openings all over that mountain, and they have .51-caliber machine guns. Don't get too close, over!"

"Roger, I've got purple smoke. You got no friendlies on that cliff, is that right? Over."

"That's correct, over," I answered.

The Seawolves went to work, and 2.75mm rockets began to slam into the mountain, along with 7.62 and .50-caliber machine-gun slugs. The VC returned fire with RPD and heavy machine guns, narrowly missing the lead ship. The trail ship rolled in to engage the enemy gunners to ensure they didn't get the lead chopper as it rolled out of its run. Then the gunships came around again for another pass.

Under cover of the gunship strikes, Major Thi ordered the forward Ranger companies to withdraw back to our position. *Dai Uy* Yen, still hidden in the cave with the survivors of the climbing party, never got the word. They couldn't get out safely anyway, and would have to wait all day until darkness fell to evacuate their dead and wounded, and perhaps make another effort to climb the cliff face. The attack had begun badly.

Twenty minutes later the leading companies reached our location with their dead and wounded. The first Ranger I saw had been hit with B-40 rocket shrapnel in the thighs and groin. The battalion's doctor, Bac Si, examined the man's private parts, stuffed some gauze into the front of his trousers, and tagged him with a medevac tag. Another soldier assisted him in the walk back to the ACAVs. Groups of wounded continued to arrive, some walking, some on stretchers. After checking their wounds, the medics either bandaged them up and sent them back to their company, or ordered them to the rear. My lieutenant and sergeant arrived with one group. Neither of them was wounded, but they looked spent. Lieutenant Morris said the lead company arrived at the base of the cliff just before dawn.

Dai Uy Yen and a climbing party immediately began to ascend the cliff. The VC spotted them almost immediately and began tossing grenades over the edge of the cliff, and firing down on them with small arms and RPGs. The attack was over before the climbers got 20 feet up the cliff. The Rangers were going to have to find another way to gain the top of the mountain.

Major Thi and his lieutenant conferred over a map as their radios crackled with the sing-song voices of their distant commanders. Thi finally called me over and confided that his Rangers would not climb the northern cliff face of the mountain. Pointing his finger at a map, he traced a route that led out of the swampy area and continued south, paralleling the eastern side of the mountain until he found an area that was climbable. I knew that once we left the mangrove swamp, we'd be sitting ducks for the enemy on the mountaintop, but there weren't any better options.

"What about *Dai Uy* Yen," I asked.

"Never mind *Dai Uy* Yen," Thi snapped. "He hides in cave. Very bad officer."

It was obvious that there was no love lost between the two Vietnamese Ranger officers.

We moved in a single column headed out of the swamp. After only a few minutes, my legs felt like they were made of rubber. The water was up to my knees and I stumbled over submerged roots and vines. Before long, I swallowed half a canteen of water and sucked on a piece of hard candy for energy. Damn soft living in Germany ruined me, I thought, as I struggled along. Thi's operations officer, *Trung Uy* Nghi walked ahead of me, and he moved like a cat without breaking a sweat. Finally, we broke out into the open where the going was slightly easier, as there were fewer roots hidden beneath the water in the waist-high marsh grass.

During a short halt, I refilled my canteens in a bomb crater filled with milky, tepid water. After dropping a couple of iodine tablets into my canteen I quenched my thirst, but the water left an iodine and cordite aftertaste in my mouth. The column began to move again.

Moments later the VC spotted us and sniper fire erupted from the mountain. We were out of maximum-effective range for their AK-47s, but they had snipers armed with SKS rifles, a more accurate weapon at longer ranges. With telescopic scopes, they were deadly accurate. A Ranger a few yards ahead of me took a head shot that blew his brains out. A mixture of gray matter, blood, and bone fragments blew from his head as he pitched sideways. I crouched down in the waist-high marsh grass, not wanting to be the sniper's next kill. Two Rangers grabbed the dead soldier's rifle and web gear, while two others picked up the body and continued on through the mud-bottom marsh. I shoved my map case under my fatigue shirt, so as not to stand out as an officer.

Bui, my radio operator, was still keeping his distance from me. He'd switched antennas on the radio, replacing the long antenna with the short whip to avoid detection by the snipers. Major Thi's radio operators kept the long antennas on their radios; I kept my distance from them. At 500-plus yards, there was no point in returning fire. Besides, the snipers were firing from covered and concealed positions among the numerous rock outcroppings on the mountain, and were almost impossible to spot.

Lieutenant Morris and Sergeant Roberts were moving toward the rear of the column. If I got hit, I hoped they'd radio for a medevac chopper. I radioed Morris to ensure they knew correct frequency. Glancing to the east, I saw that the ACAVs were paralleling our route about a half a kilometer away. The stretcher-bearers carrying the wounded began to veer off toward the ACAVs. Moments later, the vehicles came to a halt and took up firing positions facing toward the mountain. The 106mm recoilless rifle track moved forward to a firing position and fired a HEAT round at a cave entrance halfway up the mountain slope. The gun roared and the round slammed into the slope above the cave entrance, sending a shower of rocks down the mountain. As the gunner was loading another shell, the VC returned fire with two RPG rounds aimed at the 106mm track. The rounds fell way short, but the driver of the ACAV put his vehicle in reverse and rolled back another 200 yards to ensure he was out of harms way.

Major Thi began moving our column closer to the mountain. To our south, I could see groups of Vietnamese soldiers clustered around some rocks about 50 yards up a slope. There was a gaping cave entrance nearby. The mountainside was slightly concave and the enemy atop the mountain could not fire directly down at the attackers. The soldiers clustered among the rocks were from the 16th Regiment, whose mission was to attack and seize the southern portion of the mountain. Major Thi saw them too, and he ordered his Rangers forward toward the rocks. I pushed myself beyond the point of exhaustion as we closed the distance to the base of the mountain. Near the base, we skirted around two huge 750-pound bomb craters. Apparently, not all the Aussie bombs were on target. Finally, we reached some cover among some large boulders right at the mountain base. I don't know if the huge boulders were blown down the mountainside during the bombing, or were the result of an earlier rockslide. The area reminded me of the Devil's Den and forward slope of Little Roundtop on the Gettysburg battlefield.

Moving up the slope, we finally made it to the cave entrance where the 9th ARVN Division infantrymen were clustered among the rocks. There were smiles on their faces, and they traded insults with the

Rangers since they had gained the first foothold on the mountain. Major Thi wasn't smiling and his glare soon silenced the men.

I sat down on a flat rock and checked my map. I knew we had crossed the boundary meant to separate the Ranger sector from the 9th Division sector, but Major Thi apparently didn't give a damn, and at this point neither did I. Boundaries were established primarily to control and coordinate supporting fires, and in reality are nothing more than grease pencil lines drawn on a map. Our primary mission was to seize the northern portion of the mountaintop; how we gained the heights mattered little at that point in time.

My head began to ache as I sat in the hot sun. I was thirsty, but my canteens were empty. Yon, my batboy, pointed toward the cave entrance and said, "*Dai Uy, Nuc!*" I knew what *nuc* meant; it was the Vietnamese word for water. Yon and I walked toward the cave to fill our canteens. Inside the mouth of the cave was a rather large room that was close enough to the entrance to allow in sunlight. The roof of the cave was about 15 feet high, with limestone stalactites dropping down from the ceiling. Several Rangers were catching the drippings from the stalactites. It was damp and cool in the cave, and I noticed some ashes from a recent VC campfire on the floor. There were some small tunnel entrances at the back of the cave, just large enough for a small person to squeeze through on his belly. The Rangers displayed little interest in these natural escape tunnels.

I caught a few drips of water from one of the stalactites and tasted it. The water was cool, but had a bitter-lime taste. I left Yon to fill our canteens and walked out of the cave, where I saw Lieutenant Morris and Sergeant Roberts conversing with two advisors from the ARVN infantry battalion, a heavy-set captain and a middle-aged sergeant. They both wore flak jackets and looked more bushed than we were. We had left our flak jackets behind in the trailer, as they were too heavy as far as I was concerned. I joined the conversation and we discussed our progress thus far. Having wished the pair luck, I walked over to Major Thi's location to figure out our next move.

As the Major and I studied his map, we were suddenly distracted by the shouts of the Rangers and infantrymen. They were pointing toward a lone figure that was moving among the rocks 100 or so meters to our south. The man reached the bottom of the mountain, and started running through the marsh grass toward a canal 200 meters away. We could clearly see he was wearing black pajamas, with a pistol belt around his waste. A couple of hand grenades were hanging from his waist, but he was carrying no other weapons. He was obviously a VC.

The enemy soldier stopped for a second when he heard the shouting and stared up at us, then took off again. The Rangers and infantrymen opened fire on the man. Miraculously, the volley of fire from more than 100 soldiers didn't hit him—I was astounded by their poor marksmanship. Finally, one of the Rangers found his mark and the VC went down in the marsh grass. I thought it was all over, but the man popped up again and made a dash for the canal. There were some bushes growing along the canal bank and if he reached them, he could slip into the canal and make his escape. The soldiers opened up once more and again he went down, only to appear once again. I've always sort of favored the underdog. In this case, the VC was probably in the process of deserting his unit, and he posed no threat to us. I began to hope the poor bastard would reach the safety of the canal.

About that time, Major Thi was getting a little bent out of shape about the marksmanship in his battalion and ordered his operations sergeant, a mean looking Cambodian, to take a small patrol and run the VC down. By this time, the wounded VC started running in circles in the marsh grass, trying to get his bearings.

The Ranger patrol got on line and began to sweep through the grass toward him, all the while firing short bursts from the hip. The VC got no support from his buddies on the mountaintop, where they were no doubt watching the whole episode. This convinced me even more that the man was a deserter. He finally went down about five feet short of the canal. As the Rangers cautiously approached him, there was a muffled explosion that lifted the man's body from the grass. The VC had pulled the pin from one of the grenades he was carrying and shoved it under his body as he fell. They stripped what was left of the body and tossed the corpse into the canal as the other Rangers cheered. Just to let us know the truce was over, the VC on the mountaintop started firing on the patrol as the Rangers dashed back toward the rocks.

That was one of the few times I actually caught more than a fleeting glimpse of an enemy soldier over the next weeks. A few years later, I talked to one of my uncles who fought as a 19-year-old Marine on Iwo Jima. My uncle said that he saw only a few Japanese during the fighting, since they fought from their caves during the day, inflicting terrible casualties on the attacking Marines. They almost always launched their Banzai attacks at night. Since he had a few scars to prove it, I took him at his word. He also said that the Japanese always fought to the death; surrender was not in their playbook.

Major Thi called me over and pointed to a break in the cliffs that led to a saddle in the mountaintop. I'd spotted the same area on our aerial reconnaissance the day before. The slope was steep and pocked with boulders, but it was not so impossible a climb as it appeared from the air. It was a stairway, but not an easy one to ascend, particularly when the guys at the top were shooting at you.

The major intended to send a patrol up the slope to seize the saddle. Once that was secure, the battalion would follow. He wanted me to radio for gunships to keep the VC on the mountaintop busy while his men maneuvered up the slope. It was a gamble, but there were no other viable options. I radioed the regimental advisers to request the gunship support. Thus far, they had provided excellent support.

The Ranger patrol wound its way up the slope, exchanging shots with a small group of VC who were firing from positions in the rocky saddle. The large rocks and boulders that lay strewn along the slope offered the soldiers excellent cover, and they knew how to use the tactic of fire and movement to seize the saddle. An air-cavalry fire team arrived and I directed their attack. The OH-6 scout helicopters spotted the enemy positions for the circling AH-1 Cobra gunships, which then swooped in low and fast to strafe the mountain top with rockets and mini-gun fire. The VC opened fire at the Cobras as they rolled in on their targets, but with their thin fuselages the attack helicopters were difficult to hit head on. The critical moment came after the pilot flew over the target and went into a steep turn, gaining altitude. That's when the trail ship had to be in position to cover the lead ship with its fires. I watched the strikes with great admiration for the Cobra pilots and their gunners.

As the Ranger patrol assaulted the enemy in the saddle, driving them down the steep, almost vertical, western slope of the mountain, Major Thi ordered the remainder of the soldiers to move out. We began to ascend the slope. Halfway up I could feel my thigh muscles tightening, and I had to stop every ten yards or so to catch my breath before continuing. Stepping over even the smallest of rocks was an exhausting effort, and it took all my resolve to toil upward a few yards at a time.

When we reached the saddle, the Ranger patrol was still blasting away with rifle and M-79 grenade fire, trying to drop the retreating VC. The enemy soldiers knew the mountain like the back of their hands and they soon disappeared like rats, crawling into small cave entrances on the rocky mountainside.

I peered down the western slope that was much steeper than the one we had just climbed. Looking across the valley, I had a good view of the mountain to our west and the Gulf of Thailand. The Rangers began consolidating their positions on the mountain.

The gunships shifted their strikes to the western slope of the mountain. An enemy machine gun returned fire from the rocks near the base of the slope, shattering the canopy of the lead Cobra gunship, but missing the pilot and gunner. I borrowed an M-79 grenade launcher from one of the Rangers and fired several 40mm grenades at the enemy position. The machine gun went silent, and the OH-6 scout helicopters flew over the position and drew no fire.

Our position in the saddle was little more than a notch in the mountain's rocky, zigzagging spine. The rocky shelf we had seized was about 150 square feet, and on the north and south sides were steep rock walls that led to the highest points on the mountain. The wall leading up to our south was about 25 feet, and to our north was a steeper cliff, about 45 feet, that went almost straight up. I was convinced that experienced climbers could scale both cliffs. Since Major Thi had decided to set up his CP in the saddle, he was going to have to get some men up both those cliffs. Otherwise, our position was untenable, since the enemy could crawl to the top edges of these cliffs and drop grenades down among us. The gunships had kept the VC pinned down, but once the attack helicopters left station, the VC would likely mount a counterattack to drive us from the mountain.

Major Thi agreed with my assessment and ordered his Rangers to scale both rock walls.

The commanders selected their most agile climbers to scale the cliffs. Each of the men carried a length of rope that would be secured to the top of the cliff and dropped over the ledge to assist follow-on climbers. With their M-16 rifles and coils of rope slung over their shoulders, they began to ascend the cliffs. Moving from handhold to toehold, they felt their way up the steep cliffs. Both teams reached the top and disappeared over the ledges. Seconds later, the Rangers atop the cliffs tossed their ropes to the climbers waiting below. Thus far, not a shot had been fired. Apparently, the VC thought the cliffs were unassailable. Additional squads of Rangers began to climb and most were skilled and swift, their light, sinewy frames being ideal for this sort of thing. After each squad reached the top they hauled their rucksacks up by rope, along with their M-60 machine guns. The Rangers now had toeholds on both sides of the mountaintop and our position was relatively secure, except for mortar and recoilless rifle fire from the adjacent mountain.

Major Thi's small command group began setting up in the saddle. The platoons and squads that had not scaled the cliffs took up positions on the slope that we had just climbed. The major's batboys strung a poncho about a foot and a half off the ground, lining the earth beneath it with straw mats and a U.S. air mattress. The major took off his fatigues and crawled into the shelter for his mid-afternoon nap.

By now the sun had broken through the clouds and was shining on the western slope of the mountain, turning the dark purple hues of the gullies and defiles into shades of lavender and blue. Heat rose from the rocky shelf and cliffs, and the mountain to our west seemed to shimmer in the superheated atmosphere.

Yon dug into my rucksack and using my poncho, began to rig a similar shelter for me. Since I didn't carry an air mattress, I told him to string my Vietnamese nylon hammock low to the ground under the poncho. I'd had the hammock made in Can Tho and used it throughout my tour. Yon strung it low to the ground, securing the suspension lines to a rock on one end, and a stubby dead tree on the other.

Yon then began preparing our evening meal, cooking over a small stove made from a C-ration can and some heat tablets that he found in my rucksack. He also found a small jar of instant coffee that I'd purchased in the Eakin Compound PX. After pouring about six teaspoons of the instant coffee into a canteen cup of boiling water, he tasted the brew, then added another two teaspoons. "Whoa, beaucoup strong!" I scolded him. I never could break him of that habit, even after I showed him how to measure the crystals using a plastic spoon.

Yon also discovered a small transistor radio that I carried. He smiled like a kid who just found his present under the Christmas tree. Putting it next to his ear, he turned it on, and tuned it to a Cambodian radio station. Later, he jerry-rigged a field expedient antenna for the radio, and wired it to a PRC-25 radio battery. From our mountain, the radio could then pull in stations as far away as Saigon, including the Armed Forces Network (AFN) station. Every morning, I listened to Cronauer's morning wake-up call, "Gooood morninng Vietnaaam!"

As darkness enshrouded the mountain, I crawled into my hammock for a few minutes of sleep. It started to rain, and I had the feeling that it was going to be a long first night on the mountain; I wasn't wrong.

Around midnight, the VC to our west began registering their 82mm mortars on our position. Since the saddle was very narrow in width, it was a difficult target for the VC mortars. Despite the high-angle trajectory of the mortar shells, the rounds either fell short or overshot our position, exploding among the boulders on the slopes. If a single round exploded in the saddle it would have killed all of us, since it was impossible to dig foxholes in the limestone rock. The shelling lasted about 30 minutes, wounding four Rangers on the eastern slope of the mountain. I tried to pinpoint the mortar positions on the mountain opposite us, but couldn't determine their exact location. Nevertheless, I called for counter-battery artillery fires on a suspected firing location in the "punchbowl" of the adjacent mountain.

It began to rain heavily, and sheets of rain blown by a brisk, westerly breeze swept through the saddle. As lighting streaked across the pitch-black sky, I could barely make out the silhouettes of the ACAVs parked in the wetlands to the east.

Thunderclaps, much louder than the exploding mortar shells,

shook the mountain. I must be an idiot, I thought to myself. I could be drinking beer at the Oktoberfest in Munich. Beneath my hammock, I could hear Yon playing my transistor radio on low volume. I could barely make out the refrain of the tune, *Detroit City*: "*I wanna go home, I wanna go home, O how I wanna go home.*" I wondered if he grasped the meaning of the words.

About 2 a.m., we began receiving 75mm recoilless rifle fire from our friends on the mountain opposite us. One round slammed into a rock outcropping about 20 feet above our heads, showering us with fragments of rock and hot bits of shrapnel. I wasn't hit, but looking up at my poncho shelter, I saw several holes. I reached under the hammock and shook Yon, who was curled up underneath. "Yon, Yon, ok?" I whispered. "Ok, Ok, *Dai Uy*," he replied. Then I then realized that my body would have protected him from any shrapnel, just like a layer of sandbags.

The shelling was followed by the sharp crack of AK-47 fire on top of the cliffs above us, followed by bursts of automatic M-16 fire. The VC was trying to drive the Rangers atop the spine of the mountain back over the cliffs. The situation suddenly became very serious, so I radioed the regimental advisers to request a flare ship and gunships. I was told that there were "Black Ponies" on strip alert at Binh Thuy that could respond.

"What are Black Ponies?" I queried the voice on the other end of my radio, "Never heard of them, over."

"They're Navy fixed-wing OV-10 aircraft modified to carry machine guns, rockets, and flares, and they fly a helluva lot faster than helicopters," he answered, adding, "and they'll fly in just about any kind of weather, over."

"Scramble them, over," I answered.

About 20 minutes later, I heard the whine of the OV-10 engines in the darkened sky above. My radio crackled to life.

"Gallant Bishop, this is Black Pony 19, over."

"Black Pony one-niner, this Gallant Bishop," I replied.

"Good evening Sir, this is Black Pony one-niner. We're five minutes from your location, how can we assist you? Over."

I'd worked with all types of Army and Air Force air support during my first tour in Vietnam, and I'd never heard any pilot talk so calm, cool, collected, and politely on the radio. It had a calming effect on me.

"This is Gallant Bishop, we're taking recoilless rifle fire, mortar fire, and small arms fire. We're located two and a half miles south of the cement plant on Nui Ba Voi." I continued.

"Roger sir, we're familiar with that area. Can you mark your position, sir?" the lead pilot asked.

"Affirmative, I have a strobe light, over."

"Roger, and where the friendlies are, over."

I radioed a description of where the Ranger companies were located, and the suspected VC positions on both mountains.

"Can your friendlies mark their positions, over?"

"Affirmative. They'll have to use trip flares, over."

"Roger sir, I've got your strobe."

By this time the two Black Pony OV-10s were orbiting over the mountain dropping illumination flares that cast long shadows among the rocks. I asked Major Thi to have his Rangers mark their positions with trip flares.

On their first pass, the lead OV-10 drew a steam of green tracers as he pulled out of his strafing run. The sister ship spotted the source of fire and dove on the enemy machine gun and its crew, firing two salvos of rockets. The drill was repeated several times, and I'm sure we knocked out at least one of the machine guns. I then directed the Black Ponies to the punch bowl area on the opposite mountain. The lead aircraft made a low pass trying to draw fire, but the enemy were silent. They're back in their caves I thought. The Ponies stuck around for a while, dropping flares until they began to run low on fuel. Finally, the lead pilot radioed me to let me know they were leaving station.

"Gallant Bishop this is Pony one-niner. We're departing the area. We have another team of ponies on call if you require further assistance, Sir."

"Black Pony one-niner this is Gallant Bishop. No, that's not necessary. I'd like to buy you guys a beer if I ever get up your way, over."

"Glad we could be of assistance Sir. Call us if you need us. Have a good night, out."

Hand salute to the U.S. Navy Black Ponies, I said to myself.

* * *

The next morning, Yon cooked some rice and I sipped a canteen cup of coffee that he'd prepared. The brew was still too strong, but it cleared my head. Major Thi moved his command post area to a narrow ledge about ten meters down the mountain, and wanted me to do the same. I saw there wasn't room, and besides, I wasn't about to roll off that ledge in my sleep and kill myself in a 15-foot fall. Even to reach his new location, I had to climb down some tricky rocks to his mountain perch.

Later that morning I directed two air strikes on the other mountain. Thi called me over to his CP to announce that *Dai Uy* Yen and his men had left their cave under the cover of darkness, and climbed the sheer northern cliff face. As a result of *Dai Uy* Yen's daring feat, the Ranger battalion now had a foothold on both ends of their portion of the mountain. For the moment at least, the *Dai Uy* had redeemed himself with Major Thi.

About 3 o'clock that same afternoon, the outpost on the cliff top to our south was ready to be relieved. Replacements scaled the cliffs using ropes, and those who had spent the night atop the cliff began to descend, hand over hand, on the same ropes. I watched as the first Ranger started down. Suddenly, a machine gun raked the cliff face from across the valley. The soldier slipped from the rope, and I watched bone chips and brain explode from his head. He fell about six feet, and his body came to rest on a ledge directly above us. The next man in line peered over the edge, preparing to make his descent. The shouts of his comrades below warned him of his folly, and he backed off the edge of the cliff. The soldier's lifeless body stayed on the ledge until darkness fell. Two of his buddies climbed up the ledge and brought his body down into the saddle, where they laid the corpse on a stretcher and wrapped it in a poncho. The dead soldier's comrades kept a death vigil beside his body that night.

In the faint light of the coming dawn, the Rangers carried their comrade's body down the mountain. The only traces that remained of the soldier were some dried blood and brain matter that had drained from his head onto some rocks beneath the stretcher. Flies buzzed around the mess until the battalion's *Bac Si,* senior medic, doused it with lighter fluid and struck a match burning, away all traces of the fallen warrior. The battle continued.

CHAPTER 5

"DON'T LET THE SUN CATCH YOU CRYING"

The bloody, life-and-death struggle for control of Nui Bai Voi and its cave complexes continued through October. As the Ranger casualties continued to mount, Major Thi became less and less aggressive in pressing the attacks on the VC, who continued to fight from their caves. It was apparent that Thi was under significant pressure from the 4th Ranger Group commander to minimize his losses. Using the battalions ANGRC/87 Radio Set, MajorThi was able to send and receive messages from his boss in Can Tho. I really had to push him to try to break the stalemate on the mountain.

After two weeks of heavy fighting, we knew that a major VC strongpoint on the mountain was a cave on the eastern slope of the mountain. The mouth of the cave was about halfway between the base and the top of the mountain. For days, helicopter gunships dueled with the VC anti-aircraft gunners firing from positions near the mouth of the cave. The gunship pilots and their gunners were never successful in firing a rocket directly into the cave's entrance. There were some close misses that impacted into the limestone cliffs, but there was never a direct hit. In addition to those gunship strikes, the armored cav troops' 106mm recoilless rifle track fired round after round at the cave, never scoring a direct hit. The damn thing probably wasn't properly bore sighted, I thought. The .50-caliber spotting rifle mounted on top of the gun was accurate to a range of 1,100 meters, and if both the main gun and the spotting rifle were properly aligned, the gunner should have been able to put a 106mm high-explosive round right into the mouth of the cave. I doubted if the Vietnamese knew how to properly bore sight the weapon system. It was a rare occasion to see an ARVN officer inspecting individual or crew served weapons.

From the mouth of the cave, the enemy could also pick off the stretcher-bearers carrying the dead and wounded off the mountain. The VC snipers were also able to pick off the Rangers who were detailed to carry supplies up the mountain. Sampans transported the supplies from the village down the canal to a drop off point near the mountain. The ACAVs then transported the supplies to a position near the base of the mountain, where they were met by soldiers who carried the supplies back up the mountain. The sniper fire was deadly accurate, and almost every kill was a headshot. The cave had to be cleared of enemy by a ground assault—there was no way around it.

I conferred with Major Thi, trying to convince him that the VC in the cave were costing him more casualties than any other enemy position on the mountain. He argued that a direct frontal assault was impossible, either from the top of the mountain with the Rangers rappelling down to the cave mouth, or attacking up the cliff from the base. In either case, he argued that the VC would easily pick off his men. I suggested that we could use smoke to conceal the attackers, but Major Thi believed that smoke would give the VC a warning that an attack was underway and eliminate the possibility of surprise. After reviewing all options, we both agreed that the only chance of success was a night attack by a small group of handpicked Rangers. *Dai Uy* Yen was the most qualified officer to lead the attack, but Yen had been wounded the day before and evacuated. The major assigned the mission to *Thieu Uy* Hop's 1st Ranger Company.

The 1st Ranger Company commander selected about two dozen of his best men for the night assault that he would personally lead. The men would only carry their M-16 rifles, hand grenades, and LAWs; rucksacks, flak vests, protective masks, and any other items that would rattle, jangle, or reflect light were left behind. Noise and light discipline were critical to achieve the element of surprise. I concluded that the assault had a 50/50 chance of success.

Taking advantage of a cloudy, rainy night, the Rangers quietly began to climb toward the cave entrance. I made sure that no artillery flares were fired as the phantom- like figures climbed the mountain slope. After a 45-minute climb, the soldiers reached the mouth of the cave without being detected. They entered the cave and cautiously inched their way forward in the pitch-black darkness. As the attackers crept forward, they heard geese hissing and chickens squawking. Suddenly, an RPG round whooshed out of the dark recesses of the cave and exploded near the entrance, wounding the six men who were inside the cave. The rocket blast was followed by bursts of AK-47 fire. The soldiers began to withdraw, dragging their dead and wounded with them. The attack was repelled, and the assault team quickly retreated down the steep slope amid a hail of small-arms fire. Two Rangers were killed, and seven more were wounded in the failed assault.

It was later determined that the Rangers entered one of the main entrances of the Mo So cave complex that housed the VC headquarters in the Kien Luong District. In addition to the main entrance, there were numerous small entrances located all over the mountain that were connected to tunnels leading to the inner recesses of the mountain. Therefore, the enemy was able to pop-up in any number of locations on the mountain to engage the Rangers at will. Under the cover of darkness, it was not difficult for small groups of enemy soldiers to escape the mountains, and similarly it was possible for reinforcements to slip undetected into the cave-riddled mountains.

The caverns were large enough to accommodate a VC regiment, and the caves were fully stocked with enough supplies and food, including live poultry and hogs, to sustain a large force for months at a time. The cave was recognized as a historic relic in April 1995, by the Vietnamese Ministry of Culture and Information. A modern-day tourist guide now invites tourists to take "a two-hour, five-kilometer walk through shrimp breeding grounds, paddy fields, and canals to reach the magnificent cave." A more recent guide advises the traveler that, "a new road has been built right to the cave entrance." We had no idea of the size and complexity of these caves in 1970, but the Communists certainly did.

Two nights later, the soldiers mounted another attack. Sentries at the cave entrance spotted the soldiers as they maneuvered up the steep slope in the darkness, and tossed several grenades down the slope. To our complete surprise, some of the grenades were CS gas grenades. The soldiers were not carrying protective masks and retreated down the slope, choking on the fumes. A breeze blew a cloud of the gas toward our location, and I suddenly regretted leaving my M-17 Protective Mask back at the village. I took a cloth handkerchief, soaked it in water from my canteen, and placed it over my nose and mouth. That worked fairly well, but I could feel the gas burning the skin on my face and forearms. It only lasted a minute or two, but we got the message. The VC had a stockpile of all types of ammunition in the cave.

During the first week of October, Lieutenant Colonel Witek, the 4th Ranger Group Senior Advisor, flew over the mountain in his UH-1D command and control ship and radioed me to mark my location with smoke. He'd come to pick up Lieutenant Morris, who was being reassigned to Chi Lang. Morris was near the end of his 12-month tour and the colonel wanted him moved out of harms way. The lieutenant quickly gathered up his gear and prepared to head down the mountain. Before he departed, I gave him a daily journal that I kept during the operation and instructed him to deliver it to Lieutenant Colonel Witek.

The chopper landed in the lowlands near the ACAV lager area and the lieutenant climbed aboard. It was the last time I ever saw him. Sergeant Roberts and I were the only Ranger advisors remaining on the mountain.

Two days after Lieutenant Morris was extracted, the Ranger battalion experienced a terrible tragedy. About 4 p.m. of that blistering-hot day, most of the Rangers were trying to find some shade on the mountainside. Some napped in the shade of large boulders, while others lay beneath their poncho shelters. Nothing much was going on and all was quiet. Suddenly, two jet fighters dove out of the sky, releasing their bombs on the 1st Ranger Company. Six men were killed and several more were wounded. Major Thi screamed at me from his location to stop the air strike. He apparently thought that I was directing the strike, and that the aircraft were U.S. jets. He was wrong on both counts. The aircraft were Vietnamese Air Force (VNAF) jets. I pointed out their markings to Major Thi and, still furious, he radioed the ARVN regimental headquarters to get them to contact the aircraft and abort the mission. As far as I knew, there was no forward air controller in our area at that time, so I concluded that the VNAF aircraft were just dumping their ordnance before returning to base. The Vietnamese pilot had not cleared their strike on the mountain with anyone.

The U.S. advisors with the ARVN regiment could not provide information on the strike; they knew nothing about it. It was Lieutenant Morris' good fortune that he'd been extracted, since he'd been with 1st Ranger company during most of the operation.

The longer we stayed on the mountain, the more sanitation and hygiene became a problem. There were no areas where slit trenches could be dug in the rocky ground, and the soldiers relieved themselves wherever they could find cover. Drinking water was also a major problem, because no supply of fresh water was moved forward to the mountain. Our only sources of water were the rain-filled bomb craters at the base of the mountain. The Rangers organized water patrols that carried empty canteens down to the craters during the hours of darkness; it was too dangerous during daylight due to the snipers.

Sergeant Roberts and I drank the water after purifying it with iodine tables, or boiling it our canteen cups—it tasted awful in either case. In spite of these precautions, Roberts came down with a serious fever. Late one afternoon, I noticed that his face was taut and sallow, and by nightfall his temperature soared well above 100 degrees. The Vietnamese doctor examined him, and we all knew that he'd have to be evacuated from the mountain the next day. The Vietnamese doctor thought it might be typhus, so I asked the sergeant when he had his last typhoid shot, and he replied: "Well...ah... I can't really recollect Sir," adding, "maybe when I was with the Wolfhounds in '68. I don't care much about gettin stuck with them needles."

The next morning, accompanied by two Rangers, Sergeant Roberts stumbled down the mountain and out into the wetlands, where a medevac chopper picked him up. Roberts later told me that when he reached the hospital, he was running a temperature of 104 degrees, and medics quickly put him in a series of ice baths to bring down his fever. Roberts stayed in the hospital for several weeks and nearly lost his life to what the American doctors referred to as, "a fever of unknown origin."

After Sergeant Roberts was evacuated, I was the only American adviser with the battalion for several days. By that time, I trusted the soldiers to watch my back, but I still worried about what would happen if I was seriously wounded and couldn't radio for my own medevac. My fears were allayed a couple of days later when Lieutenant Colonel Witek flew to the area to insert another Ranger advisor, Specialist Gary Lockwood. Gary had completed a tour with the U.S. 4th Infantry Division, and for some reason had extended to serve as a Ranger advisor.

I watched as the new arrival climbed the mountain in the stifling afternoon heat and noted that he moved agilely, taking advantage of the cover and concealment afforded by the boulders on the slope. Lockwood had the instinctive knowledge of the ground that only a natural born infantryman possesses. When he arrived at my position, I saw that he was very young, probably about 20 years of age, with still-boyish features. I was impressed that he was not overly taxed by the long climb. Although he wore neither jump wings nor a Ranger tab on his uniform, he did wear a Combat Infantry Badge (CIB), and that was good enough for me. Gary Lockwood was an infantryman, and a good one at that. I didn't have the time to retrain or baby-sit a typist or supply room clerk, and if they sent me one of those, I'd have sent him back to Can Tho on the next flight out. After briefing the new arrival on the battalion and on-going operation, I spent the rest of the afternoon reading and rereading the stack of letters from home that Gary delivered to me. When I finished, I burned them all. Gary took to the younger Vietnamese Rangers right off the bat, and they liked him as well. He was a welcome addition to the team.

* * *

By mid-October, we were still on the mountain trying to root the VC out of their caves, and losing a few men every day. The ARVN infantry battalions to our south weren't making much progress either. On 16 October, after tuning my transistor radio to the AFN station, I heard that the Baltimore Orioles had won the 1970 World Series, sweeping the series from the Cincinnati Reds. I didn't feel sorry for the Reds, since they'd defeated my beloved Pittsburgh Pirates in the National League playoff. Later that same day, I left the mountain for the first time to attend a meeting of all U.S. senior advisors involved in the operation. Lieutenant Colonel Witek was to be in attendance as well.

I didn't have any problems during my extraction by helicopter. After a trek down the mountain, I slogged east through the marshy lowlands until I was out of small arms range of the mountain. Then I radioed for a helicopter to pick me up. I didn't learn much at the meeting, except that the 44th Ranger Battalion was scheduled to be relieved by the end of the month. After the meeting, I gave Witek my personal assessment of the operation.

I told the colonel that in my opinion, it would take more than one ARVN regiment reinforced by a Ranger battalion to clear the two mountains. This size force was insufficient to cordon off the two mountains and simultaneously clear them. I remained convinced that the enemy was able to reinforce and resupply the units defending the two mountain bastions. There was never a concerted effort to cut off the enemy's routes of reinforcement or retreat. Carl Von Clausewitz devoted a chapter in his book *On War* to attacks on a mountainous area. In that chapter he wrote that, "The fastest way of getting results is always to give the enemy reason to fear having his line of retreat cut...one must therefore aim at really cutting him off." In the case of Nui Bai Voi, this could have been accomplished with the commitment of a division-size force, but not with a reinforced regiment. I think the colonel agreed with me, but the ARVN generals thought otherwise.

After receiving new SOIs (signal frequency and code information) for our radio communications, I boarded Witek's Huey, along with Ranger Eddy Moreno and a couple of Vietnamese Ranger officers who had flown in with the colonel for the meeting.

The C&C ship flew south toward the mountain, and Lieutenant Colonel Witek ordered the pilot to land the ship about 100 meters from the base of the mountain. I was seated on the floor of the ship with no safety belt, and the Huey's doors were wide open. When I saw where the ship was heading, I shouted over the roar of the Huey's engine to Witek that we were too close to the mountain, and the cave that was giving us so much trouble was just up the mountain from the landing zone. My warnings came too late; the VC opened up on the C&C ship with a 12.75mm machine gun. I could hear the rounds ripping though the tail boom of the aircraft. When the pilot banked sharply to the right in an attempt to gain altitude, machine gun rounds began piercing the underbelly of the aircraft, wounding one of the Vietnamese officers in the foot. At the same time, because the ship was in such a steep bank, I was sliding across the floor toward the open door. We were a couple of hundred feet in the air, and I could see the emerald-green marsh grass below. I thought I'd had it as I neared the door, trying to grab hold of something. Suddenly, someone grabbed the cross strap on my web gear that ran horizontally across my back, and I stopped inches from the door. My guardian angel that day was Ranger Eddy Moreno, who shouted at me, "Where you tryin' to go *Dai Uy*, you got no parachute."

The pilot gained control of the Huey and made a low-level beeline back to the regimental CP landing pad, where we landed safely. I checked myself out to see if I'd been hit, or if I needed to change my shorts. The boom of the helicopter was riddled with holes, and there were two holes in the floor of the troop compartment. Witek had to radio for a replacement ship and we spent the night with the regimental advisors. The following day we flew the same mission with a replacement ship, only this time Witek ordered the pilot to land far out into the wetlands, which he did without incident.

I jumped out of the chopper as it hovered above the marsh grass, hoping Major Thi was watching my insertion from the mountain. There was no way I could radio Specialist Lockwood, since I left our only radio with him when I left the mountain. At the same time, I was also hoping the VC snipers were napping. As the chopper flew off, I was on my own in the marsh. I made my way slowly through the chest-high marsh grass, deliberately not walking in a straight line. Every 30 yards or so, I squatted down in the grass to confuse any sniper who might have me in his sights, waiting for me to come within range. Then, I began to worry about the Rangers who might mistake me for a VC as I approached one of their outposts at the base of the mountain. I never felt so alone. Fortunately, Major Thi watched the whole episode from his rocky ledge on the mountainside, and sent a patrol down the mountain to meet me. Yon, my batboy, was with the patrol and he took my rucksack for the climb back up the mountain. At least I'd had a couple of good meals and a beer or two during my one day off the mountain, but that's about all I accomplished.

A couple of days later, Major Thi wanted to see if we could direct some helicopter rocket fire into that large cave entrance. We moved to a position below the entrance, and to my knowledge that was the first time Major Thi left his CP area. Accompanied by a squad of Rangers, the major and I and his radio operators made our way to a forward position. I brought along Buey, my own radio operator. I'd alerted a U.S. gunship team that was working the area and they flew toward our position. After I pointed out the target, they had no problem identifying it from the air. I popped a yellow smoke grenade to mark our location, just to let them know where we were in relation to the cave. The lead ship headed straight for the cave, unleashing a salvo of 2.75-inch rockets directed straight at its mouth. One of the rockets went haywire and veered off course—they can be erratic at times—and slammed into some rock right next to us. Unfortunately, one of the Rangers was severely wounded with shrapnel and I cancelled the rest of the strike. The incident wasn't the fault of the gunship crews, or anyone else. Fortunately, Major Thi understood this.

* * *

As the end of the month approached, the rainy season was on the wane. There were sporadic downpours, but on some nights we actually saw the stars and moon. The situation on the mountain was a stalemate. The Rangers tried every trick in the book to drive the VC from the caves. I began to think of the cavernous mountain as a treacherous living thing out to destroy us all. Only by burning out its guts could we kill the beast. I was convinced that flame weapons were the solution, but my repeated requests for flamethrowers went unanswered. I'd read somewhere that the Marines on Iwo poured barrels of gasoline down into the Japanese caves, but we had no barrels or gasoline. Lobbing a napalm canister from a jet into the mouth of a cave on an almost vertical cliff face was also so statistically improbable, so we didn't try it. Besides, the flaming napalm would likely spread all over the mountain face and take out some friendlies. We did capture some smaller caves, but the Rangers never were able to penetrate the primary cave system.

One day during our last week on the mountain, a U.S. Navy destroyer arrived on station, just off shore to our west in the Gulf of

Thailand. We could even see it from our mountain. The Navy wanted to shell the mountain with its five-inch guns. Not having any experience with naval gunfire, I decided to select a target on the mountain opposite us. We were still taking mortar and recoilless rifle fire from that adjacent mountain. The Navy destroyer had a forward observer in a fixed wing observation aircraft to direct its fire on specific targets. I radioed to give him the grid coordinates of a couple of targets on the adjacent mountain.

Naval gunfire is exceedingly accurate, but has a low-angle trajectory, almost direct fire. Deflection is almost never a problem with naval gunfire, but range can be. The airborne FAC passed the list of targets to the destroyer's fire direction center, and seconds later we heard the "boom" of the ships five-inch guns. They overshot the target and hit our mountain. Fortunately, the rounds exploded on the western slope where the Rangers had no outposts.

"The FAC radioed me and said, "Any friendlies hit down there, over."

"That's a negative, but you hit the wrong mountain," I answered.

"I know, but the next salvo will be right on target."

I guess the gun crews used fewer powder bags on the next salvo, or whatever they do to adjust for range, because the next salvo was right on target. Nonetheless, I concluded that howitzers, because of their high-angle fire, are much more useful than naval gunfire in mountainous terrain.

* * *
•

Finally, after 28 long days and nights, Major Thi called me over to his CP on the morning of 24 October and informed me that he was moving his CP to the base of the mountain. The 44th Ranger Battalion was to be relieved by the 42d Ranger Battalion early that same afternoon. The Rangers from the 42d would take up the positions held by the 44th's companies on the mountain, and we would depart the following morning. By this time Major Thi looked sick and exhausted. Apparently like many others, he had come down with some type of tropical fever.

During mid-afternoon, I spotted a long column of Rangers from the 42d Battalion trudging their way through the wetlands toward our mountain. We packed our gear and headed down, anxious to meet and greet them.

About three p.m., the command group from the 42d Rangers reached our position near the base of the mountain. I was surprised see Captain George Crocker, who had arrived in country with me leading the advisor team. The last I'd heard, George was still assigned to the Ranger border camp at Tho Chow.

"Thought you were at Tho Chow with the border Rangers, George." I exclaimed.

With a wide grin on his face George replied, "Life was too soft up there for me, and I convinced Witek to reassign me to a maneuver battalion."

"You'll be sorry," I said.

I gave George a summary of all that had transpired in the past month, and pointed out the 44th's positions and enemy-held caves on his map, putting special emphasis on the danger posed by enemy snipers. George's senior NCO adviser said, "I came prepared, Sir," holding up an M-1 Garand rifle, caliber .30 with a leather sling and shoulder pad on the stock.

"Great!" I said. "I haven't fired one of those since 1963, when I was in ROTC summer camp. I'd like to try a shot or two after we're done here."

The M-1 rifle was the primary infantryman's weapon during World War II and the Korean War. It was a clip-fed, semi-automatic, shoulder-fired weapon with a muzzle velocity of 28,000 feet per second, and it was exceedingly accurate at ranges out to 500 yards (and well beyond depending who was firing it). With a little "Kentucky windage" and a gentle trigger squeeze, I'd seen expert marksmen plug a bull's eye at 700 yards. The M-1 also had an adjustable rear sight that was much easier to adjust than the front and rear sights of the M-16. But it had two major disadvantages. First, it fired only an eight-round clip of ammo. When that clip was empty and ejected, you had to quickly jam another clip down into the receiver with your right thumb, and quickly remove the thumb before releasing the bolt. If you didn't get your thumb out of the way before the bolt slammed forward, you got what was referred to in the old army as an "M-1 thumb." Very messy. The rifle was also a bit heavy, weighing nine and a half pounds.

The M-1 was phased out of the Army inventory in the early 1960s, replaced by the M-14. The M-14 fired a 7.62mm round that was supposed to be the standard for all NATO armies. It was also a pretty accurate weapon, designed primarily for the plains of central Europe. When the Vietnam War began, the "experts" at the Pentagon decided the troops needed a lighter weapon that was capable of both semi-automatic and full automatic fire.

The AR-15 rifle, later modified to become the M-16, was sold to the Army and later the Marine Corps. Despite claims and a lot of data to the contrary, I never believed the weapon was as accurate as either the M-1 or the M-14. However, the ammo was much lighter, and the individual soldier could carry 15 or more 20-round magazines. The M-16 added quite a bit of firepower to the infantry squad, and it was a match for the Russian and Chinese AK-47 rifle, which was less accurate than the M-16. Of course, the M-16 was a much better rifle for the South Vietnamese given its lighter weight.

Later that afternoon, George, his sergeant and I took turns trying to pick off a particularly annoying sniper on the mountain. I doubt that any of us got him, but he almost took out George a few days after we left the mountain.

George was advancing with the Rangers when he was shot in the side of the head, knocking him to the ground and almost ending what turned out to be a brilliant career. The side of his head was grazed by the bullet, but when he saw it wasn't serious he remained on the mountain until ordered off for medical treatment the following day by our boss, Lt. Colonel Witek. George returned to his battalion soon after his treatment, only to later contract typhus. Once he recovered he wanted to return to the Rangers, but MACV reassigned him instead as an aide-de-camp to General McCaffrey at Long Binh.

George went on to a brilliant career leading an airborne battalion during the U.S. invasion of Grenada, and later became the Commanding General of the 82d Airborne Division. Prior to his retirement from active duty, he was promoted to three-star lieutenant general, and commanded I Corps at Ft Lewis, Washington. George

Crocker was one of the Army's most respected officers and infantry-man of his generation.

That night we sat among the rocks beneath a cloudless starry sky, watching artillery flares rock beneath their tiny white parachutes as they descended toward the earth. I wondered where each of our own stars would lead us.

* * *

Early on the morning of 21 October 1970, the 44th Ranger Battalion with its advisors pulled off the mountain identified as Nui Ba Voi on the U.S. maps. Major Thi was carried by stretcher. His fever was raging through his body, and he looked like he was at "death's door." We marched out into the wetlands and drew a few parting shots from the mountain. No one was hit. Perhaps we had killed a few of the VC's best marksmen over the past weeks. The armored cav's 106mm recoilless rifle slammed a few more rounds into the mountain as we approached the ACAVs.

The tracks gave us a lift back to the canal, where a fleet of sampans waited to ferry us back to the town. I glanced over my shoulder for one last look at the defiant giant limestone mountain rising out of the wetlands. The battle for the two mountains lasted until the following May of 1971. During the ensuing months, from November to May, the ARVN lost more than 900 men killed trying to take those strongholds, along with an untold number of wounded. By my count, the 44th ARVN Ranger Battalion lost 28 men killed, and 74 Rangers were evacuated with serious wounds. I had no way of knowing how many of the wounded later died from their injuries.

The ARVN kept throwing regiment after regiment into that meat grinder. When the Mo So cave was finally captured, the ARVN found inside a large quantity of live poultry, pigs, and rice; enough to hold out for months. A modern day tour of the Mo So mountains and caves is not high on my list of top 20 places to visit or revisit before I die. In fact, it's not even on the list. My first visit will suffice, but occasionally I return there in my worst nightmares.

CHAPTER 6

"WE'VE ONLY JUST BEGUN"

After returning from Kien Giang, the battalion returned to its main base at Cai Rang for a two-week stand down period. When I was a company commander with the 4/12th Infantry in 1968, we never spent more than two consecutive nights at our main base at Long Binh. Nonetheless, I didn't begrudge the Rangers for their opportunity to rest, refit, and retrain. Theirs was a long war; much longer than ours.

On the first Saturday afternoon of the stand down, Major Thi threw a large outdoor barbecue, Vietnamese style, for the troops. The men consumed a palette of beer along with generous amounts of beef, chicken, and other assorted Vietnamese dishes. As far as I could determine, Major Thi and his officers paid for all of it. I knew he didn't pick up the tab on his pay as a major, and he wasn't independently wealthy. However, there were other means to gain compensation in the South Vietnamese army. Although I was hard pressed to prove it, I was sure there were "ghosts" on the battalion's payroll, and the major probably received kickbacks from wealthy families who wanted their sons to serve in rear echelon jobs in the battalion. There was also the black market, where I'm sure some of the supplies issued to the battalion ended up. Such practices were common in South Vietnamese military units.

In addition to throwing a party for the troops, Major Thi also hosted a dinner for his officers and the advisory team at a restaurant in Can Tho. There were five or six courses served during the meal, along with countless bottles of Vietnamese beer, *Ba Moui Ba-Bierre 33* and *Bierre LaRue*. The long restaurant table was covered with a variety of dishes and bowls, with everything from Spicy and Sour Prawn soup, to various side dishes of wraps, dumplings, and spicy rolls stuffed with pork and chicken, and of course small dishes of *nuc mam* (fish) sauce. The waiters kept refilling large bowls of sticky rice. I was always amazed at the amount of rice the average Vietnamese could consume during a meal.

After just about every dish was empty, the major had to test the level of our cultural assimilation by offering each of us a traditional 100-year egg. Preserving a duck or chicken egg in a mixture of clay, salt, lime, and rice straw for several months makes the main ingredient of this Vietnamese delicacy. As a result of the process, the yolk becomes a dark green, cream-like substance with a pungent odor of sulfur and ammonia, while the egg white becomes a dark brown, transparent jelly-like substance with practically no flavor at all. I got mine down in two bites, and washed away the flavor with a long pull on a bottle of La Rue beer. We ended the meal with glasses of Hennessy French cognac, the major's favorite drink. Many South Vietnamese officers still had an attraction for all things French.

The dinner was very enjoyable, and I think it was Major Thi's way of showing that he and the officers of his battalion accepted our team as battle tested *Co-Vans*. We had built a foundation of mutual trust and respect on Nui Bai Voi, and I thought our relationship was off to a good start.

* * *

I had a long discussion with my boss, Lieutenant Colonel Witek, about the performance of the battalion during the battle for Nui Bai Voi. During the operation, I wrote a series of situation reports and sent them back to Can Tho. I ran out of paper after the first week, and thereafter I wrote them on cardboard boxes that C-rations came in. Usually, I handed them to the U.S. chopper pilots who flew in our supplies and asked them to mail the letters to Can Tho. Witek indicated that he appreciated my timely battlefield reports, especially the ones written on C-ration boxes.

Lieutenant Colonel Witek was particularly interested in my

appraisal of Major Thi and his executive officer, *Dai Uy* Yen. I told him that Major Thi was not a "hard charging," aggressive battalion commander, but he got the job done. I also mentioned that Thi was receptive to innovative ideas, and he was definitely not overly concerned with his own personal safety. He led his battalion throughout our time on the mountain, even when he was ill. Hell, I thought, few U.S. battalion commanders moved and fought with their battalions on the ground. Typically, most U.S. battalion commanders controlled their units from command-and-control (C&C) helicopters orbiting hundreds of feet above the battlefield.

I also gave my appraisal of the battalion executive officer, *Dai Uy* Yen. The *Dai Uy* was courageous, sometimes to the point of recklessness. However, he led by example from the front, and was a good role model for the junior officers. He had strong potential for a battalion command, if he lived that long. His relationship with Major Thi was strained, but the two could work together on the battlefield.

The roles of the battalion commander and the battalion executive officer were quite different than those in most U.S infantry battalions in Vietnam. In the latter case, the battalion executive officer usually spent most of his time supervising the activities of the battalion staff, particularly in the areas of personnel and logistics, and to a lesser extent, in operational and intelligence matters. The exec, however, was always prepared to take command of the battalion in the absence or incapacitation of the commander. In the ARVN Ranger battalions, the executive officer typically was responsible for two of the companies moving on the ground with them, and personally directed their operations, while the battalion commander accompanied the other two companies. In a sense, it was almost a dual command arrangement, but one in which the battalion commander retained overall command authority.

All of the company commanders in the battalion were mid-level and senior lieutenants. By way of comparison, captains almost always commanded U.S. Army infantry companies in Vietnam, while U.S. Marine rifle companies sometimes had majors as commanding officers. The Vietnamese Ranger company commanders needed quite a bit of supervision, much like the second lieutenants that led U.S. platoons in Vietnam. Some were better than others, but most displayed little initiative and had little tactical expertise.

Unfortunately, non-commissioned officers were in short supply, particularly senior NCOs. The junior officers were not generally receptive to taking advice from their NCOs, unlike U.S. lieutenants. There was simply too much class distinction between the two.

As far as the individual Rangers were concerned, I told Lieutenant Colonel Witek that I had witnessed acts of heroism, but had seen no cowardice on the part of the troops. The soldiers could endure hardship and deprivation without complaint. There were skills that needed improvement, such as rifle marksmanship and noise and light discipline, but overall they were good soldiers with remarkable endurance and forbearance.

Overall, I reported that the 44th Ranger Battalion was a combat effective unit. However, the battalion needed more training in mountain warfare and cave clearing operations. If the battalion received more training for those types of operations, and had the proper equipment, it would be able to perform at a much higher level of effectiveness.

Lieutenant Colonel Witek appeared satisfied with my debriefing, and said he'd pass my comments and recommendations on to the U.S. generals in IV Corps, Major General Hal McCown, the CG of the Delta Regional Advisory Command (DRAC), and Major General John Cushman, the deputy CG. I'd talked to General Cushman by radio once during the fighting on Nui Ba Voi. He over flew the mountain at about 2,000 feet and asked me to have each company pop smoke to mark their positions on the mountain. He seemed pleased when he saw some smoke rising from rocky precipices at the very top of Nui Ba Voi; perhaps he was unaware that the enemy still held the interior of the cavernous mountain.

* * *

Since my arrival in Can Tho, several other U.S. officers arrived to serve in assignments within the Ranger command, and Witek used the newcomers to fill staff positions at his headquarters. All of these officers had previous tours in Vietnam. A Major Rothelsberger became the operations officer (S-3), and three captains filled the adjutant (S-

1), intelligence (S-2), and logistics (S-4) positions. I asked Lt. Colonel Witek if he planned to rotate these officers into the Ranger battalion advisor positions after six-months, to give the field advisors a break, and he said yes. I took him at his word, but that never happened. As far as I know, those officers spent their entire tours as staff officers in Can Tho, never having to get their spit-shined jungle boots muddy.

Witek and his staff liked to play up their advisor roles in Can Tho, so every Friday night he'd stage what he termed a "Ranger Strike," which meant a trip to Ben Ze Moi, a particularly notorious section of Can Tho. In that section of the city there were a number of bars, massage parlors, and whorehouses frequented by both ARVN and U.S. rear-echelon troops. I thought the practice was rather immature, as did the other battalion advisors, but Witek and his staff appeared to enjoy those forays. Maybe he instituted the practice to offset the tedium of staff work.

* * *

A few days after my debriefing with Lieutenant Colonel Witek, all the advisors were told to report to the nearest U.S. installation. In my team's case, this was the Can Tho airfield where the Group headquarters advisory team was located. We had no idea what was going on. That evening the whole U.S. portion of the airfield, including the Ranger compound, was placed under lockdown; no one could enter or leave the base. The following morning we were informed that it was "C-day" throughout South Vietnam. It was a day declared every six months or so, when a new series of Military Payment Certificates (MPC) were issued to the troops. (Note: U.S. servicemen were paid in MPC while stationed in South Vietnam, and regulations forbade the use of regular U.S. currency in Vietnam.) Every U.S. serviceman was required to convert whatever MPC notes he had in his possession for the new notes. The newer notes were always printed in a different color and design than the old ones.

The reason for this exchange was to cut down on black marketeering. The South Vietnamese economy suffered from high inflation and the local currency, the *piaster*, was under constant devaluation. As a result, the U.S. MPC was becoming the primary currency for major

Detachment A-4631, 46th Special Forces Company, Thailand, 1966–67.
Author is standing second from right. (All photos are from the
author's collection unless otherwise noted.)

2d Airborne
Battalion Senior
Advisor, Captain
Tonsetic, during
field training exer-
cise at Van Kiep
training center.

B-52 conducting an Arc Light strike. (NARA)

44th Ranger
Battalion Advisor,
Staff Sergeant
Roberts, and
Captain Tonsetic.
December 1970,
U Minh opera-
tion.

Lieutenant Colonel Harry Ball, Senior Advisor, 4th Ranger Group in background.

44th Ranger Battalion main attack route on Nui Ba Voi.

Major Thi, 44th Ranger Battalion commander, seated at right at Moc Hoa.

Ranger Advisor Sergeant Lopez enjoys a barbecue.

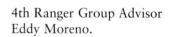

4th Ranger Group Advisor Eddy Moreno.

View of the Hau Giang River from the 44th Ranger Battalion headquarters at Cai Rang.

44th Ranger Battalion Senior Advisor's batboy, Yon, with Radio Operator Bui, at left.

44th Ranger Battalion Advisor, Sergeant Gary Lockwood, right, and South Vietnamese interpreter Hai.

South Vietnamese Navy river craft at anchor in U Minh area, December 1970.

Troops from the 44th Ranger Battalion disembark on south bank of Cua Lon River opposite Solid Anchor base, February 1971.

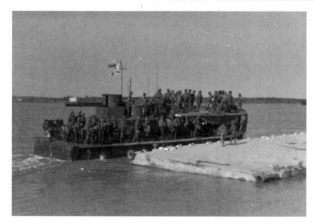

44th Battalion Rangers aboard Vietnamese river craft at Sold Anchor base, February 1971.

South Vietnamese
river craft en route to
landing area south of
Solid Anchor base,
February 1971.

44th Battalion
Rangers disembark
from river craft en
route to night
ambush position,
February 1971.

South Vietnamese boats
at anchor after landing
Rangers south of Solid
Anchor base, February
1971.

Rangers from 41st Ranger Battalion receive instruction from Mobile Combat Training Team during a break, April 1971.

Ranger MCTT leader (left), and 41st Ranger Company commander (right) prior to night VC attack. The VC are dug in along distant tree line, April 1971.

2d Airborne Battalion Senior Advisor, Captain Tonsetic, prepares for airborne operation at Van Kiep, 21 July 1971.

2d Airborne Battalion NCO Advisors. SSG Pilon is at right, 21 July 1971.

2d Airborne Battalion mass tactical parachute drop at Van Kiep,
21 July 1971.

2d Airborne Battalion Senior NCO Advisor, after water landing at Van
Kiep drop zone, 21 July 1971.

Airborne Division 105mm howitzer fires registration mission in northern III Corps, August 1971.

2d Airborne Battalion fire support base in III Corps, August 1971.

2d Airborne Battalion troopers trade with Montagnard tribesmen in northern III Corps, August 1971.

Montagnard tribesman with crossbow in III Corps, August 1971.

175mm artillery piece fires off a twilight round from a hilltop position. (NARA)

CH-54 Skycrane helicopter delivers bulldozer to 2d Airborne Battalion in War Zone D, August 1971.

2d Airborne Battalion convoy prepares for movement in northern III Corps, August 1971.

2d Airborne Battalion combat assault in War Zone D. August 1971.

2d Airborne Battalion commander, July 1971.

B-57B "Canberra" twin-engined bomber. (NARA)

OV-10A "Bronco" aircraft, U.S. Navy's VAL-4 squadron, on a fire-support mission. (NARA)

Author during a 3d Vietnamese Airborne Brigade operation in northern III Corps, August 1971.

portions of the South Vietnamese economy. Although it was forbidden by U.S. regulations to use MPC for transactions on the local economy, most GIs ignored the ban. Vietnamese civilian establishments—local bars, restaurants, brothels, and markets—eagerly accepted the MPC, as it was more stable than the South Vietnamese piaster. Consequently, many local businessmen and women typically held thousands of dollars worth of U.S. MPC.

The actual date of the C-day was kept secret from military personnel below the rank of general, and no Vietnamese were told when they were scheduled. Such precautions were necessary because the Vietnamese holding huge amounts of the certificates would attempt to find one or more GIs to exchange the MPC for them. Of course, the GIs would get a cut, sometimes returning only one dollar on every ten exchanged. The Vietnamese were desperate, and would take any deal offered since the old MPC notes would no longer have value.

On C-day, no Vietnamese workers or ARVN personnel could enter the U.S. bases. On this particular C-day, a couple hundred angry Vietnamese tried to storm the U.S. MP gate at our compound, and the MPs had to dispatch reinforcements in riot control gear to disperse the mob. I never carried more than 50 dollars worth of MPC anyway, but I dutifully exchanged my old notes for the new ones.

* * *

A few days after C-Day, the 44th Ranger Battalion received an order to move to the Moc Hoa District of Long An Province. The area is south of the Parrot's Beak border region. The battalion moved by U.S. CH-47 helicopters, landing at the Moc Hoa airstrip. Upon arrival, the battalion established a base of operations in a small village nearby. In typical fashion, the battalion command post was located in a civilian dwelling and as usual, Major Thi selected one of the larger houses in the village. The dwelling had a large room that the family used as a living and dining area. Like almost all Vietnamese homes, there was a shrine in the living area, with photographs of dead ancestors and joss sticks burning in small vases. In keeping with a long established tradition, the Vietnamese family welcomed and served their unexpected guests. I asked Major Thi about the owner of this particular house, and he said the man was a relative of one of his Rangers. I was to hear this same explanation time and time again when the battalion occupied a village. Article III of our own Constitution's Bill of Rights stipulates that,

"No soldier shall, in time of peace be quartered in any house, without the consent of the owner, nor in time of war, but in a manner to be prescribed by law."

I asked myself how an American family might react if uninvited soldiers occupied their home.

As it turned out, the battalion's deployment to Moc Hoa wasn't much of an operation. During the day, the companies conducted sweep operations in the vicinity of the village, and at night the soldiers established ambush positions in the same terrain. Major Thi and his staff officers spent most of the day lounging in their hammocks and playing cards. The card games continued long into the night, and relatively large amounts of *piasters* changed hands. Many Vietnamese were addicted to gambling. When Major Thi became bored with the game, or had a streak of bad luck, he'd invite me to dine with him at the local restaurant.

The major confided in me that there were no major VC units in the vicinity, just some local cadre. The primary threat to the Rangers was booby traps emplaced by the local VC. I reminded Major Thi that the soldiers had not sprung a single night ambush since our arrival in the area, and suggested that the battalion should conduct refresher night-ambush training. I also offered to give a class to his officers on night-ambush techniques. Additionally, I wanted to accompany one of his patrols since I had a gut feeling they weren't using stealth techniques to reach the ambush positions, and that perhaps the troops were "playing possum" when the VC approached. Unlike their adversaries, the South Vietnamese were not great night fighters. On the other hand, the VC and NVA were accustomed to moving and fighting at night. They had to be experts in night operations, since moving about during daylight hours imposed a high risk of being spotted, particularly from the air, and the allies owned the skies. Unfortunately, the Rangers had no Starlight Scopes or other night vision devices, so they were on a level playing field with the enemy during the hours of darkness.

Major Thi agreed to the classes, but explicitly forbade me, or any of my team, to accompany any night ambush patrols. His reason was that he was accountable to his superiors for our personal safety, and night ambushes were just too risky. I gave a series of classes to his officers, and they proved their worth on the next operation when the battalion conducted several successful night ambushes.

I never learned the purpose of the Moc Hoa operation, but I speculated that the ARVN high command was positioning forces for another incursion into Cambodia. The Moc Hoa area was not far from the border. As it turned out, I was wrong; we were headed in another direction. In late November 1970, the ARVN high command set its sights on two Communist sanctuaries in South Vietnam. One was the A Shau Valley in the northernmost I Corps, and the other was the U Minh Forest deep in the Mekong Delta. The 4th Ranger Group was headed for the latter area.

CHAPTER 7

"INTO THE FOREST PRIMEVAL"

The U Minh Forest, or "Forest of Darkness" as it's sometimes called, served as a sanctuary for pirates, fugitives, and guerrillas throughout Vietnamese history. During the French Indochina War, the forest was a Viet Minh sanctuary and base area, and in the more recent Vietnam War, it became a Viet Cong stronghold. Covering some 1,550 square miles, the U Minh is an extensive peat swamp forest stretching northward along the western half of Cam Mau Peninsula. The forest encompasses large portions of Ca Mau, Kien Giang, and An Xuyen Provinces. The northern portion of the forest is called U Minh Thuong, while the southern area is called the U Minh Ha.

Within the forest's tangled swamps is an abundance of wildlife, tropical birds, snakes, otters, boar, and tigers. In recent decades, however, the latter species has all but disappeared from the area. Next to the Amazon, the U Minh is said to be the largest area of its type in the world.

The forest itself is crisscrossed with hidden canals and streams that are almost invisible from the air due to thick vegetation. In the dense interior of the forest, the *Melaleuca* species of trees grow to a height of five meters. In areas near the coast, the U Minh is flooded on a daily basis by tidal waters, and the entire forest and surrounding areas are inundated during the monsoon season. Consequently, military operations in the area are extremely difficult from May to December.

Along the fringes of the forest, there is a mosaic of grasslands, rice fields, pineapple fields, small villages, and canals. The people inhabiting the areas surrounding the forest had strong ties to both the Viet Minh, and later the Viet Cong. Few non-Communist troops ever ventured into the depths of the forest, and even the villagers living along the fringes kept their distance from the sanctuaries hidden deep within the forest.

* * *

Attempts to deprive the Communists of their U Minh sanctuary dated back to the French Indochina War. In 1952, some 500 French and Vietnamese paratroopers dropped into the U Minh and, according to legend, disappeared forever in the mangrove swamps. Throughout the First Indochina War, the forest remained an important logistic training area and sanctuary for the Viet Minh troops, many of who were indigenous to the surrounding areas.

In 1967, a battalion of South Vietnamese airborne troops parachuted into a drop zone on the edge of the forest and assaulted nearby VC base camps. Some 4,800 ARVN infantrymen reinforced the paratroopers. The reinforcements made multiple airmobile assaults into landing zones (LZs) and conducted search and destroy operations. Although the South Vietnamese forces killed 89 insurgents and captured large caches of weapons, they did not pursue the VC forces when they retreated into the depths of the forest. This, however, was not the last attempt to destroy the enemy sanctuary.

In March of 1968, a group of Vietnamese fishermen became enraged when the Viet Cong forbade them from fishing in the forest's ponds, and in an act of revenge set it on fire. At almost the same time, fires accidentally broke out in other parts of the forest. Fanned by gusty winds, the fires merged and swept through 85 percent of the forested area over a five-week period.

After the fires burned off much of the foliage, U.S. and RVNAF aerial observers were able to pinpoint the Communist base camps deep within the forest. The observers also saw Viet Cong soldiers trying desperately to dig firebreaks to protect their camps and supply dumps. Seizing the opportunity, the observers called in air strikes to destroy the enemy base camps, and kept the fires burning by dropping additional ordnance. U.S. Navy ships offshore in the Gulf of Thailand also fired hundreds of rockets at suspected enemy positions.

As a result of the air strikes, naval bombardment, and the fire itself, vast quantities of supplies, ammunition, and shelters were destroyed, and the jungle foliage and canopy no longer offered concealment for the enemy. It would take another rainy season to turn the forest green again. Thereafter, the burning and defoliation of the U Minh became routine military policy, doing considerable harm to the forest's fragile ecosystem. Despite these measures, the Communists continued to use the U Minh as a sanctuary, moving into unburned areas of the forest.

Except for a number of U.S. Navy Seal missions into the forest, the only U.S. ground force to conduct operations in the U Minh was the 9th Infantry Division's Mobile Riverine Force. Taking advantage of a huge fire in the spring of 1968, the U.S. Naval Assault Flotilla One transported troops from the 9th Division's 2d Brigade into the U Minh on 30 July 1968. Less than half an hour after landing, the troops uncovered a large cache of weapons, medical supplies, and documents. During the ensuing ten-day operation the brigade's two infantry battalions, reinforced by the 5th Vietnamese Marines, made frequent contact with the enemy, capturing cache after cache of weapons and supplies. The operation was considered a success, but the VC did not abandon their huge sanctuary. Instead, they withdrew to the unburned areas of the forest, preparing to fight another day.

On 31 December 1968, a U.S. gunship team working in the U Minh spotted a figure in black pajamas running through a relatively open swampy area. The Cobras swooped in to engage the VC, but before they made their firing pass, Major Dave Thompson of the "Dutch Masters" called them off. Thompson, orbiting overhead in a command and control ship, wanted to take a prisoner. When the major's ship descended to pick up the suspected VC, the crew saw that the man was not Vietnamese, but American. Under covering fire from the circling gunships, Major Thompson's huey touched down and picked the man up.

The American extracted from the U Minh was Nick Rowe, a Special Forces officer who had been captured by the VC five years earlier. In October of 1963, Rowe and two other Americans were captured in an ambush near Tan Phu in Thoi Binh District. The VC held Nick captive for five years in the forest, under the worst imaginable conditions. Nick Rowe was a true American hero and patriot, as was

Captain Humbert "Rocky" Versace, who was captured with Nick. The Viet Cong executed Captain Versace during his captivity, and he was posthumously awarded the Congressional Medal of Honor in 2002. Nick Rowe resumed his Army career after his captivity and was promoted to full colonel. Tragically, Colonel Rowe was assassinated in the Philippines in 1986, one of the first casualties in the War on Terror.

Intelligence reports on American POW sightings at camps throughout the U Minh continued in the late 1960s and early 1970s. Later in my tour with the Vietnamese Rangers, I participated in a raid on a suspected POW camp, but that comes later in this story.

* * *

In October 1970, the last brigade of the U.S. 9th Infantry Division departed Vietnam. Thereafter, major military operations in Military Region 4 were totally under the control of ARVN forces, with support provided by U.S. Army Aviation and U.S. Navy forces. The war had entered its Vietnamization phase. The U.S. and South Vietnamese governments touted the success and progress of this phase, particularly in the Mekong Delta region. The enemy was deceptively inactive, leading some to conclude that progress was indeed being made. Roads were open throughout the Delta, and there were no major attacks on government installations. It was assumed that the U.S. and South Vietnamese attacks into Cambodia in May of 1970 had knocked the enemy off balance, and disrupted the supply routes from the Cambodian ports to the border regions. The war seemed to be going well, and Vietnamization appeared to be making progress.

Facing a re-election campaign in 1971, President Theiu wanted to demonstrate that his government was firmly in control of the countryside, including the enemy's sanctuaries in the U Minh forest. A decision was made to mount a major offensive in the U Minh in December of 1970. The ARVN's 21st Division, arguably its best division in the Mekong Delta, was given the mission of driving the enemy from that sanctuary. At that time, an estimated 3,000 VC were believed to be hiding in the forest and the areas around its periphery. To insure success, four battalions from the 4th Ranger Group reinforced the 21st

ARVN Division. They had just undergone a major reorganization.

During the month of November 1970, the conversion of the Special Forces CIDG border troops to ARVN border Rangers was completed, while the forces in the Delta were reorganized under a Regional Ranger Command. An ARVN Ranger full colonel was selected to command the new organization. The MR-4 Ranger commander exercised command and control over three groups: the 4th Ranger Group and two border Ranger Groups, each commanded by a lieutenant colonel.

With the reorganization of the Rangers, Lt. Colonel Witek became the senior advisor to the newly organized MR-4 Ranger Command. Lt. Colonel Harry Ball replaced Witek as senior advisor to the 4th Ranger Group, and thus became my new boss. Ball, a mature man graying at the temples, turned out to be a great boss. He had served as a company commander in the 187th Regimental Combat Team during the Korean War. He was a tough, no-nonsense commander and a deeply religious man who read the Bible every night. When he flew missions in his command and control helicopter, he carried an M-16 and M-79 grenade launcher, along with a basic load of ammo for both weapons. If he spotted a VC, he would order his pilot to fly low over the enemy so he could get a clean shot. His assistant senior advisor, Major Leon Constantine, on the other hand, was a difficult officer to work with, but Ball kept the major under control.

Major Eugene Hawkins took charge of one of the border Ranger advisory groups. The "Hawk," as we dubbed him, had served a previous tour in Vietnam with the 101st Airborne Division and was a real professional. Hawkins was promoted to full colonel after the war, and later commanded the Army Ranger School at Fort Benning before his retirement. Major Wayne Chittenden was assigned to the other border Ranger group and he, too, was a real professional who had commanded a company in the U.S. 1st Cavalry Division on his first tour in Vietnam. I had nothing but respect for both of them.

I was also surprised to learn that an old friend of mine had taken over as senior advisor to the 42d Ranger Battalion. Captain Marty Tovar and I were both in the same class at the Special Forces Officers Course at Fort Bragg in 1966. Marty was raised in El Paso, Texas, and was commissioned through the OCS program. He spent his first tour in the 101st Airborne Division in Hank "Gunfighter" Emerson's battalion, and married a Red Cross "Donut Dolly" that he'd met in country during his tour. It was through Marty and his wife that I met my future wife, Polly, in 1972. She also served with the Red Cross in Vietnam in 1970–71, but our paths never crossed in Vietnam.

* * *

Lieutenant Colonel Ball briefed us on the details of the upcoming U Minh operation. The 4th Ranger Group, including the 41st, 42d, 43d, and 44th Ranger Battalions, were attached to the 21st ARVN Division for the operation that was scheduled to begin on 1 December. Major General Nguyen Vinh Nghi, the commander of the 21st ARVN Division, was designated the overall commander of the operation. The 21st ARVN Division and the Rangers would commit a total force of about 7,500 men to the operation.

The fire-support plan for the operations included: the U.S. Army, U.S. Navy and Australian helicopter and fixed-wing gunships, U.S. Navy offshore bombardment, VNAF and U.S. strike aircraft, and U.S. B-52 bomber support. According to ARVN intelligence sources, two NVA Regiments and five Viet Cong battalions, plus local guerilla forces, were based in the forest sanctuaries and surrounding areas. The NVA units were thought to have moved into the U Minh after they were driven out of the Seven Mountains region near the Cambodian border. We were also informed that there were some 10,000 civilians living around the edges of the forest, and that many of the civilians were Communist sympathizers.

The 4th Ranger Group was assigned an operational area on the eastern fringes of the forest just north of Thoi Binh in Ca Mau Province. The battalions were ordered to arrive in Ca Mau no later than 30 November, and commence airmobile assaults into their respective areas of operation on 1 December 1970. Battalion advisory teams were to move with their battalions to Ca Mau and accompany their units during the airmobile assaults and follow-on operations. As usual, advisors would receive logistic support from their counterparts.

Lieutenant Colonel Ball finished his briefing by indicating that he and his team would deploy with the 4th Ranger command group led by Lieutenant Colonel *Trung Ta* Pham (not his real name). Great, I thought; at least I wouldn't have to keep in touch with my boss by writing letters to the headquarters in Can Tho.

The 44th Ranger Battalion received a number of replacements to restore their losses incurred during the October attack on Nui Ba Voi, and morale within the battalion improved considerably. I was confident that I had a good relationship with Major Thi, and he was receptive to my recommendations on how to improve his battalion's performance in the field.

* * *

The 44th Ranger Battalion departed its base at Cai Rang on 28 November, headed for Ca Mau. Similar to the Nui Ba Voi operation, this one began with a truck convoy, but this time we knew our destination in advance. I was still uneasy about road movement due of the possibility of ambush. We had no air cover during the movement, and this disturbed me as well.

Our convoy headed south on Highway 4 toward Soc Trang on the first leg of our journey. Soc Trang is located about 60 kilometers south of Can Tho. Driving through the town, I noted a strong Khmer cultural influence, as evidenced by the architecture and temples. The condition of the highway between Can Tho and Soc Trang was generally good, but the road worsened after we passed through the town and drove south toward Bac Lieu. The rains had almost stopped by late November, but the highway was heavily pitted from five months of daily downpours.

Bac Lieu sits on the Song My Thanh River, only a few miles inland on the South China Sea. There was a steady stream of sampans moving agricultural products to the town's markets. After passing through Bac Lieu, we drove past large, open fields flooded with seawater. The seawater was undergoing evaporation, leaving the salt to be gathered up and sold at market.

The final leg of our journey took us to our destination, Ca Mau. The highway paralleled a large canal, the *Ca Mau di Bac Lieu*. On this stretch of highway, we had to cross a number of bridges spanning small canals that flowed into the main inland channel. These crossings slowed our progress considerably, since the bridges accommodated only one lane of traffic—and there was a substantial amount of civilian and military traffic. The final 15 kilometers of the road were torturous for us. This portion was unpaved, partially washed out, and filled with numerous potholes. Finally at about 6 p.m., we rolled into Ca Mau totally worn out.

Major Thi selected a house on the outskirts of the city for his CP, and we set up camp for the night. My advisory team slept on cots outside the dwelling. While I never felt comfortable as an uninvited guest in a Vietnamese home, it didn't seem to bother our ARVN counterparts. Major Thi always had the same story: A relative of one of his Rangers always owned the house in which he set up his headquarters, and he and his staff were invited guests.

The next morning, I accompanied Major Thi to the forward command post in Ca Mau. The dreary town was built on the muddy shores of the Ganh Hao River that winds through the city. Wartime Ca Mau was a dirty, dull, and unappealing town in the middle of a swampy wasteland, lacking the frenetic hustle and bustle of Saigon and Can Tho. The majority of the vehicles driving along the trash-littered streets were motor scooters, three-wheeled taxis, and military vehicles. We found the Ranger command post that was co-located with the 21st ARVN Division.

Lieutenant Colonel Ball indicated that we would fly an aerial reconnaissance of the Ranger operational area north, or Thoi Binh, later that morning. Ball's counterpart *Trung Tha* Pham, Major Thi's immediate superior, was at the CP that morning. It was my first meeting with him and my initial impression was not a good one. Pham was a small, slender man with narrow eyes and sneering lips. He had a serpentine look about him, and I found his high-pitched voice annoying when he snapped at his subordinate officers. On the other hand he was ubiquitous, almost fawning, when he spoke with American officers.

Lieutenant Colonel Ball, Trung Tha Pham, Major Thi, and I boarded a UH-1D command and control ship and flew north to recon the landing zone that we tentatively selected for the 44th Ranger battalion air assault. The 4th Ranger Group's area of operations was on the east side of the Song Trem Trem River, about ten miles north of Thoi Binh. The western boundary was the Kinh Song Teem canal that flowed into the aforementioned river. It was in this same area that then Special Forces Lieutenant Nick Rowe was taken prisoner in 1963. The area was on the eastern periphery of the U Minh forest, where there were open patches of marshlands and a network of small canals, along which were small groups of thatched, brown huts surrounded by coconut palms and banana trees. The area looked deceptively peaceful from 1,000 feet, but from my prior experience in the northern Delta in 1968, I knew that there were probably packed mud VC bunkers along the canals, well hidden in the nipa palm growth. Additionally, I knew the paths and trails that connected the small settlements were likely to be booby trapped with trip wires that would detonate powerful explosive devices.

The landing zone was a large, open area with a covering of marsh grass and clumps of reeds. Since the rainy season had just ended, I knew there was likely to be several inches of water covering the soft muck. Other than a tree line about a kilometer east of the landing zone, there were no areas in the immediate vicinity of the LZ that could conceal a large enemy force. Our armed Huey made only one low pass over the LZ, so as not to give away our intentions. The door gunners were ready to respond to any ground fire, but we drew none. As we flew back to Ca Mau, B-52 bombers pounded the area west of the Trem Trem River deep in the U Minh Forest. We could hear the muffled explosions and see the smoke from the powerful bombs.

After we landed at Ca Mau, I queried Lieutenant Colonel Ball on what type of airmobile lift, gunship, and artillery support we'd have for the operation. Ball confirmed that the lift ships would be U.S., and that we'd have U.S. Army, U.S. Navy, and Australian gunships, the "EMUs," in support of the operation, as well as U.S. tactical air support. The ARVN 21st Division was responsible for artillery support, and I was particularly concerned with hitting the tree line about a kilometer away from our LZ. If there were large enemy forces in the vicinity, that is where they would be hidden.

Lieutenant Colonel Ball also filled me in on the overall plan for the 4th Ranger Group. The plan was to insert two battalions, the 44th and 43d, into the area we had flown over. The remaining two battalions, the 41st and 42d, along with the 4th Ranger command group, would occupy a fire support base on the Song Trem Trem River, about ten miles north of Thoi Binh. They would conduct daylight riverine operations up river and west into the forest. The 44th and 43d battalions were to rotate with the battalions operating from the firebase after a week or two. A brigade of the 21st ARVN Division was going to conduct operations from a firebase further north on the Song Trem Trem River.

I had one additional concern that I discussed with Lieutenant Colonel Ball: my advisory team had only two members assigned in addition to myself, Staff Sergeant Roberts, and newly promoted Sergeant Lockwood. The two sergeants were both doing a superb job, but I needed a lieutenant. With a lieutenant, I had the capability to split the team when the situation warranted, sending two team members with the executive officer and two Ranger companies, while I remained with the battalion commander and the other two companies. My intent was, if at all possible, never to have just one U.S. team member moving with one of the battalion's maneuver elements. Ball told me that he expected to have two new lieutenants assigned by mid-December, and one of them would be assigned to my team.

Tuesday, 1 December 1970
Downdrafts from the UH-1D helicopters rotor blades churned the marsh grass, mud, and surface water into a wet spray that stung our faces as we leapt into the murky water of the marsh and began slogging toward the distant tree line. We continued moving as dozens of artillery rounds screeched overhead and exploded in fiery flashes among the coconut palms and banana trees. A second later, as the sounds of muffled explosions reached our ears, columns of smoke, mud, and debris erupted from the tree line. On the far horizon, a pair of AH-1 Cobra gunships circled like hawks, waiting to pounce on their prey once the barrage lifted. Although the hellish preparatory fires appeared to devastate our first objective in the tree line, I knew from previous experience that the enemy hunkered down in their mud-packed bunkers would, save for an unlikely direct hit by a 155mm round, survive the shelling. Still, I would not have traded places with them.

As we neared the tree line, Major Thi ordered his lead company to deploy a line of skirmishers in front of our advancing column. *Dai Uy*

Yen, leading two companies, veered toward the left edge of the tree line, while Major Thi and the remaining two companies veered to the right in a pincer-like movement on the objective. Occasionally, long-range sniper fire cracked and popped over our heads. I'd long ago learned that, unless you heard a sound like a hornet buzzing past your ears, the rounds weren't actually that close. As usual Bui, my radioman, kept his distance from me.

A pair of AH-1G Cobra gunships, with a line of sharks teeth painted below their nose, swooped down and blasted the tree line with salvos of 2.75" rockets. I summoned Bui toward me so I could radio the gunships. I wanted to know if they spotted any bunkers in the tree line, and they had indeed. Not good I thought. On the positive side, I knew that the artillery fire had most likely detonated any booby traps that may have been strung in those trees. The skirmishers began to lob 40mm grenades into the tree line using their M-79 grenade launchers, as the battalion's two maneuver forces entered the left and right flanks of the 200 meters of tree line. I radioed the gunships again, and instructed them to cease-fire as the Rangers entered the area.

A pair of egg-shaped OH-6A scout helicopters nicknamed "Loaches," for Light Observation Helicopters (LOHs), continued to perform their part of the mission. The small, light OH-6s buzzed the enemy bunkers, marking them with colored smoke and engaging them with its side mounted 7.62" mini-gun and 40mm grenade launcher. Occasionally, if the scouts suspected a bunker was occupied, the pilots would hover a couple of dozen feet above the bunker and a crewmember would attempt to toss a hand grenade into the entrance. As the "Loaches" worked the center of the tree line, the Rangers moved in on the flanks.

My legs were beginning to feel like lead weights by the time we reached the more solid ground of the tree line, but I was in better shape than I was when I arrived three months earlier, and weighed about ten pounds less, so I wasn't short of breath. There was some shouting in Vietnamese, and I heard the muffled explosions of hand grenades as the soldiers went about clearing bunkers. Staccato bursts of M-16 automatic fire added to the noise of the continuing detonations. A few bunkers in our sector were occupied, but most were empty. In the former case, the Rangers dragged the shattered VC bodies from the charred interiors of the bunkers and put them on display for their battalion commander, who was following with his command group. Suddenly, we heard a huge explosion on the other end of the bunker line where *Dai Uy* Yen's two companies were advancing. Booby trap, I thought immediately, and I was right. The VC had rigged a howitzer shell with a small block of TNT and an electric blasting cap, hung it on a tree branch, and ran a firing wire into one of their bunkers. They exploded the device as a Ranger squad approached their bunker, killing six of the men and wounding four more.

The mopping-up operation continued until all of the bunkers were destroyed. There were a sufficient number of bunkers for a company size force, but we only counted about ten bodies, although it was hard to tell from the bits and pieces. Counting weapons was probably more accurate. The soldiers collected only half a dozen badly damaged AK-47 rifles, and a RPD-50 light machine gun. The enemy is dispersing into small groups, I reasoned—I'd read Mao's book on guerilla warfare cover to cover.

I radioed for a dustoff for the Ranger KIA and wounded, and updated Lieutenant Colonel Ball on the battalion's progress. As I radioed in my report, I saw Major Thi in an animated conversation with *Dai Uy* Yen. From the tone of Thi's snarling voice, I knew he was chewing Yen's ass for losing ten Rangers. There was no love lost between those two officers, but Major Thi knew he needed *Dai Uy* Yen. Besides, it wasn't anyone's fault but the enemy's.

After we loaded the casualties on the medevac helicopter, Major Thi ordered the battalion to move out toward a long canal about three kilometers from the tree line. There were some clusters of small, thatched huts along the canal that we needed to search. Long columns of men plodded through the marshy terrain like they had webbed feet. After awhile, I no longer noticed my wet feet and the slippery mud beneath my jungle boots. A couple of times, the major called the battalion to a halt and checked his map, which was carried by his operation's lieutenant. Then he conferred via radio with his lead company commanders before we moved out again.

About four in the afternoon, the battalion halted about 300 meters short of a canal that ran northwest to southeast and intersected our line of march. I could make out the shapes of about half a dozen huts among the banana trees that grew along the canal bank. The major ordered a squad from the lead company to check out the small group of huts. I could hear a dog barking in the distance, and it turned out that the small village was inhabited, but there were no VC in the hamlet—at least not at that moment. While we moved out toward the small group of huts with the lead company, Major Thi ordered *Dai Uy* Yen to take his two companies northwest up the canal bank to search another group of huts.

It wasn't much of a village; around eight brown, thatched huts inhabited by about 30 or 40 people—women, children, and a few old men with wispy beards. The major ordered all the people outside while his men searched the huts. The people clustered in small groups beneath the shade of some palm trees while the Rangers went about their work. Most of the women wore cautious smiles on their faces, displaying their betel nut stained teeth. The curious kids were adorable. They were all barefoot, but the boys wore shorts and shirts that buttoned up the front while the girls wore short black pants and white tunics. The kids looked well-fed, and pretty clean considering the environment. At the time, I was more worried about what the older brothers and fathers of the children had planned for us.

The thatched huts were primitive, but adequate for the climate. The structures were constructed with readily available local materials. First, a frame of timber and bamboo poles was built over a pounded earth floor. The frame was then covered with layers of dried palm fronds, and a thatched roof made from the same materials completed the dwelling. The steep roofs overhung the sides of the "hootches" so that the rainwater would run off, and in the dry season served to shade the house from the tropical sun. The interiors consisted of a single room with a cooking area, including a few pots and bowls, a couple of sacks of rice, and a sleeping platform. Beneath the sleeping platform was a bunker where the family could take cover from mortar or artillery fire, or when some trigger-happy gunship pilot thought he saw a VC enter the hut. It was a frightening existence for the women and kids.

Major Thi called me aside to inform me that we'd spend the night in the small village. I recommended that he allow the civilians to go back in their homes for the night, since his men had found nothing incriminating in the huts. He agreed, and ordered his own men to dig in for the night in a perimeter around the area and along the canal banks. I didn't think the VC would mortar us that night, since I was pretty sure that some the locals had family in the tiny village. The women returned to their huts to prepare the evening meal, while my team members passed out some candy bars to the kids.

I watched curiously as a couple of Major Thi's batboys rigged some small blocs of C-4 with blasting caps and time fuses. When they were done, the batboys lit the fuses and flung the blocs of C-4 into the canal where they detonated underwater, sending geysers of water into the air, showering the canal bank. The boys and some of the kids then ran excitedly to canal to scoop up the catfish that were floating belly up on top of the water. My batboy joined the fishermen.

We finished digging our shallow foxholes along the muddy bank of the canal while Yon prepared our supper of rice, catfish, heart of palm, and pineapple. The pineapples grew in green-topped fields across the canal. The Rangers found a couple of small sampans and crossed the waterway, returning with several dozen fresh pineapples. It wasn't my idea of a gourmet meal, but it wasn't bad. I was to grow mighty tired of such fare over the next three weeks.

Darkness was coming on. After a radio check with Lt. Colonel Ball's location, I strung my VC hammock between two palm trees and settled in for the night. The first day of the operation was a long one, and the only attack we suffered that night was repeated attacks by swarms of mosquitoes. Since I didn't carry a mosquito net, I kept dousing my exposed skin with insect repellent all through the night. With the mosquitoes, plus the artillery firing H&I missions in the surrounding area, I got little sleep that night.

2–12 December 1970

The following morning the 44th Ranger Battalion was ordered to sweep west toward the Trem Trem River, a map distance of approximately ten miles. Of course, the distance we would travel would probably be at least twice that, since we never moved in a direct line. The heart of the U Minh forest lay to the west of the Trem Trem River. Two major canals and various smaller ones led from the river into the heart of the forest itself. After downing a leftover breakfast of rice, heart of palm, and pineapple, we stared off on our journey. As we began our trek, I recalled four of the Standing Orders that Major Robert Rogers issued to his Rangers in 1759, during the French and Indian War.

> When we're on the march we march single file, far enough apart so one shot can't go through two men.
> If we strike swamps or soft ground, we spread out abreast, so it's hard to track us.
> When we march, we keep moving till dark, so as to give the enemy the least possible chance at us.
> When we camp, half the party stays awake while the other half sleeps.

Major Rogers's orders were applicable for the terrain we encountered over the next several days.

Major Thi followed my advice to deploy night ambush patrols every evening. On the night of 4 December, this paid off when a patrol killed four VC who were apparently following our column during the day. Of all the Rangers in the battalion, the Cambodians were the most adept at these ambushes. The ethnic Khmers loved to fight at night. They were a close-knit fraternity within the battalion and most were assigned to second company, the only one commanded by an ethnic Cambodian *Trung Uy* (first lieutenant). The dark skinned, slightly overweight officer was unimpressive in appearance, but his men were intensely loyal to him.

Some evenings when we halted for the night, I was able to reclaim my transistor radio from Yon and try to tune in to the AFN station. The reception was poor, but I did hear one report that the 21st ARVN Division and Rangers were credited with killing 28 Communists on the second day of the U Minh operation. That was not remarkable since over 7,000 men were involved in the operation.

Cross-country movement through the marshes was very difficult. We always had to be alert for the possibility of booby traps and ambush. It was slow going, and in some areas we had to cross a number of small canals and ditches. Sometimes, I could clear these with a good leap, but on least one occasion I didn't make it and ended up in a ditch full of water, much to the amusement of the Vietnamese. So it went day after day.

One evening we moved into a night defensive position that was on a piece of relatively dry ground. It was overgrown with bushes and there were a number of trees. The night was uneventful, but the next morning a Ranger about 50 meters away from us triggered a booby trap and was seriously wounded. I reported the incident by radio to Major Constantin at Lieutenant Colonel Ball's CP. Constantin wanted to send a dust-off helicopter to evacuate the wounded man, but Major Thi had already ordered the battalion to move out—he was concerned there were more booby traps in the area. We gingerly packed up our gear and cautiously left the bivouac area. The wounded man was carried on a stretcher.

For the next hour or so, Major Constantin was on the radio every ten minutes, demanding to know when we planned to evacuate the wounded man. I tried to explain to him that we were in an area that was heavily booby trapped, and it was too risky to bring in a medevac chopper. Besides, the man's wounds were not life threatening. Constantin became more irate with each radio call, and eventually I just stopped answering. We finally reached an open area and I called in a dust off. The next time I saw the major, he was still upset that I hadn't called in the dust off sooner.

The 44th Ranger Battalion finally reached the 4th Ranger Group CP situated on the Trem Trem River on 12 December 1970. The command post was located in a large field that was cleared for the cultivation of pineapples. Irrigation ditches ran from the river through the area. A large general purpose (GP) army tent was erected in the center of the field for the headquarters staff and command group. Inside the tent was a working area for the staff, and a couple of sandbagged bunkers where the officers could take cover in the event of a mortar attack. Two days prior to our arrival, a 21st Division Regimental CP located a few miles upriver had come under a VC mortar attack, killing and wounding a number of staff personnel.

The 41st Ranger battalion manned the mud bunkers around the perimeter of the area, but was scheduled to depart the base on a riverine operation on 14 December. When we arrived, our battalion took over the southern portion of the perimeter.

The ground was still soft from the rainy season, but it was quickly drying out in the blazing tropical sun. Except for an occasional light shower, the rainy season was just about over. We took the opportunity to dry ourselves and our clothing out after our long march through the wetlands. I kept checking to see that my team member's feet showed no signs of immersion foot, a constant medical problem for U.S. personnel in this type of terrain. U.S. units that operated in the Mekong Delta had a rule of thumb: A rifle company should be kept in the field for no more than five days at a time. We far exceeded that, and never suffered from immersion foot.

Monday, 14 December 1970

After two days rest, our battalion was prepared to assume complete responsibility for the security of the base. A small flotilla of South Vietnamese brown water Navy boats was scheduled to arrive at about noon. The plan was for the 41st Ranger Battalion to embark on the vessels and proceed upriver to a canal that led westward into the heart of the U Minh forest. This was the first foray directed at its interior. During the preceding two weeks, the soldiers operated along the eastern periphery of the forest.

At about 10 o'clock, a UH-1D landed on the PSP helipad at our base to off load two young U.S. Army lieutenants—our long awaited deputy senior advisors. Lieutenant Colonel Ball briefed the new arrivals on the operations, and assigned one of the lieutenants to my advisory team, and the other to Captain Malone's 41st Battalion Advisory team. Both lieutenants were new in country. They'd arrived in Saigon on the same flight on 4 December, and shipped out to Can Tho a few days later. Captain Malone and I were more than pleased to have a deputy on our team, despite their inexperience. First Lieutenant Bill Harrison (not his real name) was assigned to my team, and First Lieutenant Gordon Cordiner went to Captain Malone's team. The pair bid each other farewell and joined their respective battalions.

I spent the next two hours briefing Lieutenant Harrison on the 44th Battalion and what had transpired thus far on this operation. When the boats arrived to pick up the 41st battalion, we walked down to the river to see them off. As we watched the Rangers embark, I chided Lieutenant Harrison,

"Looks like your friend will be getting his Combat Infantryman's Badge, CIB, a few days before you get yours."

"Guess so," the lieutenant replied.

We watched for a few minutes as the boats got underway before returning to our command post.

Afterwards, we sat around and monitored our PRC-25 radio to track the progress of the riverine operation. About 30 minutes after the flotilla left base, they turned west into one of the long canals that ran into the forest. The boats were less than a kilometer into the canal when all hell broke loose. We could hear the explosions of B-40 and B-50 rockets as they slammed into the boats, and the *thud, thud, thud* of heavy machine gun fire. The boats returned fire with heavy machine guns and cannon, as they tried to reverse their course and escape the kill zone of the ambush.

Captain Malone was on the radio screaming for gunship support when his boat took a direct hit from a B-50 rocket. The radio went silent for a moment, and then the captain was back on screaming that he'd been wounded by the shrapnel, and that his lieutenant was seriously wounded. A piece of shrapnel had pierced the lieutenant's chest and he was bleeding profusely. Lieutenant Colonel Ball told Captain Malone to calm down, and that gunships were on the way. Other than the U.S. gunships, the ARVN Ranger Group commander showed no intention of mounting a rescue operation, or committing more troops to destroy the enemy force.

When the gunships arrived to suppress the enemy fire, the boats managed to reverse course and steam back into the Trem Trem River. The flotilla then headed south toward the Ranger base with their dead and wounded. My lieutenant and I ran to the river's edge to meet them.

Captain Malone's boat had been hit several times with rockets. We climbed aboard along with some men from our battalion to administer first aid and unload the casualties. He had been hit in the back with several small pieces of shrapnel, but his wounds were not serious. I took one look at the lieutenant's crumpled form and knew immediately by his coloring that he was dead. We could detect no pulse or breathing. With the assistance of a couple soldiers, we carried the dead and wounded off the boat. In addition to Lieutenant Cordiner, there were six other KIAs, and at least a dozen wounded on the boat. The deck was slippery with blood and gore. Dust offs were already arriving at the base helipad. We wrapped the bodies in ponchos and laid them out on the riverbank to wait for the stretcher-bearers to carry them to the helipad. My lieutenant walked over to watch the medical evacuation. The wounded were taken out on the first dust off, followed by the KIAs. I returned to our battalion area leaving Lieutenant Harrison at the helipad with his friend's body.

When Harrison returned to our CP, I could see that he was in a state of shock. It was understandable. I tried to calm him down as best I could, given the circumstances, but he kept repeating,

"It could have been me, it could have been me."

Then he revealed something that really disturbed me.

"They took his watch and wallet," he said.

"Who took his watch and wallet?" I asked.

"I don't know, the Vietnamese I guess, but when I checked for his personal effects, they were missing." The lieutenant said.

"Don't worry, I'll get them back!" I exclaimed as I stormed off to find Lieutenant Colonel Ball.

I figured it must have been one of the ARVN medics who lifted the lieutenant's watch and wallet. When I found Ball, we both went to find his counterpart Lieutenant Colonel Pham; my boss was as angry as I was.

When we found Pham, Colonel Ball told him that he wanted the lieutenant's wallet and watch returned within the next 30 minutes, or there would be hell to pay. The group commander must have seen the fire in Ball's eyes, because the lieutenant's property was found and returned in a matter of minutes. It was an ugly incident that my lieutenant never quite got over. Thereafter, he neither trusted nor liked any of the Vietnamese.

Lieutenant Harrison told me later that Lieutenant Cordiner's wife was expecting their first child. Ranger Lieutenant Duane Gordon Cordiner was twenty-four years old, and had been in Vietnam for one week and two days when he gave his life for his country. It was a sad day for all of us.

That night a large enemy force attacked one of the three 21st ARVN Division fire bases to the north of us. In a battle that lasted several hours, Communist gunners fired 200 rounds of 82mm mortar fire on the base, and launched a ground attack from several directions. The attack was repelled, but the South Vietnamese lost 14 men killed and 23 wounded. The U Minh operation was far from a one-sided game.

A few days later, we were notified that South Vietnamese President Nguyen Van Thieu was flying in to visit our base. Thieu was up for re-election in 1971, and he wanted to showcase the success of his pacification program. He spent a couple of days visiting his troops in the U Minh area, even spending the night at one of the 21st Division's regimental CPs. President Thieu arrived at our small riverside base by helicopter, accompanied by Major General Nghi, the 21st ARVN Division Commanding General, and Colonel Ross Franklin, the U.S. senior advisor to the division. Several other helicopters landed, unloading members of the President's entourage and members of the Vietnamese and U.S. press corps. A briefing area was set up in the large tent, along with a luncheon table complete with white tablecloths and china. I stayed clear of the whole briefing and luncheon, remaining near my radio in the unlikely event that the base was attacked during the visit. The 44th Ranger battalion was responsible for the security of the base, and helicopter gunship teams orbited the area outside the perimeter the entire time President Thieu was on the ground.

It must have been a tiresome briefing, since several members of the press fanned out across the base. A reporter from a major U.S. newspaper, which I won't name, walked over to our area with his interpreter and asked if he might have a word with me. I'd seen the same reporter talking to a couple of Vietnamese Rangers from our battalion, the men showing him something contained in a large glass jar.

"Captain, I was just talking to a couple of the Vietnamese Rangers and asked them how many VC they killed on this operation. They showed me a glass jar that had a body part in it. They said it was a liver they had removed from a dead VC. Do you know anything about that?"

I responded, "That's probably a boar's liver. They killed a wild pig yesterday and we had a feast last night."

"Is that right? Well, how many VC did your men kill since this operation began?" he asked.

"I've no idea. I'm not into counting dead bodies," I said. "That's not part of my job description." I'd had my fill of body counts on my first tour. It was meaningless, but the generals demanded them, and the press regularly reported and printed the useless statistics.

"Is that right. Well, good luck with these guys captain!" he exclaimed as he strode off.

As he walked away, I recalled that the Rangers the reporter talked to were Cambodians, and that our men had sprung an ambush on the VC the night before. There were rumors about Cambodians celebrating their prowess by eating the hearts and livers of their enemies, but I never believed it. The story about the boar was true; the soldiers had indeed killed a wild pig the day before.

Before President Thieu left the base, Lieutenant Colonel Ball brought Colonel Franklin, the senior advisor of the 21st ARVN Division, around to meet all the U.S. advisors. Franklin was a tall, bald-headed man of about 50, and he gave us the standard pitch to keep up the good work, and so forth. I later learned that the colonel was very controversial; he'd relieved a subordinate commander who later accused him of covering up war crimes. I believe he was even interviewed on one of the TV news shows back in the states. Since I really didn't know the colonel, I had no opinion one-way or the other. Later, a U.S. advisor with the 21st ARVN Division told me that Franklin was known for walking the ground with Vietnamese battalions for a day, and spending the night with them in the field. Not many U.S. full colonels serving in advisory assignments did that.

A few days after President Thieu's visit, the 43d ARVN Ranger battalion arrived at our base along the river. After a two-day overlap with the 43d, my battalion was scheduled to depart the base on another operation. I was happy to see my old friend Captain Marty Tovar, the senior adviser with the 43d battalion. One look told me that Marty wasn't well. He'd lost about ten pounds, and on his slender frame it looked worse. His color also looked jaundiced to me.

Marty and I exchanged notes on the operation to date, and I told him about Captain Malone and his lieutenant. At the time I was moody, disgruntled, and disillusioned with the U Minh operation. In my opinion, the Vietnamese were putting on a big show to impress the Americans, but they didn't really want to risk a major battle in the U Minh forest. We were nibbling around the edge, and I'd learned that the Vietnamese generals and politicians wanted to establish a large pineapple plantation in the area we were in, similar in size to the one west of Saigon. I told Marty that I was thinking of resigning my commission. When I was in Vietnam, I always became depressed around the holidays.

The day before we left the base for the last time, I received a dozen letters and a couple packages from my folks and my girlfriend Jackie. One of the packages contained a replacement University of Pittsburgh class ring from Jackie—I'd lost my first ring on my first tour in Vietnam. Suddenly, it dawned on me that I hadn't ordered any gifts for my family, or Jackie. I wrote a letter to my mother and asked her to do my Christmas shopping for me, then I borrowed a PX catalogue and ordered a string of Mikimoto Pearls for Jackie. Better late than never, I thought. Maybe the class ring was a subtle hint to me, but I wasn't ready for that step.

We also received a bunch of Pacific Stars and Stripes newspapers that came in on the mail run. I scanned the headlines. One read,

"U Minh Gains bring ARVN Smiles, Peace Talks Continue."

Another read,

"Stalking Reds in U Minh," and another, "83 Enemy Killed in Clashes with Viet GI's Militia."

I knew from my first tour in Vietnam that the Stars and Stripes always put a positive spin on the war. It was on one end of the spectrum, and the major U.S. newspapers, like the New York Times and Washington Post, were on the liberal end of the spectrum. Neither got it exactly right. Another Merry Christmas in Vietnam I thought.

* * *

The 44th Ranger Battalion departed the base on the Trem Trem River on 22 December 1970. I bid Marty Tovar farewell before we marched off into the wetlands. He was still concerned about my frame of mind and my remarks about resigning my commission. I told him not to worry about it; I'd see this thing through to the end.

The battalion moved to the northeast over the next two days without making contact with the enemy. Christmas Eve was more of the same. On Christmas day, Lieutenant Colonel Witek, the Ranger Command Senior Advisor, flew into our area to visit all the battalions. When he over flew our battalion, I popped a smoke grenade and guided his C&C ship into a LZ. The colonel jumped out of the chopper, his spit-shined jungle boots sinking into the mud. He was carrying a mailbag, and that made his visit worthwhile to us. After handing us our letters from home, he pulled a bottle of Jack Daniels and some Red Cross ditty bags out of the mailbag. After wishing us a Merry Christmas, he passed the bottle around. When the bottle came my way I said,

"No thank you colonel. I don't drink in the field." That was true, although I was far from being a tea toatler when we weren't on a combat operation.

"But, it's Christmas, go ahead. It's just one swig." The colonel said.

"Doesn't matter." I replied.

I think Witek recognized that I had developed a bit of an attitude, but he didn't pursue it. Five minutes later, the colonel boarded his helicopter and took off. It was a nice gesture, flying all the way down from Can Tho to wish us a Merry Christmas, but none of us really had the Christmas spirit. Peace on earth and good will towards men did not apply to us that year, and if a Christmas truce was declared, we were not aware of it.

Once the colonel departed, we looked into the contents of our Red Cross ditty bags. These bags were made up by the Red Cross donut dollies and contained nice to have items, like candy, a sewing kit, a ballpoint pen, a penlight, a cigarette lighter, and things like that. It soon became clear someone had gone through our bags and removed the nice to have items. Apparently, the "stay at home Rangers" in Can Tho did not want to burden us with those trinkets.

As the old year slipped away, the 44th Ranger battalion's participation in the U Minh operation neared its end. During the final days of December, we spent long luminous days searching for VC. The soldiers had one little firefight with a small group of VC during the last week of December, but the results were insignificant. I called in gunship strikes, and the VC broke contact. No men were killed or wounded, and I personally saw no enemy dead left on the field.

On the 29 December 1970, we were back at the Ranger base on the river. That same afternoon we boarded CH-47 Chinook helicopters for the flight back to Ca Mau. The Ranger's participation in the U Minh operation had come to an end. I boarded the helicopter with Major Thi and his staff. The 4th Ranger Group Commander, *Trung Ta* Pham, and several of his staff officers were also on board. The Vietnamese officers were all anxious to get back to Ca Mau, since *Trung Ta* Pham had made arrangements for a big dinner party in Ca Mau that evening. Unfortunately, the weather was not cooperative, and the Chinook could not land at Ca Mau. A sudden, severe thunderstorm came up over the city and its airfield, and the aircraft had to divert to another airstrip. When the pilot announced this on the intercom, *Trung Ta* became very angry and called me over to his seat.

"*Dai Uy*, you tell pilot to land at Ca Mau now," he instructed me.

"Sir," I said, "the weather is very bad in Ca Mau now. The pilot cannot land. It's too dangerous."

"*Dai Uy*, I tell you. We land now, you understand me," the Group Commander continued.

I spoke to the pilot on the intercom, and he again confirmed that he was diverting to another location to refuel and sit out the storm. I tried to explain to the Vietnamese colonel that the pilot always has the final say, but he was obviously beyond the point of reason, so I returned to my seat. He continued to glare at me until we landed. We left the aircraft during the refueling process and walked to the side of the runway. One of the Vietnamese officers came over and said the *Trung Ta* wanted to speak with me. As I approached him, he shouted at me in an angry voice.

"*Dai Uy*, you very bad officer. I tell you we land Can Tho. Why you no obey my order?"

By this time, I was getting pretty angry myself, and I stepped forward into the Vietnamese colonel's personal space to answer him directly. As I moved forward, one of the *Trung Ta's* bodyguards menacingly raised his M-16 in my direction. At that moment Major Thi, fearing the situation was getting out of control, stepped forward and grabbed my elbow, leading me away to the side.

"Never mind *Dai Uy*, everything ok. *Trung Ta* not mad you. Very bad pilot. I speak with *Trung Ta*, never mind," Major Thi whispered.

Bullshit I mumbled, trying to get my temper under control. By the time the refueling was complete, the weather at Ca Mau cleared, and we were able to take off and complete our journey. It was about 6:00 p.m. when we landed at Ca Mau, and I didn't get an invitation to attend *Pham's* dinner party that night; not that I wanted to go. When I next saw Lieutenant Colonel Ball, I described the incident for him. He said Pham had a temper and not to worry about it. "He doesn't hold grudges." Ball said. I later received some information that made me doubt Ball's assessment of his counterpart.

A couple of months after I left the Rangers, I heard about an incident involving *Trung Ta* Pham and a U.S. district advisor. The colonel wanted the advisor to call an artillery fire mission on a group of sampans. The U.S. officer refused due to the presence of Vietnamese civilians in the boats. A few days later, the American advisor was found shot to death under very mysterious circumstances. To tell the truth, I never trusted Pham from the first moment I laid eyes on him.

By New Year's Day, we were back in the Can Tho area. The 21st ARVN Division continued operations around the periphery of the U Minh for several months. The Division Commander, Major General Nghi, acknowledged that it would take "at least three full divisions to clear the U Minh quickly and effectively." Nghi was correct. The ARVN high command, however, had another mission for the Rangers.

CHAPTER 8

"THE LONG AND WINDING ROAD"
•

When we returned from the U Minh operation, I visited the Ranger Command Advisory headquarters at Can Tho airfield. In December 1970, Delta Company, 5th Special Forces Group, closed its headquarters at the airfield and departed Vietnam. The Civilian Irregular Defense Group (CIDG) forces, formerly under control of the Special Forces, were integrated into MR-4 Ranger Command and organized into eight border Ranger battalions. The battalions were placed under the control of two border Ranger group headquarters.

The phase-out of Special Forces in Vietnam was part of the overall Vietnamization of the war, and it was perhaps the most difficult to accomplish. The conversion of the CIDG program began when General Abrams gave the order for the gradual withdrawal of Special Forces in August of 1969. The MACV commander had little appreciation for Special Forces, or as they were more widely known to the public, the "Green Berets." Like most of the World War II generation of Army officers, Abrams was generally opposed to the formation of so-called "elite" units within the Army. A number of senior officers serving in Vietnam shared a perception that there was a lack of discipline, military appearance, and adherence to traditional practices and customs of the service in the Special Forces Group. In the author's opinion, only a relatively small number of Special Forces soldiers serving in Vietnam exhibited those traits, but they caught the eye of the generals and colonels. The Special Forces outliers wore whatever uniforms they deemed appropriate, showed little deference to rank, and failed to observe traditional military courtesies and customs. These outliers spent too many consecutive tours in Vietnam and sometimes went native, adopting the ways and trappings of the ethnic peoples with whom they lived and fought. These practices only served to exacerbate the distrust of Special Forces that existed among the conventional senior officers, and then the situation worsened in 1969, when a serious incident involving Special Forces occurred.

In June of that year, a South Vietnamese intelligence agent working for them was determined to be a double agent for the North Vietnamese. Special Forces personnel allegedly terminated the agent with "extreme prejudice." It was further alleged that a cover story was developed and approved by the 5th Special Forces Group Commander, Colonel Robert Rheault. When the cover story unraveled during an Article 32 investigation, Abrams ordered the arrest and confinement of all those involved, including Colonel Rheault. The Special Forces officers, including the colonel, were placed in confinement at the LBJ confinement facility in Long Binh, rather than being placed under arrest and confined to their quarters. Even Lieutenant Calley of My Lai notoriety was afforded the latter privilege while he was awaiting court martial at Fort Benning.

Secretary of the Army Stanley Resor eventually dropped all charges against the personnel, but General Abrams never forgot, or forgave, the 5th Special Forces. General Abrams was one of the Army's great commanders of the 20th century who understood what it would take to win the war in Vietnam. He accomplished much more than his predecessor, General Westmoreland, discarding large search and destroy operations in favor of stability operations. However, Abrams did not credit or appreciate all that the Special Forces accomplished during their ten years in Vietnam.

Many of the issues and problems that existed between Special Forces and conventional force senior commanders could have been avoided if one or more general officers had been assigned to command positions within Special Forces. When I completed my Special Forces training in 1966, there was only one general assigned to Special Forces and that was Brigadier General Joseph Stillwell Jr., the Commanding General of the JFK Center for Special Warfare located at Fort Bragg, North Carolina.

The 5th Special Forces Group in Vietnam was authorized a colonel as its commander despite the fact that those colonels who were in this command position commanded more U.S. and indigenous troops than any two star division commander in Vietnam. The assignment of a U.S. general officer to command the 5th Special Forces, and perhaps another general to oversee all special operations in the theater may have mitigated many of the aforementioned problems and perceptions.

Despite the problems encountered in standing down the CIDG program and converting the border troops to Ranger forces, the transition continued at a whirlwind pace. General Abrams was determined to end the role of Special Forces by the end of 1970, and the NVA and VC sought to exploit the difficulties involved in the transition. The enemy realized that CIDG personnel, many of whom were members of ethnic minority groups, were not eager to become assimilated into the regular South Vietnamese Army, and that the turnover of the border camps to ARVN control would invariably lead to personnel and logistic problems. Therefore, the NVA/VC launched a series of attacks against the border camps during the transition year of 1970.

Two of the first camps hit in 1970 were in the Delta. Camp Ba Xoai in the Delta's Seven Mountains area, near the Cambodian border, came under attack on January 14, 1970. The attack stalled at the camp's inner perimeter, and with the support of U.S. gunships the attackers were driven off by the mostly Cambodian/Khmer CIDG. The enemy returned to the same area in March of that year, attacking both Camp Ba Xoai and Camp Chi Lang. Once again, the CIDG forces defeated the NVA, allowing the transition process to move forward, and by year's end all of the border camps in the Delta were under ARVN Ranger command.

U.S. Special Forces officially ended their decade-long stay in Vietnam on 3 March 1971, when an honor guard boarded an aircraft in Nha Trang Airbase with the 5th Special Forces Group colors and flew home to Fort Bragg. General Abrams declined to attend the group's departure ceremony.

Without question, the Green Berets accomplished a tremendously difficult mission under the most trying conditions imaginable. They had organized, trained, and equipped South Vietnam's tribal minorities and oppressed ethnic groups, in the most remote parts of the country, to defend the border regions and other areas from the NVA/VC.

Fighting outnumbered, the CIDG and their SF advisors protected the population and disrupted the NVA infiltration routes from Cambodia and Laos. Unfortunately, their accomplishments often went unrecognized and their last two years in country were particularly difficult ones.

* * *

The U.S. Ranger advisors lacked many of the advantages that Special Forces advisors had in dealing with their Vietnamese counterparts. Although the Vietnamese Special Forces (the LLDB) officially commanded the CIDG camps, the U.S. Special Forces advisors were, for the most part, the de-facto commanders. The CIDG troops neither liked nor trusted the LLBD, but their support and loyalty to their advisors was unwavering. The U.S. SF Detachment Commanders also controlled the CIDG monthly payrolls, as well as generous intelligence funds, and around $50,000 in supplies each month. In most cases, the Special Forces teams also had little trust or confidence in their LLDB counterparts, who on many occasions refused to participate in combat operations with the CIDG troops, abrogating that responsibility to the Americans.

The MACV Ranger Battalion Combat Assistance Teams (BCATs) were much smaller than the Special Forces "A" Detachments. Each "A" Detachment was commanded by a captain assisted by a lieutenant executive officer. In addition to the officers, each "A" Detachment had ten non-commissioned officers, all experts in their Military Occupational Specialties (MOSs). The MOSs represented in the "A" Detachment included light and heavy weapons experts, demolition experts, communications specialists, medical specialists, and operations and intelligence experts. According to MACV manpower authorization documents, each Ranger BCAT was authorized only four personnel: two officers and two non-commissioned officers. Additionally, the Ranger Senior Advisors had no real leverage over their counterparts, such as control of funds or supplies. All that the Ranger advisors had to offer was their own tactical expertise and advice, and their ability to call for and direct U.S. airmobile assets and gunship and tactical air support.

* * *

Lieutenant Colonel Witek's MR4 Ranger Command advisory detachment moved into the facilities formerly occupied by the headquarters of Company D, 5th Special Forces Group at Can Tho Airfield. By 1 January 1971, Witek had a full staff of officers and NCO's on board, including an executive officer, an S-1 Personnel Officer, an S-2 Intelligence Officer, an S-3 Operations Officer, and an S-4 Logistics officer. The aforementioned were charged with providing advice and assistance to their counterparts on the Vietnamese Ranger Command staff. Additionally, Witek's staff was supposed to support the U.S. Ranger Advisory Teams in the field. While I have no idea what type of assistance they gave their counterparts, I do know that the Battalion Combat Assistance Teams received only limited support from the headquarters staff.

The staff officers at the headquarters wore the camouflage uniforms of the Rangers and maroon berets, but unlike the battalion advisors their uniforms were highly starched, and their jungle boots were spit-shined to perfection. I could have overlooked this, but for the fact that they were drawing the same combat pay as the advisors in the field who were living in the mud and laying their lives on the line almost every day of their tours.

As far as staff support to the BCATs, it was practically non-existent. I never received a detailed intelligence briefing from the MR-4 Intel officer, and we were seldom, if ever, given any useful information on upcoming operations. Logistic support was also practically non-existent, and any clothing, rations, and field gear we received during our tours was due to the scrounging abilities of our team sergeants. Fortunately, there were still some U.S. aviation and other support units at the airfield who were willing to trade just about anything in return for captured enemy weapons. We also had a good contact with a U.S. Navy type who was stationed in Can Tho, who could come up with just about anything for a price.

During the U Minh operation, I did not carry my issued M-16 rifle, but instead borrowed a .45-caliber pistol from the Ranger battalion. I was just tired of carrying the rifle and trying to keep it serviceable. Besides, I rarely fired the M-16 in a firefight since I was pre-occupied directing gunship, artillery, and air strikes. Nevertheless, I was a terrible shot with the .45 and wanted another weapon for self-protection. I talked to our Navy friend and he procured a Swedish-K submachine gun for me in return for some cash and a VC flag I'd picked up in the U Minh.

The Swedish-K, or M/45, is a fully automatic weapon that weighs about 8.5 pounds. It fires from the open bolt position and is accurate to 200 meters. It was also easy to clean and maintain. Additionally, with its short barrel and folding stock it is easy to carry. Along with the weapon, I received five 36-round magazines of 9mm ammunition. Sergeant Roberts asked me what I'd do when I ran out of ammunition since the Rangers had no weapons of 9mm caliber. "If that happens," I said, "I'll just grab an M-16 from one of the dead or wounded."

When I visited or stayed overnight at the Can Tho airfield Ranger headquarters, I always made time to work on my physical fitness. There was no organized physical training, but there was an outdoor basketball court, and I was able run around the perimeter of the air-field. We also enjoyed the U.S. food at the compound. The headquar-ters staff dined on steak about three nights a week, and for a price we could join them. It was important to eat as well as possible when we were out of the field. A steady diet of rice and anything else edible for weeks on end lowered our stamina and was not a healthy diet for a U.S. advisor. Of course, we also partook of the headquarters supply of beer when we were in Can Tho, and made regular trips downtown to visit the Vietnamese restaurants and bars. It was relatively safe in the downtown area, and the biggest nuisance was the local Can Tho cow-boys who were quiet proficient in stealing the batteries from a parked jeep in a matter of seconds. Sometimes they stole the Jeep itself. My team never lost its Jeep, but we did lose a couple of batteries.

* * *

During the second week of January 1971, the 44th Ranger Battalion was ordered to move with all possible speed to Cao Lanh, the capital of Kien Phong province. Cao Lanh is located on the left bank of the Mekong River about 75 miles southwest of Saigon on the southern edge of the Plain of Reeds. The 44th Special Tactical Zone (STZ) head-quarters was located in Cao Lanh. Colonel David H. Hackworth was senior advisor to the 44th STZ and Commander of Advisory Team 50. The 4th Ranger Group's 43d Battalion was also headquartered in Cao Lanh.

We moved from the 44th Battalion's base camp at Cai Rang to Cao Lanh by truck and jeep convoy. After arriving in Cao Lanh, the 44th Ranger Battalion established its forward headquarters in the vil-lage of Cao Lanh a few miles north of the Mekong River. Captain Giles, senor advisor to 43d Ranger Battalion, invited me to stay in his quarters, which were located in the Advisory Team 50 compound. I'd come down with a fever and a bout of dysentery on the way to Cao Lanh, and I appreciated the offer to stay with Captain Giles while the 44th Ranger Battalion waited for further orders. The Team 50 com-pound was a rectangular fort adjacent to another larger fort that housed the Vietnamese 44th Special Tactical Zone headquarters.

Since his arrival to take command of Advisory Team 50, Colonel Hackworth had made numerous improvements to the compound. There was an officers club, an NCO club, and an EM club. There was also a newly renovated Tactical Operations Center (TOC), and brief-ing room, a MARS radio station where the troops could place calls to the States, and recreation facilities. I wasn't sure which category the "Steam and Cream" parlor fit, but it was a great morale builder for the men of Advisory Team 50.

For the next two days, I was in bed with a fever that abated some-what on the third day. Feeling better I decided to attend one of Colonel Hackworth's morning briefings. From this I learned that the mission of the 44th Special Tactical Zone was to interdict NVA/VC infiltration of personnel and equipment from Cambodia into the Delta. The 44th STZ's area of operations was huge, stretching through the border area from An Giang Province in the west to the III Corps border in the east. To accomplish his mission, the STZ commander relied on attached ARVN Ranger, Airborne, Marines, Armored caval-ry, and Infantry units, augmented by local Regional and Popular Force units.

During the briefing, Colonel Hackworth sat in a leather-backed chair in the front of the briefing room. I had no doubt that the colonel knew all the information presented in the briefing ahead of time, but he wanted the information shared with all members of Team 50. It was obvious that Hackworth had a keen intellect and a sharp wit, and he probed each briefer's depth of knowledge in their area of expertise. Unlike the stodgy "afternoon follies" briefings at MACV headquarters, and other briefings that I attended during my Army career, Hackworth always managed to add a bit of levity to his, as he tried to nail the briefing officers on certain points that they covered. Additionally, he encouraged participants to present new ideas and challenge conventional thinking. It was as much a training exercise for the younger staff officers as it was an information update. In my eight months as a member of the MR4 Ranger advisory team, I never recall a daily briefing being given by the staff.

After the briefing Captain Giles introduced me to Colonel Hackworth. The colonel said that he'd like to have all the Ranger battalions in the Delta attached to his headquarters. I wouldn't have minded at all if that turned out to be the case, but it didn't work out that way.

Six months later Colonel Hackworth went public with his criticisms of the war in a no-holds-barred interview that was later aired on ABC's program, *Issues and Answers*. The colonel directed his criticisms at members of the U.S. chain of command in Vietnam and the Pentagon for their handling of the war. To no one's surprise, he incurred the wrath of the Army's hierarchy. General Abrams ordered an investigation into all aspects of Hackworth's professional and personal life during his tour in Vietnam, looking for possible grounds for court-martial. No charges were ever filed, but Hackworth was forced into retirement. The episode was particularly galling to the Army's chain of command because Colonel David Hackworth was one of the Army's rising stars and one of its most decorated officers. I didn't share all of Colonel Hackworth's views on the war, or the way he chose to air them, but he was one helluva soldier.

* * *

On 13 January 1971, the 44th Ranger Battalion was ordered to move to Hong Nhu near the Cambodian border. Movement was by

Vietnamese Navy river craft. Hong Nhu was the battalion's staging area for a planned incursion into Cambodia. The South Vietnamese named the January 1971 Cambodian operation *Cuu Long 44-02*. Forces assigned included the ARVN's 4th Armored Brigade with the 12th and 16th Armored Cavalry Regiments, three Ranger battalions, an artillery battalion, and an engineer group. A South Vietnamese Marine Corps force was also assigned to the operation. D-day for *Cuu Long 44-02* was set for 15 January 1971.

The purpose of the operation was to assist Cambodian forces in opening Highways 3 and 4 that ran from the Cambodian port of Kampong Som to the capital, Phnom Penh. Kampong Son is Cambodia's only deep-water port and was the site of the country's only oil refinery. North Vietnamese troops had cut the supply routes two months earlier in an attempt to starve the Cambodian capital of badly needed supplies and equipment, and to bring about the fall of the anti-Communist government of Premier Lon Nol. The return of a pro-Communist government in Phnom Penh would facilitate the movement of North Vietnamese troops and supplies through Cambodia and ultimately into South Vietnam.

The *Cuu Long* operation differed in significant ways from the invasion of Cambodia in May of 1970. The revised Cooper-Church amendment, enacted on 5 January 1971, forbade the use of U.S. ground troops or advisors in Cambodia. Given the fact that U.S. ground troops were in the midst of withdrawal from Vietnam, and were therefore available in ever decreasing numbers, that part of the amendment made some sense. It also doubtless saved many young American lives. South Dakota's George McGovern reflected the mood of the American public and political realities at that time when he said, "Any Senator who talks about sending American forces into Cambodia should lead the charge himself. I'm fed up with old men sending young men out to die, particularly in stupid wars of this kind." I didn't disagree entirely with the Senator.

On the other hand, the ban on the deployment of U.S. advisors on the ground in Cambodia and Laos made little sense to me. ARVN commanders relied heavily on their U.S. advisors to coordinate and direct U.S. airmobile and assault helicopter support, and tactical air support. The language barrier between the Vietnamese ground commanders and the U.S. pilots severely limited the effectiveness of this support. The accuracy of U.S. fighter-bomber and attack helicopter strikes was dependent on good communication between the airborne FACs and gunship pilots with personnel on the ground. There were few English-speaking South Vietnamese officers in most units who were capable of directing the strikes. U.S. advisors to South Vietnamese forces were professional career officers and non-commissioned officers, not 18- to 25-year-old draftees. The discreet presence of a few U.S. advisors on the ground with their units in Cambodia and Laos would have left almost no footprint, and would have saved many South Vietnamese lives. Nonetheless, by law, U.S. advisors were not permitted to accompany their units on ground operations. However, there was nothing in the Cooper-Church Amendment that specifically addressed the participation of U.S. advisors as aerial observers and controllers for air support assets, including helicopter lift and gunship support.

U.S. Army support of operation *Cuu Long 44/02* was placed under the direction of Brigadier General J. H. Cushman, the Deputy Commander of the Delta Military Assistance Command. The U.S. Navy was also tasked to support the operation, and the USS *Cleveland*, USS *Iwo Jima*, and USS *Tulare* sailed from Subic Bay in the Philippines to the Gulf of Thailand off Cambodia in support of the operations. The Navy ships were to serve as a mobile command post for General Cushman and his staff, and as a forward fueling and rearming platform for U.S. Army helicopters supporting ARVN ground operations in Cambodia. The Ranger Command's senior advisor and selected staff members were designated as aerial forward controllers for the gunships, and were also embarked on the Navy ships.

Ranger Battalion Combat Advisory Teams were permitted to accompany their units to the forward staging areas in South Vietnam, but were instructed not to cross the border with their units. When the 44th Ranger Battalion departed Cao Lanh on January 13, I was still too ill to accompany them, so I sent my Lieutenant along with Staff Sergeant Roberts and Sergeant Lockwood on ahead. The following day I'd recovered sufficiently to make the trip. I boarded a Vietnamese Navy supply vessel for the voyage up the Mekong to Hong Nhu. It was about a two-hour trip upriver. When I arrived in Hong Nhu I found the Rangers' command post in a French colonial building close to the dock. My lieutenant and Sergeant had brought the Jeep forward the prior day, but there wasn't much to see in the small river town. I visited with Major Thi, and asked if he needed anything for the operation. He had no requests. The Ranger battalion's rear CP would remain in Hong Nhu during the operation. Major Thi seemed more excited than normal about the operation. He'd been in Cambodia before, and it was common practice among the Vietnamese officers to return with captured or "liberated" booty. On a previous incursion, a South Vietnamese colonel brought a "liberated" herd of cattle all the way back to Can Tho. Captured enemy Mercedes were also highly prized. I hoped the major would not be that greedy.

When the 44th Battalion departed the following day for Cambodia, I decided that there was absolutely nothing for my team to do in Hong Nhu, so I decided to return to Can Tho. After determining that we couldn't catch a ride with a Vietnamese Navy supply ship until late in the day, I made a decision to drive overland by Jeep to Cao Lanh.

I checked my map and I saw that a secondary road paralleled the river all the way to Cao Lanh. In retrospect this was very stupid decision. I knew nothing about the condition of the road, nor did I have any intelligence on enemy activity in the area. A single Jeep with four Americans on board was a tempting target. After driving a few miles, I really began to regret my decision. Not only had I put my own life at unnecessary risk, but I also put my team members at risk by my poor decision.

We passed several burnt out hulks of ARVN trucks and Jeeps. The road was in terrible condition, but we drove at maximum speed anyway. There was no turning back since this would have only increased the risk. We got some hard looks from villagers and farmers along the way. I was glad they didn't have telephone service to call ahead and arrange a surprise for us down the road. Fortunately, we made it safely into Cao Lang before dark. The U.S. advisors at the 44th STZ headquarters couldn't believe we made the drive. "None of us have ever done that," a captain told us. They knew the area much better than we did. The following day we drove back to Can Tho, a much less risky drive at that time.

* * *

The ten-day *Cuu Long 44/02* turned out to be a relatively successful operation, no thanks to Senators Fullbright, Church, and Cooper. If their original legislation had been passed, there would have been no U.S. Air Force or U.S. Army helicopter gunship support for the South Vietnamese troops, and no logistical support to Cambodian forces.

Upon their arrival, the ARVN Rangers supported the 4th Armor Brigade as it pushed its way north along Routes 3 and 4. The NVA's crack 101st Regiment set up a series of ambushes on a mountainous 25-mile stretch of highway north of Kompong Som to halt their drive. The first ambushing force was literally blown away by the 16th Armored Cavalry Regiment's firepower.

A second ambush farther north was directed at the 12th Armored Cavalry Regiment. Determined to stop the armored column in its tracks, the NVA attempted to isolate the regiment's lead squadron by knocking out the lead and rear vehicles. The lead track commander's vehicle was hit and set afire, but he managed to keep it moving forward. With his .50-caliber machine gun blazing away at the enemy, the vehicle commander managed to get clear of the kill zone, before the vehicle blew up killing all of the crew. This heroic action allowed the remaining squadron vehicles to escape the enemy firing lanes and the column continued up the road until they found firing positions that enabled them to turn their guns on the ambushers. The Ranger battalion moving behind the cavalry squadron deployed and opened fire on the ambushers who were then caught in a crossfire. As the battle continued, two U.S. helicopter gunship teams arrived to seal off the NVA escape routes.

When the battle was over, some 200 NVA lay dead, and a total of 75 enemy weapons, including two 75-mm recoilless rifles, and three 12.75 heavy machine guns were captured. The ARVN troops lost five killed and twenty wounded, and a total of three ACAVs were destroyed.

Another significant battle occurred on 17 January 1971, when Cambodian forces supported by South Vietnamese Marine forces, secured the strategically important Pic Nil Pass, while the Vietnamese 4th Armored Brigade cleared Route 4 as far north as Route 18.

Cambodia's lifeline to the sea was once again open.

Insofar as possible, U.S. advisors complied with the cross border restrictions that were imposed by the Cooper Church Amendment, with one possible exception. An American civilian journalist covering the operation from the ground spotted a U.S. helicopter landing close to a Ranger command post, and directed his photographer to snap a picture of a U.S. Army major in Ranger camouflage fatigues as he jumped from the helicopter and ran to the nearby CP with a package under his arm. The photograph appeared in one of the nation's leading periodicals, and set off a firestorm in the Congress. Although, it was not possible to positively identify the individual in the photograph as an American, we all knew who it was.

The Ranger advisor in the photograph had instructed his pilot to land so that he could deliver a supply of radio batteries to the Vietnamese unit commander. The incident was a violation of the Cooper-Church Amendment, and had the potential, at a minimum, to embarrass the Pentagon and the Nixon administration. We sweated that one out for a few weeks after the article and accompanying photograph were published, but there was never a formal inquiry or investigation that I know of.

After helping the Cambodians set up strongpoints on Highways 3 and 4, all South Vietnamese forces participating in *Cuu Long 44-02* withdrew from Cambodia and returned to Vietnam by 25 January1971. The politically sensitive incursion into Cambodia was the deepest to that date in the war, and it accomplished all of its limited objectives. Moreover, it gave the Lon Nol government four more years in power. A much larger operation, *Lam Son 719*, was planned for February 1971. This cross-border operation called for a deep penetration into Laos to disrupt the Ho Chi Minh trail. Unfortunately, this operation, which will be described in a subsequent chapter, did not end as well as the Cambodian venture.

CHAPTER 9

"ANCHORS AWAY",

The 44th Ranger Battalion withdrew from Cambodia on 22 January 1971 and returned to their base camp at Cai Rang. By all reports, the battalion had performed well during the Cambodian operation, and the Rangers were looking forward to a well-earned stand down prior to their next mission. It was not to be. On 24 January the battalion was alerted for a new mission that was scheduled to commence two days later. The disagreeable news came as a great disappointment to the Rangers, since they were looking forward to spending the Tet holiday period with their families. Morale sunk to a new low when all leaves were cancelled, and the men were restricted to their base for the next two days.

The new mission would require the Rangers to deploy to the extreme southern tip of Vietnam in the Ca Mau Peninsula. It was an unusual mission even for the Rangers. Rather than operating under ARVN control, the 44th Battalion would be under the operational control of the U.S. Navy operating from its "Solid Anchor" base at Nam Can. Solid Anchor was located on the north bank of the Cau Lon River some 180 miles southwest of Saigon, in one of the most remote and contested areas in Vietnam. Nam Can fell to the Communists during the Tet Offensive of 1968, and the area remained under their control until the spring of 1969. At that time, a decision was made to challenge the VC's dominance over the area by establishing a pontoon-floating base that was anchored on the Cua Lon River adjacent to Nam Can. The base, called Sea Float, was established to support U.S. Navy riverine craft that were assigned the mission of disrupting enemy supply lines, hindering waterborne movement, and assisting the South Vietnamese government in regaining control of the region.

Riverine operations conducted from the Sea Float mobile facility enhanced the security in the Nam Can area, and a decision was made to construct a more permanent shore-based installation. Construction problems were monumental due to the swampy nature of the terrain. Dredged fill from the Cau Lon River was unsuitable, and sand had to be barged in to build the base. Additionally, all building material had to be brought in by air or boat, since there was no road access into the area.

The construction of a permanent naval base did not go unchallenged by the enemy. Seabee Battalion One was under repeated mortar and rocket attack as they struggled to complete the project, and boats bringing in supplies to the base had to run a gauntlet of mines and riverine ambushes. There was also an ever-present threat of swimmer sapper attacks on Allied boats docked at the base. Despite these obstacles, the Solid Anchor base became functional by the end of October 1970.

At the end of December 1970, the U.S. Navy completed the transfer of 650 small combat craft to the Vietnamese Navy, including those operating from the Nam Can Solid Anchor base. The U.S. Navy was ending its surface combat role on the rivers of Vietnam. However, the base at Solid Anchor temporarily remained under control of the U.S. Navy during the transition period. Throughout the transition, the VC stubbornly refused to concede control of the area to the South Vietnamese, and intensified their efforts to isolate and destroy the base.

During January of 1971, the Solid Anchor base suffered from supply, maintenance, and repair difficulties, all the while suffering from almost continual Communist harassment. Battles in the surrounding canals and rivers resulted in heavy damage to the South Vietnamese river craft as the enemy continued to interdict military and civilian traffic. Allied riverboats were ambushed seven times during the month of January, and the Vietnamese Navy cancelled its regular supply runs to the isolated base. As a stopgap measure, vital stores were airlifted in, and a U.S. Navy LST was tasked to make a risky run to resupply the base with artillery ammunition and fuel.

The Solid Anchor base was under mortar attack on four different occasions during January, with the heaviest barrage occurring on the 25th, one day before our arrival. On that date, the Communists fired close to a hundred 82mm rounds into the base, wounding two Americans and six Vietnamese sailors. The rounds impacted throughout the base, but most were concentrated in the waterfront area where two South Vietnamese boats were badly damaged. The security situation in the area surrounding the base was deteriorating day by day.

U.S. Navy SEAL Teams, supported by Seawolf and Sea Lord helicopters, conducted daring raids into the heart of the VC/NVA strongholds to blunt the enemy's offensive capabilities. While, the SEALs inflicted heavy casualties on the enemy, they suffered significant casualties during these operations, experiencing their most costly month to date.

South Vietnamese ground forces operating in the area during the month of January included the Sixth Vietnamese Marine Battalion, the Biet Hai (Naval Rangers), and local PF units. The ground forces were supported by a section of ARVN 105mm howitzers, and U.S. Navy helicopter and fixed wing gunships.

When the Marines departed on 23 January, a battalion of the 21st Division's 32d ARVN Regiment replaced them. It was quickly determined that the ARVN infantry battalion that had just returned from the U Minh operation was not up to the task, and the mission was passed to the 44th Ranger Battalion on 26 January 1971. It was not until later in the operation that I learned the reasons behind the withdrawal of the Vietnamese Marines and subsequent withdrawal of the infantry battalion from the 21st ARVN Division.

Since the Solid Anchor base was an advanced tactical support base for U.S. and South Vietnamese Navy units operating in the Ca Mau Peninsula, the mission of securing the base and conducting riverine operations in the surrounding area was initially assigned to the South Vietnamese Marines. This did not sit well with the Marines, since the base was under U.S. Navy command. Nevertheless an arrangement was worked out whereby the U.S. Navy base commander was given operational control of the 6th Vietnamese Marines, but he did not have command authority of the unit. The arrangement did not work out well. There was friction between the Vietnamese Marine battalion commander and the Vietnamese Navy contingent at the base, and between the battalion commander and the U.S. Navy Captain commanding Solid Anchor. After a friendly fire incident involving a U.S. Navy Seawolf gunship team and the Vietnamese Marines, and several incidents of Vietnamese Navy gunboats firing indiscriminately into Vietnamese Marine positions, the situation came to a head. The U.S. Navy three-star admiral in Saigon decided to replace his Solid Anchor commander with a hard-charging U.S. Marine Corps colonel.

The Marine colonel cracked down hard on what he perceived was a lack of discipline and poor attitudes among the disparate mix of U.S. Navy and South Vietnamese Navy at the base, as well as the civilian work force. He also organized a fully functional staff organization to run day-to-day operations. Additionally, the colonel attempted to rein in the Navy SEAL teams operating from the Solid Anchor base, believing that they operated too independently. He also lobbied hard to get a second Vietnamese Marine battalion assigned to Solid Anchor in order to enhance security, increase the operational tempo, and extend the range of operations around the base. In the end, the well-intentioned colonel "rocked the boat" a bit too hard. The Vietnamese Marine Corps was proud of their elite status as part of the RVNAF strategic reserve, and never fully embraced the base security mission at Solid Anchor. They weren't about to commit a second battalion, and worked to extricate the battalion already stationed there. On 23 January, the 6th Vietnamese Marines were relieved of their mission at Solid Anchor and replaced by a battalion from General Nghi's 21st ARVN Division.

Relations between the Marine commander of Solid Anchor and General Nghi's staff soon deteriorated to the point where it reached the ears of the generals at MACV headquarters. Since the base was scheduled for turnover to the South Vietnamese Navy in a few months, MACV decided to replace the U.S. Marine Corps colonel commanding Solid Anchor with a U.S. Navy Captain for the interim period. Concurrently, General Nghi of the 21st ARVN Division thought it wise to tamper down the ill will between his division and the base by removing his own battalion, replacing it with a battalion of the 4th Ranger Group that still remained under his operational control. I had no prior knowledge of the aforementioned command and control problems at the Solid Anchor base. We would soon experience our own difficulties with the convoluted arrangements between the U.S. and South Vietnamese forces stationed there.

* * *

On 26 January 1971, the 44th Ranger Battalion was airlifted by CH-46 Sea Knight Helicopters from Can Tho to the Solid Anchor base. It was my first trip to the extreme southern tip of the Ca Mau peninsula, and while flying in I had a good view of the terrain. The panorama below was a vast area of mangrove swamps laced with serpentine rivers and canals. Since it was low tide, I saw large mud flats along the rivers littered with trunks of dead and rotting trees. Save for a pair of egrets circling below us, I saw no sign of life, much less human habitation. It looked to me like a vast primordial swamp. As our aircraft approached the base, I caught a bird's eye view of the newly constructed facility and the surrounding area.

The base sat on the north bank of the Cau Lon River approximately eighteen miles northeast of the river's mouth on the Gulf of Thailand. The river was approximately a kilometer in width at this point. A canal running east off the river separated the main base from a small PF fort that sat on the intersection of the river and the canal. The area immediately surrounding the base had been defoliated with Agent Orange and turned into vast stretches of open mudflats. A considerable number of bomb craters dotted the area around the base.

On our final approach I saw a number of newly constructed buildings built by the U.S. Navy Seabees. There were WABTOC barracks, mess halls, maintenance buildings, and a sandbagged Tactical Operations Center. Along the shoreline, there were two docking areas for the various riverine craft assigned to the base. Our CH-46 Sea Knight touched down at the base's newly constructed Perforated Steel Plate (PSP) runway, and our operation with the U.S. and South Vietnamese Navies began.

* * *

Major Thi and I made our way to the Navy's Tactical Operations

Center where the base's N-3 operations officer, a U.S. Marine Corps major, briefed us. The major was a holdover from the period when the base was commanded by the Marine colonel, but he didn't look like a field Marine to me. I could tell that by his new unfaded utilities and spit-shined jungle boots. He was also a bit overweight, and didn't have the typical Marine high and tight haircut. The major informed us that the 44th Ranger Battalion would occupy an area on the south bank of the river across from the base. There were two wooden tent frame structures built on raised wooden platforms in the mud flats, and that was about it except for a small floating dock. Continuing the briefing, the major said that he'd have a water trailer airlifted by helicopter across the river to provide a supply of fresh water. There was no natural fresh water anywhere in the vicinity of the base. The river, streams, and canals were all saltwater due to the tidal flow.

Continuing his briefing, the Marine major said that he wanted the Rangers to conduct riverine operations with the South Vietnamese Navy to locate and destroy the enemy forces that were launching mortar and rocket attacks on the base, and interdicting river and canal traffic. In addition, he wanted the Rangers to conduct night ambushes in the surrounding areas. When I asked a few questions about the enemy situation, the major could provide few specifics.

After the briefing, Major Thi sought out the senior Vietnamese Navy officer at the base, and I tried to locate my lieutenant and sergeants. I found them in the Navy SEAL Detachment's team house. I'd never worked with the SEALs, but knew the Navy's Special Operations troops by reputation. There was a lieutenant and several petty officer types in the team house shooting pool and lifting weights. I introduced myself, and the lieutenant offered me a cold beer from the refrigerator. He said we were welcome to visit the team house anytime, but we'd have to chip in for any beers and sodas we consumed.

"Fair enough," I said. "Appreciate the hospitality."

"How'd it go with the jarhead?" the lieutenant asked.

"Who?" I answered.

"Major Ingram (not his real name), the base ops officer," he continued.

"Ok, I guess, why?" I replied.

"Watch your back with that guy, captain. He's never set foot outside this base since he's been here, and he doesn't know shit about this area. Rumor has it he sleeps with a loaded .45 pistol under his pillow every night. We don't know if he's worried about the VC or the Navy types he's pissed off since he's been here," the lieutenant said.

"How do you work with him?" I asked.

"I don't," he answered, adding, "we get our orders directly from Saigon. If we need any support from the base, I go straight to the Commodore."

"The Commodore?"

"Captain Spruit, the Navy captain who commands this base, and all of our Navy Forces in the Delta. He's a Navy aviator, and a good man," the SEAL lieutenant replied.

"I'll keep that in mind, and I appreciate the info," I said, finishing my beer.

Special Operations types regardless of their parent service tend to be very candid, especially with each other. Their lives often depend on it.

We walked down to the dock where we found Major Thi. He finished his meeting with a Vietnamese Navy commander who ordered a Swift boat crew to ferry us across the river to our new home. As we pulled away from the dock we passed the Assault Support Patrol Boat (ASPB) and the Armored Troop Carrier (ATC) that were damaged in the previous night's mortar attack. Both were heavily damaged, and probably wouldn't be sailing anywhere anytime soon. The helmsman struggled to keep the Swift boat on course as it fought the strong tidal flow of the river. After a fifteen-minute crossing, the Swift boat pulled up to the floating dock on the south side of the river and we disembarked.

The entire area was defoliated and was little more than a vast mudflat. Major Thi set up his command post in one of the two wooden tent frame structures that was erected on a platform raising it about three feet out of the mud. *Dai Uy* Yen, the battalion executive officer, moved into the other structure that was located about fifty meters away. Thi's headquarters personnel immediately began constructing a sandbag bunker beside his CP.

The remainder of the Ranger battalion was due to arrive late that afternoon, and we had to set up an LZ on the south side of the river.

I hoped the battalion would have time to consolidate its defensive positions before nightfall and the anticipated enemy mortar attacks.

We established a landing zone in the mudflats, and I tasked Lieutenant Harrison and Sergeant Lockwood to run the LZ operation. The U.S. CH-46 Sea Knight helicopters began to arrive with the Ranger companies at 3:00 p.m., and by 4:00 p.m. they were on the ground and preparing their defensive positions. Due to the high water table, the bunkers had to be built above ground and we soon ran out of sandbags. We had to radio the base to secure more from the Seabees. By nightfall most of the work was complete, and we hunkered down fully expecting a mortar attack. It didn't come that night.

Other than local daylight patrolling and night ambushes in the immediate vicinity of the base, the Ranger battalion was not called upon to conduct any riverine operations during the last week of January. The lull in operations was in large measure the result of problems with the South Vietnamese Navy boats that could be traced to the failure of the boat crews to perform necessary preventive maintenance. Maintenance crews ashore lacked the necessary spare parts, creating a backlog of boats awaiting repair. During the month of January 1971, only 44 percent of the boats operating out of Solid Anchor were available for combat operations. Further degrading the capability for offensive operations was a shortage of POL at the base.

On 30 January, the 4th Ranger Group Advisory Detachment notified me that Lieutenant Harrison had been designated payroll officer for that month. This required him to fly to Can Tho, pick up the monthly cash for the 4th Group advisors, and then fly by helicopter to each of the Group's battalions in the field to deliver the pay to the battalion advisors. Sergeant Lockwood also had to accompany the lieutenant, because Army finance regulations specified that each pay officer had to have an armed guard when he made his rounds. It was a good break for the lieutenant and sergeant, but it left my advisory team at half strength for several days. The fact that there were a sufficient number of officers and NCOs at the Can Tho headquarters who could have performed the duty irritated me even more. Nonetheless, this assignment probably saved the lieutenant's life.

The Rangers had no opportunity to celebrate the Tet Holiday on 31 January, but the VC was not about to let the holiday pass unnoticed. During the early morning hours of 31 January, we received a brief but intense 82mm mortar barrage. I was asleep on the floor of the CP structure, as was my team sergeant, when the first rounds impacted in the mud flats outside. Major Thi and his staff were also asleep on the wooden floor. We all scrambled out of the structure and took cover in the nearby bunker. The Rangers in *Dai Uy* Yen's structure were not so lucky. One of the first rounds exploded into the tent frame structure seriously wounding six men who were asleep on the floor. Fortunately, *Dai Uy* Yen was sleeping inside the bunker and was uninjured. When I surveyed the damage the next morning, I saw that the round impacted on the exact spot where Lieutenant Harrison had slept the night before. His guardian angel was doing a good job.

The 44th Ranger battalion made its first enemy contact on 3 February. On that date, a company was inserted by a River Interdiction Craft on the east bank of the Rach Ong Quyen, one of the many small streams that flowed into the river. As the company swept through the dense mangroves, it flushed a small VC unit and a brief firefight ensued in which one Ranger was KIA. The enemy quickly withdrew deeper into the swamp. No enemy bodies were recovered, but there were blood trails indicating that one or more VC was wounded in the exchange of fire.

Riverine operations in the Solid Anchor area were extremely dangerous, as we were to find out. Most of the smaller rivers and streams were constricted, winding waterways with narrow banks overgrown with mangroves. It was quite easy for the enemy to conceal their bunkers in the dense vegetation near the riverbanks. From their bunkers, the VC could hear any approaching river craft before it passed their position. A favorite tactic of the enemy was to emplace B40/41 rockets in homemade wooden "V"-shaped firing troughs along the riverbank, and fire the rockets remotely from their bunkers. Given the narrowness of the canals and streams most of these rockets scored direct hits on the boats. Neither the boat crews nor the Rangers knew what awaited them around the next bend in the meandering waterways.

In the days that followed, we conducted only a few company-size daylight operations in the contested areas surrounding the base. An oil tanker that was scheduled to make a POL supply run to the isolated location was delayed forcing the curtailment in combat operations.

The Rangers did, however, continue to insert small night ambush patrols by boat into areas where suspected enemy mortar sites were located. We received the grid coordinates for these ambush sites from the base operations officer, the Marine major. Whether he had specific intelligence that led him to select particular sites, or he just picked them off a map, I never found out but I suspected the latter. A single boat would then be dispatched to insert the ambush teams. I often rode along with Major Thi's operations officer to insure the teams were inserted into the proper areas. Late one afternoon when we were inserting several ambush teams north of the base, we found one of the sites to be in an area that would be completely flooded by the tidal flow in a few hours. Major Thi, who was also on the boat that day, made a decision to move the ambush a couple of hundred meters to some higher ground. I concurred thinking it was a sensible thing to do, but it resulted in a major flap.

When we returned to the Ranger CP, I radioed in the grid coordinates of the ambush sites to the base operations officer who would post them on his situation maps and pass them on to the artillery and helicopter gunship teams on alert status. A few minutes after I radioed in the locations, I got a call from Major Ingram saying that he wanted Major Thi and me to report immediately to the base TOC. At the time I thought that we would receive orders for a high priority mission.

When we arrived at the TOC, we were ushered into the briefing room where the Marine major was waiting. He then proceeded to read us the riot act for changing one of his ambush sites. I tried to explain that the area he selected on the map was chest deep in water even as we spoke. His face then turned crimson red and he in exploded in a rage.

"I'm going to see that the both of you are court-martialed for not following my orders," he said, raising the level of his voice about ten decibels. "You don't have the authority to countermand my orders, captain."

By this time Major Thi, who didn't like the tone of the major's voice or his bellicose threats, had gotten up and walked out of the room in a huff, cursing all the while in Vietnamese.

"Captain, you and your counterpart haven't heard the last of this," the major threatened.

I reminded the Marine major that he certainly had no UCMJ authority over any of the Vietnamese, and that I intended to report this incident to my boss, Lieutenant Colonel Ball. Furthermore, I told him that it was Major Thi's prerogative as battalion commander to make whatever changes he deemed necessary so long as the mission was carried out. With great effort I kept my temper under control, and stood my ground. When I finished my argument, the major said, "You are dismissed captain." I glared at him for a moment, then turned heel and left the briefing room.

After leaving the meeting, I grew angrier by the minute. As soon as we were back on our side of the river, Major Thi made radio contact with his Group Commander in Ca Mau, and related the incident. Afterwards, I spoke with my boss, Lt. Colonel Ball, who was at the same location. The colonel said he'd fly down the next day with the 4th Ranger Group Commander to get the situation sorted out with the base commander.

True to his word, Lt. Colonel Ball and his counterpart arrived at the base the next morning and had a private meeting with the base commander, Captain Spruit. Before he departed, Ball met with me and said he didn't think we'd be having any future problems with Major Ingram, and he was right. The next time we met with the major he was all smiles and never mentioned the incident again; he was some personality. We continued the night ambushes, and changed the recommended sites that the major chose from the map as necessary.

* * *

The pace of operations began to pick up after the first week of February, when a supply of POL finally arrived at the base. During the second week of February, the Ranger battalion was assigned a mission of making a landing on an island in a tributary of the Cua Lon River south of the base. Intelligence reports indicated that a VC POW camp was located on the island. Two companies of Rangers were embarked on armored troop carriers that were part of a small flotilla of other

Vietnamese river craft. Major Thi and I boarded the flotilla commander's craft for the operation.

As our boats steamed down the Cua Lon River, I was "pumped" for the operation. It was exhilarating to know that we just might be able to liberate some U.S. and ARVN prisoners. In addition to the two armored troop carriers (ATCs), our flotilla included two Swift boats, a Monitor, and two Assault Support Patrol Boats. Two Navy Seawolf gunship teams flew overhead to protect the convoy. When the island came into view, the column of boats moved into a line formation, and the Assault Support Boats opened fire on the landing area with their deck guns as the troop carriers ploughed through the mud-brown waters headed for the landing beach. As the shells exploded in the island's dense growth of salt-bearing trees and vegetation, large flocks of seabirds noisily took to the air.

As the troop carriers neared their landing area, the Seawolves pounded the area with rockets. *Dai Uy* Yen led the two Ranger companies during the landing on the mud-crusted beach. There was no opposition to the landing, and the Rangers soon melted into the foliage searching for the POW camp. At high tide, the floor of the island would be completely flooded by the salty river water, but it was now low tide and all the Rangers had to contend with was the sucking brown mud. They found the camp near the middle of the island, but it was deserted.

There were several thatched huts built on stilts, some bamboo cages, and elevated walkways. The only sign of any previous occupants were some broken cooking pots, animal bones, a couple of 55-gallon drums used to collect rainwater, and a few tattered rags. *Day Uy* Yen reported that it appeared that no one had occupied the camp in the past several weeks. We were disappointed, but it was worth the effort nonetheless. According to intelligence reports, the VC had constructed a number of these camps in the southern portion of the Ca Mau Peninsula, and routinely moved prisoners to various ones to keep them disoriented and to prevent their liberation by Allied forces. After burning the VC hootches and POW cages and shooting the rain barrels full of holes, the Rangers returned to the boats, and the flotilla headed back to the Solid Anchor base.

* * *

A few days later, I decided to accompany a Ranger company on a one-day operation. Normally, I only went out on battalion-size operations, and left the company-size ones to my lieutenant or one of my sergeants. My job was to be at the battalion commander's side, giving him advice and coordinating fire support. However, Lieutenant Harrison was having problems with immersion foot, and Staff Sergeant Roberts's tour was coming to an end. I knew Major Thi would never sanction my going out with a single company, so I never asked his permission. Instead I just hopped aboard the boat with the Ranger company, accompanied by Bui, my radio operator, and Hai, my interpreter.

I knew the Ranger company's mission was to search an area about a kilometer inland from a landing site on a small canal north of the base. We made it to the landing site without any problems and the men disembarked without incident. The lieutenant moved his company inland about four hundred meters then called a halt to the march. I thought he was only giving his men a rest, since the terrain was extremely overgrown with mangroves. After an hour had passed, I had my interpreter ask the *Trung Uy* when we were going to move out to our objective. The *Trung Uy* replied that we had reached our assigned objective, and that we were going to return to the boats. I pointed to the company's objective on my map then pointed to where we were actually located. He responded in Vietnamese that I'd gotten it wrong on my map, and that he'd completed his mission. Arguing with him was pointless. I told him I'd take it up with Major Thi when we returned to the base that afternoon.

When we returned, Major Thi was waiting for me and I knew he was not happy to see me. In fact, he was fuming.

"*Dai Uy*, why you go with second company? Very bad idea you have," he said angrily.

"My lieutenant was not able to go, and I couldn't send Roberts or Lockwood," I replied.

"Why you no tell me you go *Dai Uy*? N'est pas necessaire," he continued breaking into French.

By this time, I thought I had a good working relationship with

Major Thi, but knew I'd crossed a line.

Thi continued: "*Dai Uy*, if VC kill you, I have beaucoup trouble. Maybe I no command *Biet Dong Quan* no more. You die; I die. Maybe I go jail."

I knew the major was using a bit of hyperbole to make his point, but I was beginning to get the message. If a senior American advisor to a Ranger battalion was killed it reflected poorly on the battalion commander, especially under the circumstances I'd put myself in. Also, I'd caused him to lose face when I told him that his company commander had pulled a fast one on him during the mission. I'm sure the *Thieu Uy* caught more than a little hell from Major Thi, but he deserved it. That was the last time I accompanied one of Major Thi's companies without his knowledge.

* * *

The number of enemy contacts continued to increase as the Solid Anchor navy and ground forces increased the tempo of their operations. On 18 February, a Biet Hai (Naval Rangers) counter-guerrilla force assigned to Solid Anchor located a VC trench line and bunker complex about nine kilometers southeast of the base. The patrol opened fire on two VC, who were lying on top of a bunker, and another who was asleep in a hammock, killing all three. The firing alerted a force of approximately 30 VC, who were inside their bunkers. They returned fire on the Naval Rangers, killing the South Vietnamese officer leading the patrol and wounding two others. Outnumbered and outgunned, the Biet Hai team withdrew with their casualties as Seawolf gunships and ARVN artillery pounded the bunker complex. The 44th Ranger Battalion was ordered to reinforce a hastily organized Biet Hai relief force that was headed for the scene of the firefight.

We quickly mounted up two companies and boarded the boats arriving at our floating docks. As soon as the men were loaded, we jumped aboard an Armored Troop Carrier (ATC) that was decked over to accommodate the landing of helicopters. The boats proceeded at full speed up the Cua Lon River before turning into a tributary that ran to the southeast. About a kilometer from our destination, we began to receive automatic weapons fire from the narrow riverbanks. When the VC opened up, we were standing on the starboard side of the ATC's upper deck. Since the enemy fire was coming from that side of the river, we dashed to the port side seeking cover. As soon as we reached the port side, VC on the opposite bank of the river opened up. It occurred to me that I was out of my element. There are no foxholes on a boat. Since there was no cover on the deck where the helicopters landed, we quickly descended a ladder to the lower deck. The ATC and other boats returned fire with 20mm cannon, .50 caliber, and M-60 machine guns, fighting their way through the hastily organized enemy ambush.

Our relief force arrived at the bunker complex without suffering any casualties or serious damage to the boats. By the time we arrived, the enemy force had withdrawn. After disarming some hastily rigged booby traps, the Rangers searched and destroyed the enemy bunkers with C-4 explosives. A number of documents and a VC flag were recovered from the bunkers. A Vietnamese Assault Support Patrol Boat (ASPB) that was blocking a nearby canal was slightly damaged by a B-40 rocket that wounded one of the crew. The boat returned fire, killing the VC with the rocket-propelled grenade launcher. After taking on board the Biet Hai and Rangers we steamed back to the Solid Anchor base without further incident.

On the evening of 18 February the VC lobbed approximately 25 82mm rounds into the Solid Anchor base. Most of the rounds fell along the waterfront and into the river, but one Vietnamese sailor was killed and three were wounded as the boats got underway during the attack. No Rangers were killed or injured during the barrage.

The following day, the 44th Ranger Battalion was ordered to conduct a riverine operation on the Rach ong Dinh waterway. The operation involved the insertion of two companies on the west bank of the tributary. Once ashore they would sweep south along the bank, searching the area as they went. Since this operation involved the commitment of two companies, Major Thi and I accompanied the force.

We boarded a Vietnamese Monitor river craft that morning accompanied by our radio operators and selected members of Thi's command group, while the two Ranger companies boarded the Armored Troop Carrier (ATC) boats. It was a beautiful cloudless morning, and the sunlight sparkled off the river. I made it a point to start wearing a flak jacket on the riverine operations. The risk of ambush was extremely high once the boats entered the narrow waterways.

The monitor boat, ATCs, and two Assault Support Patrol Boats (ASTBs) moved down the narrow, winding waterway to the designated landing area on the east bank of the river without incident. The Rangers quickly disembarked and began their sweep down the south bank of the waterway. *Dai Uy* Yen was leading the two companies that went ashore, and Major Thi and his command element stayed on board the monitor. A third Ranger company was held in reserve on an ATC. All was quiet except for the sound of small waves slapping against the boat's hull.

Suddenly, rocket and machine gun fire erupted from the west bank of the river. Two of the ASPBs were hit with enemy rockets, wounding two Vietnamese sailors and two U.S. Navy advisors. Our monitor opened up with 20mm cannon and machine gun fire, drawing the enemy's attention from the ASPBs. I noticed an unmanned M-60 machine gun lying on the deck so I picked it up and ran toward a gun turret. The gunner was not in the turret and the open top was covered with a wooden plank. I put the M-60 on top of the turret cover, and began firing short bursts at the shoreline. As I continued to fire, a B-40 rocket struck the armor-plated monitor. The force of the blast blew me and the gun off the top of the turret and onto the deck. I checked myself out. There were a few small pieces of shrapnel embedded in my flak jacket, but other than a bruised knee and a ringing in my ears, I was unhurt.

As the firing continued, a pair of Seawolf helicopters arrived overhead and began to saturate the west bank of the river with rocket and machine gun fire. When the firing subsided, Major Thi ordered his reserve company to land on the eastern bank and assault the enemy positions. The Rangers gained control of the riverbank and shot their way into a large bunker complex, as the VC withdrew into the swamps pursued by the gunships.

A search of the complex turned up four B-40 rocket launchers, several rockets, and several land mines. After destroying the bunkers with explosive charges, the Rangers withdrew to the boats. Their losses were minimal, four Rangers sustaining small shrapnel wounds. The ASPBs had moderate damage, and the monitor had light damage, but all boats were able to return to the Solid Anchor base under their own power.

The following day the two ARVN 105mm howitzers supporting Solid Anchor operations were ferried across the river to newly constructed emplacements in the expanded PF fort adjacent to the Solid Anchor base. The headquarters element and two Ranger companies of our battalion moved from the south bank of the Cua Lon River to the PF fort to secure the new firing positions. I was shocked when Major Thi's wife and two small children arrived at the base two days later. How they got there is a mystery to me; they must have caught a ride on a South Vietnamese resupply aircraft. Why he wanted his wife and kids in such a remote location was beyond my comprehension, but it was his family, not mine.

A few days later, a Ranger company operating in an area about six kilometers south of Solid Anchor engaged an enemy force of unknown size around midday. The Viet Cong withdrew after a short but intense firefight, as the Rangers killed one of the enemy and captured another. This was the last enemy contact during the 44th Ranger Battalion's attachment to the Solid Anchor base.

On the night of 28 February, the VC mortared the base again. They must have been running low on 82mm mortar ammunition since they fired only three rounds at the base and three more at the two Ranger companies that remained on the south bank. There were no friendly casualties and no material damage. I was asleep when the attack began, but awoke when the ARVN howitzers several yards away from my bunker began firing their counter-mortar fires at the suspected enemy location.

Two days later, the 42d Ranger Battalion relieved the 44th, and thus ended the 44th Ranger Battalion's combat operations in support of Solid Anchor. I hoped that I'd seen the last of the Ca Mau Peninsula. We returned to the 44th's home base at Cai Rang, and since my R&R to Australia was approved for the last week of March, I was in high spirits.

A month after our departure from Solid Anchor, the South Vietnamese Navy assumed control of the Solid Anchor mission, and in

September of 1971, the last remaining U.S. Navy personnel turned over control of the shore facility to their counter-parts. The Navy's "brown water" operations in the Delta came to an end.

CHAPTER 10

"JEREMIAH WAS A BULLFROG"

•

The 44th Ranger Battalion returned to its base at Cai Rang during the first week of March 1971, for a well deserved stand-down. The battalion's losses during the U Minh campaign, the *Cuu Long* Cambodian operation, and the Solid Anchor operation were relatively light, and its combat effectiveness had improved significantly over the prior five months. In fact, the battalion was credited with the highest kill ratio of any unit involved in the U Minh operation. Major Thi's job was secure, at least for the time being.

After we returned to Cai Rang, I was told to report to Lieutenant Colonel Witek's headquarters at Can Tho airbase. I had no idea what was afoot, but hoped that the Ranger Senior Advisor was going to rotate some of his battalion combat advisors into staff positions at his headquarters. After six months in the field with the Ranger battalion, I felt I needed a break. Additionally, I had some ideas how the staff could improve their support to the Battalion Combat Assistance Teams. Having never experienced life with a Ranger battalion in the field, Lt. Colonel Witek's staff officers displayed little empathy or support for the battalion combat advisors. Unfortunately, in my case, a staff position was not in the offing.

Unbeknownst to me, the entire MACV advisory organization was undergoing restructuring as part of the Vietnamization program. In November of 1970, the MACV Commander, General Abrams, announced a plan to restructure Division Combat Assistance Teams (DCATs), and eliminate Regimental (RCATs) and Battalion Combat Assistance Teams (BCATs). Under the plan, the BCATs would be phased out first followed by the RCATs. All BCATs were scheduled to be phased out by 1 July 1971. Within the Delta Regional Assistance Command (DRAC), the Ranger BCATs were to be some of the first to be phased out. Lt. Colonel Witek selected my team as the first to be deactivated, and that was why he summoned me to his headquarters.

The colonel went on to explain that he had selected my team because our Ranger battalion had shown great improvement over the past six months, and he considered it one of the best in Military Region 4. That's great, I thought, now maybe I'll move into a staff job, perhaps as the assistant operations officer; but that was not to be.

Witek went on to explain that MACV had authorized the organization of a three-man team in each Ranger group to be used in a mobile assistance concept to support Ranger battalion training and operations. He had selected me to lead the 4th Ranger Group team. He went on to explain that my team would work with a three-man Vietnamese training team that would do most of the actual instruction. Our role was to develop the training plan, including the curriculum and lesson plans, and to train our counterparts to deliver the instruction. A significant portion of the training was devoted to training the Ranger ground commanders on coordinating and directing tactical air, helicopter gunship, and artillery support without the assistance of U.S. advisors. Additionally, we were to provide training on orchestrating aerial medical evacuations, airmobile operations, and logistic operations. All of the training and assistance was to be delivered in a field environment while the Ranger battalions were conducting combat operations.

I didn't think that the concept of training the Ranger ground commanders during combat operations was sound. During combat operations, there are too many distractions that the commanders have to deal with other than training. An alternative was to establish a short course for the Vietnamese Ranger officers that they could attend during battalion stand downs, but the die had already been cast.

The Senior Ranger Advisor also informed me that he had already selected two non-commissioned officers for my team, and that I'd still be reporting directly to Lieutenant Colonel Ball who would provide me additional guidance and establish the priorities for training battalions within the 4th Ranger Group.

I brought up the matter of my R&R leave that was scheduled later that month. After six months in the field I thought I'd earned a rest. The colonel passed the buck, saying that I should discuss my R&R with Lt. Colonel Ball.

When I left the meeting, I felt disappointed and let down. It was apparent that the colonel's earlier promises were unfulfilled. The battalion combat advisors would not be rotated into staff assignments, which are also important to an officer's professional development. On the other hand, the staff advisors would never serve a day in the field with a Ranger battalion, but they would continue to draw the same combat pay and collect their Bronze Stars for service at the end of their tours.

I drove back to Cai Rang to break the news to my team members. We'd all be moving to the Can Tho Ranger Headquarters during the transition. My lieutenant and sergeants would be reassigned within the Ranger command for the duration of their tours. I paid a final courtesy call on Major Thi to break the news. He'd already been informed through his own chain of command that he was going to lose his advisors. The major wasn't pleased, but he had no say in it. He asked about some of the items in our team house, specifically the U.S. stove and refrigerator. I told him he could have both since they weren't on anyone's property book. This was the first time Major Thi had asked me for anything for his personal use, and I think that the request really came from his wife. On our last night with the battalion, Major Thi took us to a local restaurant for dinner. The following morning we loaded up our Jeep and trailer and headed for Can Tho.

Reflecting on the leadership within the 44th Ranger Battalion, I concluded that Major Thi was a capable battalion commander who carried out his orders to the best of his abilities. He was not a risk taker, however, and he showed a certain reluctance to finish a fight and win the day, more often than not leaving the enemy an avenue of escape. I concluded that he was under considerable pressure from higher-level commanders to keep his casualties to a minimum. Replacements seldom outpaced the casualty rates. While I was sure that there was a certain level of corruption in the administration of the battalion, there was no evidence that Major Thi was enriching himself or his family. They lived a very modest lifestyle and had few personal possessions. The major did what he had to do to survive, but nothing beyond that.

Dai Uy Yen, the battalion executive officer, was a true warrior who always led by example. He was a charismatic combat leader who was willing to "kick ass" to get the job done. While Major Thi and his exec did not have a close personal relationship—in fact it was at times extremely acrimonious—they had a command relationship that worked.

The weakest link in the officer ranks was at the junior level including the company commanders. To be fair, the Ranger company commanders did not have the authority that U.S. company commanders exercise. In a sense, the Vietnamese company commanders were more on the level of U.S. platoon leaders in terms of the amount of freedom of action they had and the number of men they commanded. The Ranger companies typically fielded between 60 to 80 men. When the Rangers participated in company-size operations away from the direct supervision of the battalion commander, the company commanders could not be relied upon to accomplish their assigned missions. Additionally, in the absence of orders, the company commanders were unlikely to take the initiative and act decisively. In fact, aggressive leadership was not rewarded or nurtured in the ARVN officer corps.

The professionalism of the ARVN Ranger NCOs was not even close to what existed in U.S. units, but the Vietnamese Ranger NCOs were on the whole better than those serving in typical ARVN infantry battalions. Also, due to the class structure of Vietnamese society, the Ranger NCOs did not have the close working relationships with their officers that existed in U.S. units. The vast majority of ARVN NCOs came from the rural peasant class, while their officers had their origins in the society's middle and upper classes.

Overall, the rank and file of the Ranger battalion were top-notch soldiers. During my six months with the battalion, I observed many selfless acts of heroism comparable to those I observed while commanding a U.S. rifle company. The ARVN Rangers fought heroically and died hard under some of the harshest conditions that I experienced during my two tours in Vietnam. Moreover, they had remarkable stamina and endurance. They deserved better leadership from the top down.

●   * * *

When we moved to the MR-4 Ranger advisory compound at the Can Tho Airfield, I was assigned a room in the billeting area. While the accommodations were well below the one-star hotel level, we did have hot showers, real U.S.-style toilets, laundry and maid service, and American food and beverages. It was a far different world from the one I just left, even though it was temporary.

The MR-4 ARVN Ranger Commander assigned a Vietnamese captain and two senior NCOs as our counterparts on the combined mobile combat training team. The *Dai Uy* was a hard worker who was well grounded in the training business. We worked together to develop a series of lesson plans that were adaptable to a field environment. After drafting the lessons in English, we had them translated into Vietnamese for our counterparts. The *Dai Uy* had his NCOs prepare the training aides. For the most part, these were prepared on butcher paper using "magic markers," and they were nothing more than outlines of the key points covered in each lesson. I wondered how well they would hold up in a field environment. It was obvious that the *Dai Uy's* background in training must have been in a classroom environment.

My concept for the training was to develop a variety of situations that could be executed over a period of time while the battalion was in the field. Each situation would require a performance-oriented bloc of training that required participation and action by the officers and NCOs, to be followed immediately by a critique of their actions. I doubted if the commanders had the latitude to devote a specific amount of time each day to training, but that didn't matter. Situational training is by definition impromptu, and need not conflict with operational requirements. In fact, it can be accomplished in support of operational requirements. I tried to explain my concept to my Vietnamese counterpart, but I'm not sure he grasped it.

The two sergeants that Lieutenant Colonel Witek assigned to the training team were ex-Special Forces NCOs, who wanted to remain in Vietnam when Special Forces left country. They were addicted to the lifestyle much like many other expatriates. These soldiers spoke enough Vietnamese to get by, loved the food, and thrived on the cheap booze and sex, and the thrill of combat. In short they were "animals" or "combat junkies." Their type was easy to identify. Typically, they wore some variation of the camouflage uniform accessorized with Montagnard brass bracelets, and a gold Buddha around their necks. Nonetheless, these NCOs were the type you wanted watching your back in a tough combat situation.

Neither Staff Sergeant Eldridge nor Sergeant Pyle (not his real name) would have lasted more than a week in the Stateside Army. They could not have adjusted to the discipline and tedium of garrison life. Eldridge had a wife and a couple of kids back in the States, but that didn't cramp his style. During the first week with the team, the pair tried to feel me out, deliberately testing my tolerance for their informality and lack of military courtesy. They were a bit disconcerted when I didn't react as they expected. I kept our relationship on a professional level, and didn't overreact to their conduct. I did, however, insist that they live on the compound rather than downtown. The two sergeants had no choice but to comply; however their room was soon decorated in a motif that could best be described as Vietnamese "cat-house chic." There were long beaded doorway curtains, black velvet artwork on the walls, and a strong odor of incense always permeated the room. I received quite a few complaints from the staff NCOs, who had adjacent rooms.

Since Eldridge and Pyle both spoke passable Vietnamese, I assigned them to work with the Vietnamese Ranger training NCOs. They seemed to get along well with their counterparts.

As the month wore on, I became more excited about my upcoming R&R that was scheduled to begin on 26 March. I'd always wanted to visit Australia. My plan was to get to Saigon a couple of days prior to that date to do some shopping at the Tan Son Nhut PX, since I had no civilian clothes to wear during my R&R. Someone had broken into the storage room at the Can Tho compound where we stored our baggage, and all my personal clothing was stolen. A deployment date for our mobile combat training team had not been determined, and I continued to hope that my R&R would not be derailed. Unfortunately, it did not work out that way.

When I brought up the matter with my boss, Lt. Colonel Ball, he put the ball squarely in my court, asking what he could do if his counterpart wanted to deploy the mobile combat training team while I was on leave in Australia. I didn't have a good answer so I reluctantly cancelled my R&R. At least I wouldn't have to explain to Jackie why I took R&R in Australia instead of meeting her in Hawaii. Maybe I'd get another chance for a leave if I managed to get myself reassigned, I thought. By this time, my attitude was half sardonic and half fatalistic.

I knew that we had to finalize the training plan, and then deploy to the field with one of the Ranger battalions to implement it. By that time at least two additional Battalion Combat Assistance Teams (BCATs), would be phased out, and there would be two captains available to take my place as leader of the training team. I had learned that the Vietnamese Airborne Division was authorized to retain their BCATs through November 1971, and I decided to pursue an advisory assignment with that unit.

By the first week of April, the mobile combat training team was ready to deploy with one of the Ranger battalions. Since the 41st Ranger Battalion was next in line to lose its advisors, our training team was attached to that unit. We flew by helicopter to the battalion's field location west of Vinh Long. The battalion was running company-size operations in an area where there had been a recent series of attacks against isolated RF/PF outposts.

Our plan called for our team to spend one week with each of the 41st Ranger Battalion's line companies. We joined the battalion's 1st Company that was commanded by a Ranger second lieutenant, *Thieu Uy*. With his tightly tailored fatigues, sunglasses, bushy haircut, and scrawny frame he looked like an aspiring teenage rock star. He must have thought himself a mandarin prince, since his entourage included about half-a-dozen batboys, cooks, and bodyguards.●

The first few days with the company were uneventful. We walked with the company during their daylight sweeps, taking advantage of breaks and evenings to present our instruction and critiques. Our team gave separate classes to the officers and NCOs covering basic tactics, and the employment of helicopter gunships and close air support. Most of the officers had a basic proficiency in English, and we had them practice radio communications with a simulated gunship team leader or Forward Air Controller. We'd pick out a tree line or other terrain feature, and had each officer direct a simulated strike on the target. I'd start the exercise scenario by making a radio call to the officer student:

"Ranger one this is Spur one-niner, we are approaching your area. Request you mark your location with smoke, over."

The student would respond, "I am at your three o'clock, and I am marking with smoke, over."

Continuing, I would answer, "Roger, I have yellow smoke. Identify target location, over."

Then the student would be required to direct the gunship to the target by the use of his location as a reference point: "From my yellow smoke, VC is two hundred meters west. VC is dug in along tree line, over."

Then I'd throw them a curveball to get them to think and react. "This is Spur one-niner. I have two yellow smokes, one in tree line, and one in rice paddy. Are there friendlies in tree line? Over."

It was pretty basic, but with the language difficulties it was challenging for the Ranger officers. We spent quite a bit of time familiarizing them with terminology and techniques used in adjusting fires onto a target.

We also tried to enhance the effectiveness of the company's night patrols by covering the basic techniques of the night ambush in a short class, and then accompanying an actual patrol. We critiqued the patrol leader on his preparations and how he moved his men into positions at the ambush site. We also critiqued the patrol's light and noise discipline, emplacement of Claymore mines, and selection of rally points and withdrawal routes.

Near the end of the first week of training, the company was searching an area along a canal that was bordered on both sides with rice paddy fields. About mid-morning, we reached a small PF outpost at an intersection of two major canals. The outpost was a mud-walled fort with a few sandbagged bunkers. We were surprised to find a three man Mobile Advisory Team (MAT) at the remote outpost. The team consisted of a U.S. Army captain and two NCOs. I asked the team leader about the enemy situation in the area. The captain said that there was a local force VC platoon operating in the vicinity. The VC platoon was not strong enough to launch a ground attack against the outpost, but had harassed the PF platoon with sniper fire and occasional 60mm mortar attacks. The most recent incident occurred the day before our arrival. A PF officer was shot and killed by a sniper as he was standing on the mud wall that surrounded the outpost.

The MAT team had an ANGR-46 radio set up in their bunker with an RC-292 antenna outside to maintain radio communication with their headquarters. We exchanged radio frequencies, since we were operating in the surrounding area. Despite the fact that the MAT team was housed in a sturdy bunker, I would not have traded places with them. They were really isolated at the outpost with fewer than 30 PF soldiers. I asked the captain if the outpost was within friendly artillery range, and he said that the fort was within range of an ARVN 155mm howitzer section located in a larger fortified outpost about ten kilometers to the north. After drinking a couple of their cold beers, we bid the MAT team members farewell, and moved out with the Ranger company.

About noon we halted for a break. As the Rangers began to prepare their noon meal, the *Thieu Uy* received a radio message from his battalion commander ordering him to prepare immediately for an airmobile pick up. The company was to conduct an airmobile assault into an LZ located about ten kilometers to the northeast. Thirty minutes later, ten U.S. UH-1D lift helicopters landed on the Ranger PZ. As I boarded the lead helicopter with the *Thieu Uy* and his command group, the U.S. pilot handed me an operations order and overlay. The order was written in Vietnamese, but I was able to decipher it by looking at the accompanying map overlay. After securing its LZ, the Ranger company was to move north and search a wooded area about a kilometer away. After posting the information on the overlay to my map, I handed the order to the *Thieu Uy*.

Our LZ was located in a dry rice paddy, and there was no preparatory artillery fire to support our assault. A gunship team covered our landing, but we took no fire on the LZ. Thus far, it was a routine airmobile operation. After disembarking from the Hueys, the company moved into an area just off the LZ where a thatched house was located. We were in clear view of the wooded area that was the company's objective, but the *Thieu Uy* ordered his men to form a perimeter in the rice paddies around the house. I advised the *Thieu Uy* that his orders were to search and clear the wooded area. He replied that his men had to prepare their noon meal before doing anything further. I received no support from my counterpart, the *Dai Uy* who led the Vietnamese half of our training team. Since he held the rank of captain, he should have taken the young company commander to task, but he didn't. It was obvious that they were both dragging their feet on completing the mission. I tried to radio the 4th Ranger Group field CP to pass this information to Lt. Colonel Ball, but we were out of radio range.

After the noon meal was consumed, I asked the company commander again when we were going to move out.

He responded, "*Dai Uy*, no VC here. We stay here. No worry *Dai Uy*."

I said, "Your orders are to search and clear that woods, *Thieu Uy*."

"Beaucoup booby traps in woods, *Dai Uy*. Very bad place. Rangers not go there," he replied.

Totally exasperated and frustrated with the young punk, I said, "*Thieu Uy*, at least send a patrol to check the woods for VC."

"Very bad idea. We stay here," he finished.

I wanted to pick the *Thieu Uy* up and start shaking him, but I restrained myself. After finishing their lunch, the *Thieu Uy* and his men moved inside the house where his batboys had set up his hammock. The afternoon wore on and it was evident that the company commander had no intention of going anywhere. The Ranger platoons began to dig in along the paddy ridges for what was to be a long night.

As darkness approached, the *Thieu Uy* and his command group as well as the Vietnamese members of our training team moved inside the house for the night. Sergeant Eldridge and I were not that foolhardy. We moved our rucksacks into a vegetable garden about twenty meters from the house. There was an irrigation ditch a few meters away. Eldridge and I both realized that, if there was an enemy force in the area, they would be ready to pounce. Since, the Ranger perimeter was clearly visible from the wood line, the VC would know exactly how many troops we had, and where all the fighting positions were located, including the M-60s. The enemy would also know that there were two Americans accompanying the Ranger company. We were right on all counts.

Shortly after midnight, a B-40 rocket slammed into the thatched hut, followed by bursts of machine gun fire. Sergeant Eldridge and I were asleep when the firefight began. We grabbed our radio and weapons and low-crawled to the irrigation ditch that had only a few inches of water flowing through it. Machine gun rounds stitched the ground around us as we crawled toward the ditch. The Rangers on the perimeter returned fire, providing us some cover. When we reached the ditch, I saw the Rangers dragging their dead and wounded from the burning hooch and heading for our irrigation ditch. After they jumped in I saw that the *Thieu Uy* was bleeding from multiple small shrapnel wounds, as were the other survivors who made it to the cover of the ditch. As the medics worked on the wounded, the enemy fire intensified. Based on the volume of incoming fire, I estimated that we were under attack by a company-size force.

Suddenly there was a lull in the firing, and we heard shouting back and forth between the Rangers on the perimeter and the VC. I asked my counterpart what they were saying. He answered, "VC are saying, 'give us the Americans'."

Pointing my Swedish K in the *Thieu Uy's* direction, I said, "Don't even think about it, *Thieu Uy*. At that point, I did not have any trust or confidence in the Ranger company commander. I told Sergeant Eldridge that we might have to escape and evade if the perimeter was overrun. In that case, we'd try to make it to the PF outpost. Neither of us intended to be taken prisoner, and we vowed to go down fighting if necessary.

Suddenly, I remembered the MAT team's radio, and quickly switched to their frequency, hoping we were in range. After three or four attempts, the MAT team responded. I think they were asleep. I gave the captain the grid coordinates of our location and the enemy location, and asked what fire support was immediately available.

He said that we were within the artillery fan of the ARVN 155mm howitzers, and that he could relay our fire mission. I plotted a fire mission on the wooded area to our north. While the ARVN artillery fire direction center was plotting the mission, the MAT team captain told me that he also had radio contact with the U.S. base at Dong Tam where U.S. Army gunships were on alert status. I requested that he pass an urgent request for gunship support to Dong Tam. Thanks to our friends on the MAT team, I thought we stood a chance of getting the situation under control.

Ten minutes later, the ARVN artillery began to fire on the wood line. The rounds were right on target and shell after shell exploded in the woods. I was fairly certain that the main enemy force was dug in on the edge of the woods, but at least one enemy platoon had moved forward to a rice paddy dike about fifty meters from our perimeter. They were too close to engage with artillery fire, and were inflicting heavy casualties on the Rangers with RPGs and automatic weapons fire. I had no idea how many Rangers were still able to continue the fight along the perimeter, but the volume of their fire was diminishing all along the line. The company had no reserve, but there were about eight Rangers in the irrigation ditch who were unwounded or only slightly wounded, so I told the commander that these men should reinforce his platoon on the northern portion of the perimeter. I knew that the total strength of the company was around sixty men, and it didn't make sense to keep eight men in the ditch where they were contributing nothing to the fight. The *Thieu Uy* refused, arguing that these men were his personal bodyguards, and some had lost their weapons when they had fled the burning house.

The firefight continued, and the *Thieu Uy* said that the Rangers were running low on ammunition. I pulled all the loaded 9mm magazines for my Swedish K from my rucksack and lined them up on the edge of the ditch, saving two that I shoved into the cargo pockets of my fatigues. If Eldridge and I had to make a break for it, we would take only our weapons and radio with us.

Moments later our radio crackled to life with a call from the leader of a Taipan gunship team. I had worked with the Taipans during the U Minh operation. They were part of a joint U.S./Australian assault helicopter company (135th Aviation) that supported U.S. and ARVN forces operating in the Mekong Delta. The lift platoons were called the Emus, and the gunships were called the Taipans, and both knew their business well.

"Marauder 6, this is Taipan one-seven over," the gunship team leader called.

"This is Marauder 6, over," I answered.

"Marauder 6 this is Taipan one-seven, we are one zero minutes from your location. Are you still in contact, over."

"This is Marauder 6, that's affirmative; we're taking RPG and small arms fire, over," I responded.

"This is Taipan one-seven, how will you be marking your location, over."

"This is Marauder 6, I'll mark my position with strobe light, over."

"This is Taipan one-seven, roger," the gunship team leader answered. "I have tracer fire at my 4 o'clock. Have your strobe in sight, over."

"This is Marauder 6, we are in a perimeter defense. VC are dug in along tree line two hundred meters to our north with forward assault platoon deployed along rice paddy dike five zero meters north of our perimeter, over." I continued.

I turned to the *Thieu Uy* and told him to have his Rangers on the northern perimeter mark their flank positions along the paddy dike with trip flares.

"This is Marauder 6, marking flanks of friendly position with trip flares, anyone north of trip flares are VC, over," I said, orienting the gunships.

The Taipans began their gunship runs blasting the wood line with rockets before shifting their fires to the VC closest to the Ranger perimeter. They dove on the paddy dike that shielded the VC, strafing it with machine gun fire. After the first run, the VC who were still alive retreated toward the tree line. The enemy were cut down in the open rice paddy by the circling Taipan gunships. It was all over in fifteen minutes. After overflying the area all around our perimeter, the gunship team leader announced:

"Marauder six, this is Taipan one-seven, we can see no more VC near your perimeter. There are bodies and weapons north of your perimeter. We'd sure appreciate a few of those weapons, if you can deliver them to Dong Tam, over."

"This is Marauder 6, you got 'em, and I'll throw in a case of your favorite brew as well, over," I promised.

"This is Taipan one-seven, roger Marauder 6; glad we could be of some help, over."

"This is Marauder 6, one more favor, could you radio Dong Tam to send us a Dust Off. We have friendly WIAs and KIAs, over."

"This is Taipan one-seven, WILCO, out," the Taipan finished.

There was no doubt about it. The Taipans saved our asses that night. After evacuating our casualties, I insisted that the Rangers sweep the area around the perimeter. The *Thieu Uy* wanted to wait until daylight, but I insisted. Sergeant Eldridge and I led the sweep ourselves. I counted thirteen enemy KIA, and we recovered ten enemy weapons, four of which we kept for the Taipans.

An airmobile unit extracted the Ranger company and our Mobile Combat Advisory Team the following morning. When we arrived at the 41st Ranger Battalion's field headquarters, Lt. Colonel Ball was already there and he wanted a full report on the firefight. I described everything that happened from the time we landed on the LZ the previous day, focusing on the Ranger company commander's actions. I stressed the fact that he had placed his men in jeopardy and ignored the mission he was assigned in the battalion's operations order. In my opinion he deserved a court-martial.

Furthermore, my Vietnamese counterpart was a captain, and as the senior officer on the ground he should have taken over when the company commander refused to comply with the battalion commander's orders. As far as I was concerned, my counterpart was as worthless as the young *Thieu Uy*. The colonel told Sergeant Eldridge and me to get some sleep, and that he'd take the matter up with his counterpart, the 4th Ranger Group Commander. I heard later that the *Thieu Uy* was relieved, but doubt that any disciplinary action was taken against him.

Sergeant Eldridge and I racked out in a Vietnamese hootch. As usual, Eldridge had his transistor radio blaring. I fell into a deep sleep with the sounds of Three Dog Night's "Joy to the World / Jeremiah Was a Bullfrog" blaring in my ears. About two hours later, an ARVN artillery battery nearby began firing, and still half asleep, I instinctively rolled off the sleeping platform and hit the floor, thinking it was incoming fire. The war was wearing on me.

The following day our team joined another Ranger company for a week. By the end of the operation our team had trained all of the 41st Ranger companies without further incident. I had no doubts that the battalion was going to falter once their advisors were phased out. The officer leadership throughout the battalion from the commander on down was weak.

The battalion ended the operation at a location about halfway between Can Tho and Vinh Long in mid-April. The companies assembled in a village on Highway 4, to await the arrival of truck transportation back to their base near Long Xuyen. The 4th Ranger Group Advisory Team radioed Can Tho for a chopper to fly our Mobile Combat Training Team back to the Ranger compound at Can Tho airfield.

When the trucks arrived to pick up the Ranger battalion, we were still waiting for the chopper. I convinced the battalion's senior advisor, Captain Malone, to stay behind with his Jeep until the chopper arrived. Several hours passed and the chopper had not arrived, so I asked Captain Malone to drive Sergeant Eldridge and myself back to Can Tho. He wasn't keen on the idea and neither was his Vietnamese driver. By this time, I'd had about enough of the 41st Battalion, and I told Sergeant Eldridge to go start the Jeep. I told Malone that he could ride along and spend the night in Can Tho, or take the next bus to Long Xuyen with his driver. Captain Malone and his driver had a sudden change of heart.

When we finally got back to the Ranger headquarters at Can Tho airfield, I went directly to the S-3's office to find out why we were never picked up by helicopter as promised. "Oh yeah," the major said, "the S-4 had some supplies that had to be delivered to one of the border camps; the chopper was supposed to pick you up on the way back. I guess someone dropped the ball. Sorry about that. Well, anyway you made it back," he finished.

"Thanks for nothing major," I said. At that moment I made up my mind that I was going to find another assignment as soon as possible.

I spent the next week writing an after-action report on the first deployment of the Ranger Mobile Combat Training Team. The concept of training a unit during a combat operation was flawed. It was like trying to train firemen in techniques while they were involved in fighting an actual fire. The ARVN Ranger junior officers needed extensive training in everything from basic infantry tactics to adjusting artillery fires and directing tactical air strikes. Trying to squeeze in a few hours of training during a combat operation was nothing but window dressing. In my report, I proposed the establishment of a modest-sized Ranger training center within the MR-4 Ranger Command that would offer short courses for officers and NCOs on the subjects previously mentioned. Forward air controllers and gunship pilots could be brought in to assist in the training. Lt. Colonel Witek reviewed the report and forwarded it to his counterpart and the Delta Regional Assistance Commander, but nothing ever came of it.

A few days after I finished my report, Captain Marty Tovar and another Ranger advisor and I decided to make a trip to Saigon for a few days of relaxation. Our boss, Lt. Colonel Ball, was on leave so we sought no one's permission. We traveled by Jeep following Highway 4 to reach the capital and checked into a Vietnamese hotel upon arrival. Later that evening we hit the bars on Thu Do Street and ended our partying at the Massachusetts's BOQ bar. When we entered the place we were shocked to see our boss, Lt. Colonel Ball, sitting at a table with three other colonels. He spotted us immediately so there was no way we could make a graceful exit.

"What are you three doing in Saigon? Are you on official Army business?" he asked.

"Well you see Sir..., we thought we'd take a little in-country R&R," I replied sheepishly.

"I see," he said. "Well then don't get into any trouble. Now go get yourselves a drink and have the bartender put it on my tab."

We didn't know at the time that the colonel had put in for retirement at the end of his tour, and was in Saigon to take his retirement physical. He was a fine officer and gentleman, and he wasn't going to make an issue of three of his captains taking a short, unauthorized leave in Saigon.

The next day we drove out to Tan Son Nhut airbase to visit the PX. I dropped my two friends off saying I had another errand to run for about an hour, giving no hint that I was job hunting. My destination was the Vietnamese Airborne Division Advisory Team 162 that was located on the base. My intention was to talk with the admin officer to see if there were any projected advisory vacancies in the detachment over the next month or two. After summarizing my qualifications to the captain in charge of personnel, he told me to hold tight while he checked with his boss. He soon returned and said that the Division's Senior Advisor, Colonel Vaught, would like to speak with me. I was quite surprised since this was strictly a "cold call" on my part.

Colonel James Vaught had taken over as Senior Advisor to the Airborne Division during the worst period of the Laotian incursion, *Operation Lam Son 719*, two months earlier. The Airborne Division had just had a major fire support base overrun, and one of their brigade commanders captured. Vaught had been hand-picked by the MACV commander to turn things around, and he did just that. He had a distinguished combat record in three wars: WWII, Korea, and Vietnam. On a tour with the First Cavalry Division in 1968, he commanded a battalion that broke the siege of Khe Sanh in the aftermath of the Tet Offensive.

I gave the colonel what I thought my qualifications were for an assignment as battalion senior advisor in the airborne advisory detachment. He said that he expected to have an opening for an advisor in one of the division's battalions in May, and that he'd check with the MACV J-1 on a possible transfer for me. I knew he'd have my officer's personnel file pulled so he could check out my qualifications before he took it to that level, and that he'd also want Lt. Colonel Witek's recommendation as well. I saluted the colonel, and left his office full of hope for a new assignment with the Airborne Division.

That evening Marty Tovar arranged a little get-together at the Tan Son Nhut Air Force Officers Club with a Red Cross girl who was a friend of his wife during her tour with the organization in 1968. We met Pat Rowan and her date, an Army Military Intelligence officer, at the Air Force Officers Club. We overstayed our welcome a bit, consuming the better part of a case of beer and stacking the cans in a pyramid on our table. We then ordered a couple bottles of champagne before we were politely invited by the club officer to leave the premises. Pat had no problem keeping up with three raucous Ranger officers on leave from the Mekong Delta, but I don't think her date enjoyed the evening as much as we did. Little did I know that Pat would be the one who would later introduce me to my wife of 36 years, once we returned to the States.

About two weeks after we returned to Can Tho, I received a phone call from the adjutant at the Delta Regional Assistance Command. He wanted me to come to his office. I drove across the airfield, and he told me that he had MACV orders reassigning me to Advisory Team 162, the Airborne Division Advisory Detachment, and demanded to know how I managed to get myself reassigned without a formal request through his office, adding that he was in charge of officer reassignments in the Delta. Since he was of equal rank, I told him that it was none of his damn business, and suggested that if he had such a big problem with it we could step outside and settle it. That shut him up in a hurry, and he shoved a copy of my orders across his desk. My reporting date to Team 162 was 28 May 1971.

To tell the truth, I had mixed feelings about leaving the Ranger Advisory Detachment. Over the past months, I had made some good friends among the captains who were battalion advisors, but the self-serving staff officers were another matter. Despite the trials and tribulations that went with the job of a battalion senior advisor, it was the job I was best qualified for within MACV. Since the battalion combat advisory teams were to be phased out in the Ranger battalions, it was time to leave. For an airborne infantry officer assigned to MACV, Team 162 was a top-notch assignment. There was a long list of captains waiting to get this post, and somehow I jumped to the top of the list. I later learned that Lt. Colonel Witek had spoken to Colonel Vaught and had strongly recommended me for the airborne.

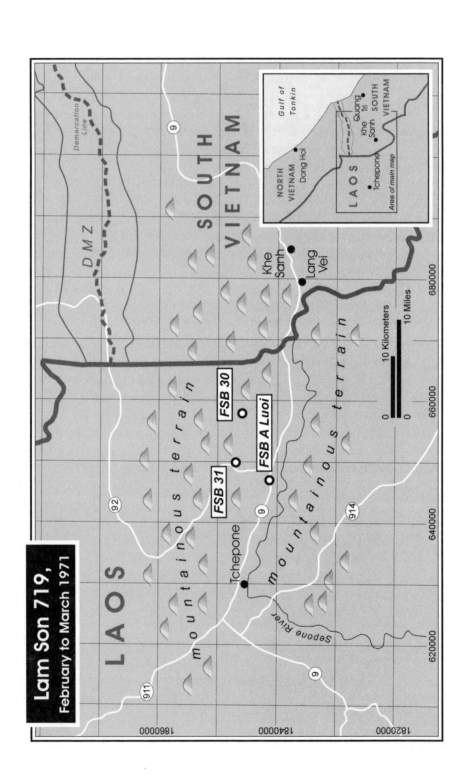

Lam Son 719,
February to March 1971

LAOS

SOUTH
VIETNAM

DMZ

Demarcation
Line

9

9

92

FSB 30

FSB 31

FSB A Luoi

Tchepone

Khe
Sanh

Lang
Vei

911

914

9

Sepone River

mountainous terrain

mountainous terrain

10 Kilometers

10 Miles

620000

640000

660000

680000

1820000

1840000

1860000

Gulf of
Tonkin

NORTH
VIETNAM

Dong Hoi

Quang
Tri

Khe
Sanh

SOUTH
VIETNAM

LAOS

Tchepone

Area of main map

CHAPTER 11

"INTO THE MIDST OF BATTLE"

•

My reporting date to the Vietnamese Airborne Division Detachment, Team 162, was 29 May1971. The day prior I packed my gear, said my goodbyes, and boarded a chopper that was headed for Saigon. At the time, I looked upon my new assignment with optimism. It was good to be going back on jump status, and I looked forward to an airborne assignment when I returned to the States in September. Ludicrous as it sounds, I actually enjoyed jumping from "perfectly good airplanes." Some officers I knew in the airborne units in which I'd served volunteered for this type of assignment for professional and career reasons, but I actually enjoyed the parachute jumps as well as the camaraderie and esprit that existed in the airborne units.

When I arrived at Tan Son Nhut airport, I ran into a soldier who had been in Charlie Company 4/12 Infantry when I commanded that unit in 1968. He was granted a compassionate reassignment after a family tragedy in the States. I was surprised to see him back in Vietnam. I didn't pry into the circumstances involved in his return, but he told me that he volunteered to complete his service in Vietnam and had decided to make a career in the Army. I was deeply touched by his dedication and patriotism.

After my chance encounter with the soldier from my old outfit, my sponsor from the Vietnamese Airborne Advisory Detachment, Captain Ed Donaldson, met me. Appointing a sponsor of equivalent rank for all incoming officers and NCOs was indicative of a high performing organization like the Airborne Advisory Team. This practice helped ensure continuity and high morale within the team. On the drive to our BOQ, Ed briefed me on the Airborne Division, its recent operations, and the inner workings of the advisory detachment. Some of the history of the Vietnamese airborne I already knew, having read Bernard Fall's books on the French war in Vietnam.

The ARVN Airborne Division traced its origins to the French Parachute forces in the First Indo-China War. Vietnamese parachute battalions were part of the general reserve of the French Expeditionary Corps. In 1954, three Vietnamese parachute battalions fought during the siege of Dien Bien Phu. Although the French suffered a devastating defeat at the hands of the Viet Minh at Dien Bien Phu, the Vietnamese parachute battalions fought heroically during the battle.

After independence, the four Vietnamese airborne battalions were formed into an Airborne Group that was activated in May of 1955 at Tan Son Nhut. Concurrently, a jump school was also organized at the same location. In December of 1959, the Airborne Group was reorganized as an Airborne Brigade and two additional battalions were added. The soldiers assigned to the brigade were all volunteers, and were required to complete nine weeks of basic combat training followed by three weeks of airborne training. There was no shortage of volunteers since the paratroopers received better pay, rations, quarters, and family benefits than the average ARVN soldier.

On 1 December 1965, the Airborne Brigade was expanded to a divisional size unit, and was designated as the ARVN high command's general reserve. In addition to participating in planned ARVN/U.S. operations, the Airborne Division was constantly on alert for short notice deployments to aid isolated ARVN outposts and beleaguered units throughout the country.

During the 1968 Tet Offensive, Airborne Division units distinguished themselves in the defense of Quang Tri City, and later in the battle to retake the Imperial City of Hue. Airborne units also fought in the battle for Saigon during the Tet Offensive and the May Offensive of 1968. In May of 1970, the Airborne Division participated in the invasion of Cambodia, and in February–March 1971 the invasion of Laos (*Operation Lam Son 719*). I was particularly interested in the Laotian operation, since it was the Airborne Division's most recent operation, and one that severely tested the Division's combat effectiveness. I followed with interest the *Stars and Stripes* coverage of the *Lam Son 719* operation while it was in progress, and I'd read a preliminary after-action report. Captain Donaldson, my sponsor, and other members of the advisory detachment were able to fill me in on many of the details on the Airborne Division's participation in the operation.

Operation Lam Son 719

The impetus for an incursion into Laos originated in the White House, specifically within President Nixon's National Security Council's (NSC) staff. Henry Kissinger, Nixon's National Security Advisor, had built a powerful political-military team within the White House that guided the conduct of the Vietnam War and the negotiations for a ceasefire, often overruling the Pentagon on policy and operational matters. The situation created a nightmare scenario for General Abrams, the commander in Vietnam, who often received conflicting guidance and orders from the White House and the Pentagon. In December of 1970, the NSC staff began planning for a military operation that would buy time for the continued withdrawal of U.S. forces and the complete Vietnamization of the war. Consideration was given to limited incursions into North Vietnam, Cambodia, and Laos. After consultations with Ambassador Bunker, General Abrams, and South Vietnamese President Thieu's government, a proposal was developed for an attack into southeastern Laos in February 1971, along Route 9, just south of the DMZ in I Corps. Concurrently, a secondary cross-border attack was to be launched from III Corps into Cambodia's Chup rubber plantation, where a major North Vietnamese logistic base area was located. Neither of these attacks was intended to lead to extended occupation of the Communist base areas. It was hoped that, if both attacks were successful, the allies would limit North Vietnamese capability to conduct offensives into South Vietnam for two or more years. A successful cross-border operation by South Vietnamese ground troops would also bolster the morale and confidence of the ARVN and increase the civilian population's support for the Thieu government.

The plan for the Laotian incursion called for the seizure of the Communist logistic complex around the town of Tchepone, some fifty kilometers west of the border between South Vietnam and Laos.

Tchepone was strategically located at the intersection of several supply routes along the Ho Chi Minh Trail. The plan called for a four-
phase operation, only one of which involved U.S. ground forces.

During phase one, U.S. forces operating in I Corps were responsible for seizing the border approaches to Laos and for conducting
diversionary operations along the DMZ to portend an attack into
North Vietnam. Phase two was an ARVN armored and infantry attack
following Route 9 into Laos to seize the area around Tchepone. A
series of airmobile assaults were planned to seize the high ground on
the northern and southern flanks of the armored/infantry column.
After landing, the airmobile forces would establish fire support bases
for the artillery that would also be airlifted in to provide supporting
fires for the armored/infantry column as it advanced on the Laotian
town. During phase three, South Vietnamese ground forces were to
locate and destroy North Vietnamese logistic base areas and supply
dumps. Phase four was the withdrawal of South Vietnamese ground
forces back across the border to South Vietnam. It was a bold plan
with substantial risks and major flaws.

Earlier U.S. plans for an invasion of Laos had called for a force
considerably larger than the one allocated for *Lam Son 719*. That plan
included U.S. and ARVN ground forces. The total ground force committed to *Lam Son 719* was only slightly larger than three South
Vietnamese divisions. This force consisted of the 1st ARVN Division,
the Vietnamese Airborne Division and the Vietnamese Marine
Division. The latter two divisions comprised Saigon's national reserve.
Other ground forces allocated for the invasion were the 1st Armored
Brigade and three Ranger battalions from the 1st Ranger Group. The
total strength of all RVNAF ground forces committed to the operation
was approximately 17,000 men. Since, the Airborne Division and
Marine Division were the major units of Saigon's strategic reserve,
there was no reserve force immediately available once those units were
committed to the battle in Laos. The size of the South Vietnamese
ground force was entirely too small considering the known enemy
forces in the area and North Vietnamese capability to quickly reinforce their units.

It was estimated that there were some 22,000 enemy troops
deployed in the southern panhandle of Laos at the beginning of the

operation, and the North Vietnamese had the ability to reinforce with up to four divisions. In addition, since the battle zone was near the North Vietnamese border, the enemy had the capability to deploy tanks, heavy artillery, and anti-aircraft into the area to counter any invasion. Unfortunately, the ARVN plan did not take into account the NVA's capability to rapidly reinforce their ground forces with heavy armor. The NVA had on occasion deployed lightly armored Soviet PT-76 amphibious tanks into South Vietnam, but had never committed its heavy armor, Soviet-made T-54 tanks. The T-54 mounted a 100mm main gun and had a top speed of 55km per hour, while the ARVN's M-41 tanks mounted a 76mm gun and had a maximum speed of 45km per hour. Thus, the North Vietnamese had a clear advantage in tank-on-tank battles. Additionally, the ARVN infantry, Rangers, and airborne units were unprepared and inadequately trained to confront the armor threat.

With the numbers of North Vietnamese forces deployed in and near the Laotian panhandle, the success of *Lam Son 719* was totally dependent on surprise, speed of movement, close coordination between the maneuver forces, and effective employment of U.S. air support. The South Vietnamese proved incapable of meeting any of those criteria.

The command and control arrangements established for *Lam Son 719* were also flawed. Lieutenant General Hoang Xuan Lam, the Vietnamese I Corps commander was given overall command of the operation. According to some senior U.S. officers, Lam was a capable organizer and administrator, but he had never commanded a large multi-division operation. Since the Vietnamese Marine Corps Commander, Lieutenant General Le Nguyen Khang, outranked General Lam he decided to remain in Saigon and delegate command of the Marine unit to a subordinate commander rather than take orders from the I Corps Commander. Lieutenant General Dong, the Airborne Division Commander, also outranked the I Corps Commander, and he gave his support to Lam only reluctantly after being pressured to do so by President Thieu. However, his cooperation with Lam and the other commanders was minimal.

Another failure in operational planning involved the missions assigned to the airborne and Ranger battalions. Along with the marines, the airborne and Ranger units were the "shock troops" of the Vietnamese armed forces. As such, they could best be used in an offensive combat role, taking the fight to the enemy rather than defending territory or bases. But in *Lam Son 719*, the Rangers and airborne forces were assigned the mission of protecting and defending the northern flank of the armor/infantry force as it moved westward along Route 9. To accomplish their missions, the units were inserted by helicopter to seize key terrain and establish artillery fire support bases and patrol bases along the northern flank of Route 9. Placing these highly mobile forces in a defensive posture in hostile enemy territory was a recipe for disaster.

Another factor working against the South Vietnamese was the absence of U.S. advisors on the ground in Laos. For security reasons, the lower echelon units were not notified of the operation until a few days prior to D-Day. The Vietnamese Airborne Division, one of the units selected to spearhead the operation, did not receive any detailed information on the plan until 2 February, less than a week before D-Day. There was a limited amount of last-minute training given to the ground commanders on procedures for requesting and controlling U.S. tactical air, assault helicopter, artillery, and logistic support, but this training was too little and too late.

The planners for *Lam Son 719* were quite aware of the risks and weaknesses in the plan, but it was approved at the highest levels of the U.S. and South Vietnamese chains of command. General Abrams understood the risks, but believed that U.S. B-52 strikes, tactical air support, tactical mobility, and assault helicopter support would even the odds. He actually had no other choice, since the Nixon administration was adamant that the cross-border operation be conducted.

On the U.S. side, Lieutenant General James W. Sutherland Jr., the XXIV Corps Commander, was given responsibility for planning and supporting the operation. In effect he was Lt. General Lam's counterpart. U.S. forces under Sutherland's command were responsible for reoccupying the Khe Sanh base and clearing the approaches to the Laotian border along Route 9. This preliminary operation was called Operation Dewey Canyon II. U.S. forces were also responsible for providing air, artillery, and logistic support to the South Vietnamese forces once they had broken over the border. While no U.S. ground forces were permitted to cross into Laos, this restriction did not apply to U.S. fixed and rotary wing aircraft flying missions in support of the South Vietnamese.

On 29 January 1971, President Nixon gave his approval for the operation to proceed, and South Vietnamese troops moved to the border on 8 February. However, the crossing was delayed until the following day due to an unfortunate incident. At sundown on 8 February, the lead armor battalion and the accompanying 8th Airborne Battalion were approaching the border when a U.S. aircraft mistakenly released a load of cluster bombs on the task force. Captain Ted Mataxis, the 8th Airborne Battalion's senior advisor, reported in a taped interview that his battalion lost 14 killed and 40 wounded in the friendly fire incident, and the armor unit lost three killed and 40 wounded. The airborne and armor units halted near the border to evacuate their casualties. The following morning (9 February), the ARVN forces crossed the border, entering Laos on Route 9. U.S. advisors accompanied them to the border crossing before returning to the support base at Khe Sanh.

Spearheading the invasion was the ARVN's 1st Armored Brigade, commanded by Colonel Nguyen Trong Luat, and the Airborne Division's 1st Airborne Brigade, under the command of Colonel Le Quang Luong. These two units moved west along Highway 9 toward their initial objective, Ban Dong/A Loui, located some 20 kilometers inside Laos. B-52 strikes and a massive artillery bombardment supported the initial advance of the armored and airborne brigades, and the column encountered no resistance.

To protect the northern flank of the attacking column, the 39th and 21st Ranger Battalions and the Airborne Division's 3d Brigade, including the 2d and 3d Airborne Battalions, conducted air assaults into LZs north of Route 9. The Ranger battalions were assigned the mission of establishing the northernmost patrol bases. The Ranger North and Ranger South bases were positioned to provide early warning of any major enemy units moving south to strike the main invasion force from the flank. The airborne units were given a similar mission, and were also tasked to establish and defend fire support bases for the artillery. The 3d Airborne Brigade headquarters and 3d Airborne Battalion established and occupied Fire Support Base (FSB)

31, while the 2d Airborne Battalion, the unit that I was soon to join as senior advisor, established and occupied FSB 30. Both fire support bases were south of the Ranger bases.

The mission of protecting the southern flank of Highway 9 was assigned to the Vietnamese 1st Infantry Division. That division conducted multiple air assaults into LZs south of Route 9, establishing three fire support bases, FSBs Hotel, Delta, and Delta 1.

The condition of Route 9 was worse than expected, slowing the armor column's advance on the first day of the invasion. To make matters worse, it began to rain on the second day, turning the highway into a quagmire and slowing progress even more. The bad weather continued for most of the day on 10 February, delaying an airmobile assault by the 9th Airborne Battalion into a landing zone near Ban Dong. The battalion had the mission of seizing the area around Ban Dong and linking up with the armor/airborne column that was advancing westward along Route 9. The weather delayed the airmobile assault until about 1700 hours on 10 February, and link-up did not occur until the afternoon of 11 February.

After link-up, the combined armor/airborne task force consolidated their positions around Ban Dong/A Luoi, and established a forward command center and the main fire support base for the operation. Although the operation's plan called for an immediate continuation of the attack to seize Tchepone, the main objective of the operation, the South Vietnamese forces held in place at Ban Dong/A Luoi. The commander of the task force was waiting for an order from the *Lam Son* commander, Lieutenant General Lam, to continue the attack. Lam, however, wanted to extend the 1st Infantry Division's strong points south of Route 9 to the west before ordering the final advance on Tchepone. That action required an additional five days, providing the North Vietnamese enough time to deploy forces to counter the South Vietnamese incursion. This delay was to prove costly to the entire operation.

The NVA response to the South Vietnamese advance developed slowly at first, but accelerated rapidly during the last two weeks of February. The ARVN Rangers operating north of Route 9 were the first to bear the brunt of the NVA counterattacks.

On 18 February, the NVA began pounding the Ranger positions at

Ranger North and Ranger South with artillery and rocket fire. On the following day, the 102d Regiment of the 308th NVA Division assaulted Ranger North. The attack was supported by Soviet-made PT-76 and T-54 tanks. Although the 39th Ranger Battalion managed to hold through the night, it abandoned its position on the afternoon of 20 February, retreating towards the Ranger South base. Only about 100 survivors of the attack on Ranger North managed to reach Ranger South. That base was next on the Communists' "hit list."

Reinforced by the Rangers who fled Ranger North, the force defending Ranger South was able to hold off the assaulting NVA for two more days before they were ordered to fight their way southeast to join the airborne troops defending FSB 30.

The savage NVA attacks against the static ARVN bases were not restricted to those on the northern flank. On 23 February, the Communists attacked the 1st ARVN Division's FSB Hotel 2 south of Route 9. The infantrymen held out one day before evacuating the base. The situation grew worse by the day.

The 3d Airborne Brigade's FSB 31 was next to bear the brunt of the NVA assaults along the northern flank. Located about eight kilometers north of A Luoi, FSB 31 was occupied by the 3d Brigade headquarters, the 3d Airborne Battalion headquarters, two airborne companies from that battalion, and a battery of 105 mm howitzers. The NVA attack against the fire support base was methodical, leaving nothing to chance. They first moved into positions all around the base, isolating it from outside support. Simultaneously, enemy antiaircraft guns were positioned near the base, making resupply by helicopter extremely hazardous. A few helicopters from the U.S. 158th Aviation Battalion braved the antiaircraft fire and flew in to the base; however, they drew such fire that further missions were cancelled. The Airborne Division's senior advisor, Colonel Arthur Pense, recommended dropping supplies by parachute, but the Division's commander vetoed the proposal, indicating that it would suggest to the defenders that their situation was near hopeless.

Anticipating an all-out assault on FSB 31, Colonel Pense recommended to his counterpart that a number of tanks from the 17th Armored Squadron, which was under the Airborne Division's control, be moved north to reinforce the FSB. General Dong, the Airborne

Division commander, approved the proposal, but for reasons never fully determined, the column of five tanks and accompanying airborne troops halted several kilometers south of FSB 31 and never resumed their advance.

The first attack on the 3d Airborne Brigade's FSB 31 began around 1100 hours on 25 February. The NVA opened with a murderous mortar and artillery barrage that included fire from heavy 130mm field guns. By 1400 hours, the base was under small arms fire from all directions, and enemy tanks were approaching the southern perimeter. The timely arrival of U.S. tactical fighter aircraft knocked out a number of NVA tanks before they could break in. The NVA, however, was not deterred by the repulse of their first attack.

Approximately an hour after the initial assault, an estimated 20 enemy tanks supported by infantry assaulted the base from the northwest and east. A single U.S. Forward Air Controller (FAC) was overhead ready to direct another air strike, but the FAC was diverted to coordinate the rescue of a downed U.S. F-4 pilot. The only aircraft remaining overhead of FSB 31 was the C&C chopper of the Airborne Division's advisory detachment, and its only armament was two M-60 machine guns. The advisor's command and control chopper circled the base and took heavy fire from NVA as the door gunners opened up on the enemy troops. The advisors could see the enemy soldiers firing straight up at them from the approach trenches they had dug right up to the perimeter wire around the firebase.

Under an umbrella of heavy artillery fire, the NVA armor and infantry pressed their attack on the outnumbered and outgunned paratroopers. Friendly artillery fire from FSB 30 and the artillery at A Luoi was unsuccessful in breaking up the Communist attack, and some forty minutes later the NVA overran the base. The 3d Airborne Brigade commander, Colonel Nguyen Van Tho, and Third Artillery Battalion commander were captured, along with most of their staff officers. The ARVN losses at FSB 31 totaled 155 paratroopers killed and missing. An unknown number of soldiers managed to break out and link up with an armored-infantry relief force that was en route to the base when it fell. The NVA lost an estimated 250 men KIA, and eleven PT-76 and T-54 tanks were destroyed. The loss of FSB 31, and the capture of the 3d Airborne Brigade commander, had a devastating impact on the morale of the Airborne Division. Within a week the captive, Colonel Tho, was making propaganda broadcasts on North Vietnamese radio.

Lieutenant General Dong of the Airborne Division and Colonel Arthur Pense, the Division's senior advisor, blamed the loss of FSB 31 on the lack of U.S. tactical air support at a critical moment during the attack, and further alleged that there was an overall failure in I Corps planning and coordination. Dong and Pence also complained that Colonel Luat, the armor commander, failed to respond to Dong's orders to reinforce FSB 31 with tanks. They voiced these concerns directly to General Frederick Weyand, the Deputy MACV commander, and Lieutenant General Sutherland when they visited the Airborne Division's field headquarters shortly after the loss of the FSB. General Sutherland, the XXIV Corps commander, apparently thought that Pense had embarrassed him in front of his counterparts and General Weyand by suggesting that U.S. air support was inadequate. In Sutherland's judgment, Colonel Pense was no longer an effective division senior advisor, and after further inquiry into the complaints of General Dong and Colonel Pense, the XXIV Corps commander decided to replace Pense as senior advisor to the Airborne Division.

General Abram's selection for a replacement was Colonel James Vaught, a South Carolinian and a Citadel graduate, who served during World War II and Korea, and had a previous tour in Vietnam as a battalion commander. With little warning, Abrams plucked Vaught from a staff job at MACV headquarters and sent him north to sort out the problems the Airborne Division was experiencing in Laos. Vaught was not intimidated by Lieutenant General Dong's rank or his political connections with the Thieu regime. Upon his arrival in I Corps on 2 March, three days after the fall of FSB 31, Colonel Vaught first met with Lt. General Sutherland at his headquarters before flying to meet with Lt. General Lam and Brigadier General Jackson, the Deputy Senior Advisor to I Corps. Lam encouraged Vaught to take all measures deemed necessary to improve the Airborne Division's tactical situation. In addition to advising the division commander, Vaught was also responsible for ensuring that the necessary U.S. support was provided to the Airborne Division, particularly air support.

On 2 March, Colonel Vaught touched down at Airborne

Division's headquarters just five kilometers from the Laotian border. Vaught's counterpart, General Dong, had served in the Vietnamese airborne units since he was a lieutenant in 1951, and had seen more than a few American advisors, but none like the straightforward Colonel Vaught. An eyewitness to the event described the scene as Colonel Vaught fixed his new counterpart with a dagger-like glare and immediately began telling him what actions he needed to take to save his division. Colonel Vaught's new, no-nonsense approach to his counterpart and the advisory team had an immediate impact when it was put to the test over the next few days.

At his next briefing, General Dong told his commanders that Colonel Vaught was authorized to make any tactical recommendations he saw fit to make, and they were "to execute them faithfully." Over the next several days, the division commander approved every tactical recommendation made by his senior U.S. advisor. When Colonel Vaught planned B-52 Arc Light strikes within the "danger close" range to friendly troops, General Dong signed the necessary waivers.

After overrunning FSB 31, the North Vietnamese focused their efforts on FSB 30 with the intent of repeating their performance at FSB 31. FSB 30 and its 105mm and 155mm howitzers was defended by the paratroopers of the 2d Airborne Battalion that I would join two months later. The terrain on which the base was situated was much more formidable than that of FSB 31. Situated on high ground, the fire support base was assailable only on its northeast side. The other three sides were near vertical drops completely unapproachable by tanks and nearly impossible for infantry. Nevertheless, the NVA remained determined to destroy the base, even if it required modifying their tactics.

Rather than launch an all-out armor and infantry assault on FSB 30, the NVA decided instead to lay siege to the base and launch a series of concentrated artillery and rocket attacks. Additionally, the NVA commander ringed the surrounding area with anti-aircraft guns making resupply, air support, and medevac missions extremely hazardous. The 2d Airborne Battalion put up a spirited defense, and morale remained high during the first several days of the siege; however, slowly but surely, the mortar and artillery fire began to take its toll. The Airborne Division's howitzers were no match for the NVA's 130mm guns, and were knocked out one by one. By the end of the week, supplies were running low, and a number of bunkers were knocked out. Only a few of the base's howitzers were still capable of firing. At this critical moment in the siege, the 2d Airborne Battalion commander cracked under pressure, and jumped aboard a dust-off chopper that had braved enemy anti-aircraft fire to evacuate wounded. The battalion executive officer took over as battalion commander.

Since practically all of the base's howitzers were out of action, there was no further reason to defend it. Colonel Vaught wanted the firebase closed. He later reported:

> Anytime they (the NVA) wanted to, they could just inundate a firebase, and if you approached it with a helicopter, they'd blow the helicopter out of the sky, if you didn't turn back. So, you couldn't stay on the firebase. There was no merit in it anyway. You were just hunkered down in a hole making a target for the enemy's counterfire.

Vaught was right and Lieutenant General Dong approved the abandonment of the fire support base. After destroying the remaining artillery pieces and all supplies and ammunition, the 2d Airborne Battalion slipped out of the base during the hours of darkness, and conducted a fighting withdrawal through rugged terrain heading for the ARVN base at Ban Dong/A Luoi. The battalion's successful withdrawal was largely the result of the new battalion commander's leadership, plus the excellent fire support from U.S. Army gun ships and U.S. Air Force tactical air support.

By 3 March the NVA controlled most of the high ground north of Route 9, but their gains were costly. In addition to the casualties suffered during the ground attacks against the Ranger and airborne bases, the B-52 strikes decimated several NVA regiments and support units operating in the area around Tchepone. Nevertheless, the enemy still had a numerical advantage over the South Vietnamese, having amassed some 35,000 troops in the battle area, including three infantry divisions, several independent infantry regiments, eight artillery regiments, three tank battalions, and six anti-aircraft battalions. The South Vietnamese high command was well aware of the NVA strength, and pondered whether to continue the cross-border operation.

After considerable prodding by General Abrams, President Thieu finally agreed to commit his last remaining reserve in an attempt to salvage something from the operation. The South Vietnamese Marine Division was assigned the mission of taking over the southern flank positions held by the 1st Infantry Division, freeing that Division to make the final push to Tchepone. Two battalions of the ARVN 1st Division's 2d Regiment conducted airmobile assaults and seized objectives north and south of the strategic road junction at Tchepone. The enemy was temporarily caught off guard by the air assaults, but by nightfall the NVA artillery began to concentrate on the 2d Regiment's positions. For the next two days the infantrymen searched the area around Tchepone, while the NVA repositioned their forces to eliminate the threat.

Instead of moving his armor/infantry force west on Route 9 to link up with the 1st Division force around Techepone, General Lam, under instructions from President Thieu, ordered a withdrawal of all forces back to South Vietnam beginning on 9 March. The move on Techepone by a minimal force of two infantry battalions was apparently nothing more than a face saving gesture by the South Vietnamese. The NVA, however, had no intentions of allowing the South Vietnamese a graceful exit from Laos, and the battle was shifting to their advantage.

A withdrawal under pressure from the enemy is one of the most difficult operations to conduct, and requires highly disciplined troops and leaders down to the lowest echelons. Although the U.S. media reported that the South Vietnamese withdrawal was a complete rout, it was not. Nonetheless, the withdrawal was difficult and costly, taking 12 days to accomplish.

The 1st Division infantrymen deployed around Tchepone were at greatest risk since they had no armor support and were furthest from the border. Some of the infantrymen were extracted by helicopter from their positions near Tchepone at heavy cost in lives and U.S. aircraft. Others fled in the direction of the airborne forces holding the northern flank of Highway 9. All together, some 28 of the 40 helicopters participating in the airmobile extraction of the 1st Division troops were damaged or destroyed.

The northernmost airborne units were also extracted under fire from pick-up zones near their positions. Concurrently, the South Vietnamese Marines on the southern flank came under extremely heavy pressure from the NVA, resulting in the forced evacuation of FSBs Delta and Hotel. Helicopter extraction of the Marine forces continued until 22 March, when the last remaining Marine unit departed Laos. Simultaneously, the airborne and armor forces along Route 9 began their own withdrawal.

Moving eastward along Route 9, the ARVN units fought their way through numerous ambushes with the support of U.S. helicopter gunships, tactical air support, and long-range artillery fires. As the armored column and accompanying airborne troops neared the border, two NVA regiments waited in ambush positions to prevent their escape. The Airborne Division commander committed his reserve to the area to clear the road, but the approaching ARVN column was never notified. Fearing the worst, the armored column left the main road to follow a jungle trail that they thought would lead them across the border to safety. Unfortunately, the trail ended on the steep western bank of the Se Pone River, and the tanks and armored personnel carriers had about run out of fuel. The NVA then attempted to move in for the final kill, but the airborne and armor fought a successful rearguard action. The 1st Armored Task Force commander, who was under the operational control of the Airborne Division, radioed the Airborne Division CP requesting permission to abandon his vehicles. Colonel Vaught, speaking on behalf of the Airborne Division commander, denied this request. He said, "Disapproved. You're not going to do that, and we'll be back in touch."

Colonel Vaught requested immediate support from the U.S. 101st Airborne Division, and got it. Helicopters from the 101st began to sling-load 55-gallon drums of gasoline to refuel the beleaguered armored unit's APCs and tanks. Meanwhile, the Division's air cavalry platoon scouted along the river to find a possible fording site for the column. They found a ford, but it had to be improved before it could be used. A U.S. Chinook helicopter and Sky Crane airlifted four small bulldozers into the area to improve the approaches to the ford. While the engineers worked on the ford, the Task Force refueled its vehicles. The crossing was completed on 23 March. In all, some 360 tanks and APCs made a safe crossing, along with the accompanying airborne troops. By 25 March, all ARVN and Marine forces were back in South Vietnam. When the allied forward base at Khe Sanh was closed on 6 April, Operation *Lam Son 719* was officially over.

Losses on both sides were heavy. Some 9,000 South Vietnamese were killed, wounded, captured, or missing. U.S. forces operating on the South Vietnamese side of the border and aircrews involved in supporting the Laotian incursion suffered a total of 1,462 casualties. Aviation units lost a total of 102 helicopters with another 618 damaged. Additionally, the USAF lost six fighter-bombers, and the U.S. Navy lost one aircraft. Losses on the North Vietnamese side were considerably higher. Some estimates put the enemy losses as high as 12,000 men; however, the exact number is impossible to determine. Suffice to say, North Vietnamese losses in manpower and weapons of all types, including artillery and tanks, required many months to replace.

Analysis of the results of *Lam Son 719* revealed many weaknesses in the South Vietnamese Armed Forces including the Airborne Division. First and foremost was the lack of a reliable and flexible command, control, and communications structure that could coordinate, control, and direct the forces involved in the operation. Throughout the operation there was inadequate coordination and cooperation between the major RVNAF commands. Lieutenant General Lam's I Corps headquarters was located in Quang Tri, while I Corps forward was in Dong Ha. The tactical command post was closer to the border at Ham Nghi, and was manned by subordinate staff officers, while senior principal staff officers remained in Dong Ha. The officers at Ham Nghi lacked sufficient authority to react to tactical emergencies when they arose, such as the attack and capture of FSB 31. Although, General Lam spent considerable time at the tactical command post during daylight hours, it was difficult to reach him for a decision at other times. During the operation there was also considerable friction between the mediocre commander, General Lam, and the other senior commanders such as General Dong of the Airborne Division and General Khang of the Marines, and this friction carried over to their staffs. Additionally, the U.S. XXIV Corps had no senior representative in the forward area to coordinate the activities of the U.S. units supporting the operation, including the 101st Aviation Group, the 1/5 Mechanized Brigade, and the 108th Artillery Group. Each of these U.S. units coordinated directly with the major South Vietnamese units involved in the operation.

A second major weakness in the South Vietnamese units was the inability of the ground commanders to effectively coordinate external support. The ARVN and Marine officers at the tactical level had insufficient training and expertise in arranging fire support, airmobile operations, and logistical support.

Another reason for the lack of success was the inability of the South Vietnamese units to fight as a combined arms team. The armor, infantry, airborne, and marine units did not share a common doctrine. In fact, up to this point in the war, the RVNAF had no combined arms doctrine that enabled infantry, armor, artillery, and air to work effectively together.

At the tactical unit level, another glaring deficiency was the inability of the ground forces to counter enemy armor threats. In the ARVN armor units, the tank commanders tended to be timid when confronting enemy tanks, often firing their main guns hastily from extended ranges, resulting in misses or deflections. Additionally, the ARVN tanks seldom fired from defilade, and they moved about in the open while the NVA tanks remained concealed in the jungle, firing at their adversaries from ambush positions.

In the infantry, airborne, and marine units, the individual soldiers and marines did not fare well when they encountered enemy tanks. The paratroopers claimed that the M-72 Light Anti-Tank Weapon (LAW) was ineffective against the Soviet-made tanks. In fact, the LAW is an effective anti-tank weapon up to ranges of 200 meters, and is quite capable of knocking out a PT-76 or T-72. Since the North Vietnamese armor often operated without infantry support in jungle terrain, it should have been quite easy for infantry to engage tanks at much shorter ranges. More training of the infantry in anti-armor tactics, including the use of tank hunter/killer teams was clearly needed.

On the U.S. side, the Army aviation units and Air Force tactical air units performed heroically and effectively in the face of an extremely dense and effective NVA air defense system within the operational area. While a significant number of aircraft and personnel were lost, the loss ratio to sorties flown was not abnormally high considering the nature of the terrain and mostly marginal weather conditions. The B-52 air strikes were executed with precision and accuracy, and no doubt saved the operation from becoming a total debacle. Colonel Vaught reported that some 152 B-52 Arc Light strikes were used in the Airborne Division's area during the period 8 February through 25 March.

Strategically, *Lam Son 719* had only a short-term effect on the eventual outcome of the war. The incursion temporarily disrupted the enemy's lines of communication and supply in the Laotian panhandle, delaying the next major NVA offensive operation in South Vietnam for about a year. The next large-scale Communist offensive in South Vietnam did not occur until the spring of 1972, when the North Vietnamese launched their *Easter Offensive*. This lull provided time for the ARVN to retrain and correct many of the operational deficiencies noted during *Lam Son 719*. As a result, the South Vietnamese, with the assistance of massive U.S. fire support, were able to counter the enemy's massive *Easter Offensive*, and survive for another three years.

CHAPTER 12

"FIGHTING SOLDIERS FROM THE SKY"

•

When I signed in at the Airborne Advisory Detachment at Tan Son Nhut Airbase, I was told that my specific assignment was Senior Advisor to the Airborne Division's 2d Battalion. This was the battalion that defended Fire Support Base 30 during Operation *Lam Son 719*. The battalion commander, *Thieu Ta* Manh, assumed command of the battalion when the former commander cracked under pressure. Manh then led a breakout from the besieged base, and maneuvered the battalion through the mountainous terrain north of Route 9, taking the fight to enemy units operating in the area. After linking up with the 7th Airborne Battalion, the two units fought as a rearguard during the withdrawal phase of *Lam Son 719*, until they were extracted by helicopter on 20 March. After the conclusion of the operation, *Dai Uy* Manh was put on the fast promotion track to major, and remained in command of the battered battalion. The 2d Airborne Battalion sustained heavy losses in Laos, and was still receiving replacements when I became senior advisor at the end of May.

After completing my in-processing with Team 162, I reported to Lieutenant Colonel Tom Ulvenes, the 3d Brigade's Senior Advisor. After welcoming me aboard, the colonel informed me that my battalion was scheduled to remain in the Saigon area until it's fill of new replacements completed their basic combat and airborne training. The battalion would then deploy to the Van Kiep National Training Center near Vung Tau to undergo unit training. Colonel Ulvenes suggested that I get to know my counterpart and monitor the battalion's training, adding that I could also participate in training jumps with the battalion's new replacements to earn my own Vietnamese paratrooper wings. It was a status symbol among airborne soldiers to wear one or more sets of foreign jump wings. I'd already been awarded Thai jump wings, and looked forward to earning my ARVN paratrooper wings.

The Team 162 Airborne Division advisors were billeted at the Missouri BOQ in Saigon near the airbase. The BOQ had several floors of rooms that opened onto a balcony that overlooked the parking lot where we kept our Jeeps. A sandbagged checkpoint manned by Vietnamese guards was the only security at the facility, so we kept our weapons close at hand in our rooms.

Ed Donaldson, my sponsor, said I could share his two-man room at the BOQ, and I took him up on it. It was a change of lifestyle after my nine months with the Rangers; clean starched uniforms every day, spit-shined boots, a private bathroom, and three U.S. hot meals a day at the cafeteria on the top floor, not to mention a fully stocked bar and nightly live entertainment. After stowing my gear in Ed's room, he suggested that I have my five sets of newly issued airborne camouflage fatigues tailored in the Vietnamese style before I met my new counterpart for the first time. All of the airborne advisors wore tailored camouflage fatigues with cloth insignia of the U.S. Army and Vietnamese Airborne sewn on the uniforms. Worn with the Vietnamese Airborne red beret, spit-shine jump boots, and U.S. aviator sunglasses, we all looked like young John Waynes. That afternoon we dropped my fatigues off at a tailor shop to be altered, and I was told that I could pick them up the next morning; that was customer service.

Since it was Saturday and we didn't work on Sundays, when our battalions were at home station in Saigon, Ed suggested that we sample Saigon's nightlife that evening. After enjoying a Saturday night steak dinner in the BOQ's dining facility, we were ready to head downtown. I assumed we'd be driving in Ed's Jeep that evening, but he said we'd be better off taking a Vietnamese taxi. A Jeep parked on a darkened Saigon street was likely to be stolen minutes after it was parked, even if the steering wheel was secured with a heavy chain and lock. In Saigon, crime was normally more of a threat than acts of terror perpetrated by the Communists. So called "Saigon cowboys" riding on Honda motorbikes sped down darkened streets and alleyways in search of drunken and disoriented GIs to mug. Without even slowing down on their Hondas, they could snap a Rolex off your wrist or snatch an expensive camera off your shoulder in a microsecond.

Our first stop was the *Hoa Binh* Bar on Le Loi Street, a favorite hangout of the airborne advisors. By 8 p.m. the bar was crowded with American and Vietnamese paratroopers along with Marine advisors. After downing a *Ba Moi Ba* beer, I spotted a couple of black soldiers wearing airborne camouflage fatigues at the end of the bar. I walked over to introduce myself to the pair, and was surprised when they greeted me in Vietnamese. I thought they were pulling my leg, but I smiled and bought them a beer anyway. When I returned to my seat at the bar, Ed laughingly explained to me that the men were Vietnamese airborne troopers who were the offspring of French African Colonial troops who fought in the first Indo-China War.

After quenching our thirst at the *Hoa Binh*, we hailed another taxi and headed for the well-known Pink Pussycat Bar. Ed warned me not to buy any Saigon tea for the bar girls. That could set you back ten or more dollars per tea. We had no trouble enticing a couple of bar girls to our table after we ordered our drinks. We ordered them a couple of cokes, but they began to lose interest in us when we refused to follow up with a couple of Saigon teas. When we got up to leave, one of the girls suggested that if we returned at closing time they would, "love us longtime" when they got off duty at the bar. They'd go for a one-night stand for a price, but what they really wanted was a long-term relationship with an apartment and unlimited spending privileges out of our paychecks.

It was approaching the curfew hour so I suggested to Ed that we head back to the BOQ, but he assured me that we wouldn't be apprehended for the violating the curfew. The 716th Battalion MPs never bothered the Airborne Division's advisors after they fought side by side with the Airborne during the Tet Offensive of 1968, and the Vietnamese White Mice (Vietnamese civilian police) knew better than to try to arrest any American wearing the uniform of the Vietnamese airborne. Our final stop that night was Mimi's Bar Lounge and Restaurant where we had a few more drinks and a late night supper. I was glad that we could sleep in the next morning since I could already feel the effects of the formaldehyde in the Vietnamese beer.

Monday morning the captain that I was replacing and I drove to the 2d Airborne Battalion's area on the southwestern corner of Tan Son Nhut airbase. Captain Griffin (not his real name) was leaving the Army and returning to West Virginia to run the family business. The advisor's office was located in a one-story building that housed the battalion's staff offices. My outgoing protégé suggested that I sign the leather bound sign-in book on his desk. I was surprised to see that the first two names in the book were French officers. Apparently the battalion had a seamless transition from French to American advisors after independence.

As Captain Griffin was filling me in on some details about the batalion, the enlisted members of the 2d Battalion's advisory team showed up. Each battalion advisory team was authorized two officers and three NCOs. Sergeant First Class Garrison was the senior NCO. Like most of the NCO airborne advisors, Garrison had served multiple tours in the 82d and 101st Airborne Divisions. He was a master parachutist with a "Screaming Eagle" combat patch on his right shoulder, signifying that he'd served a combat tour with the 101st Airborn Division. The other two NCOs were Staff Sergeants Pilon and Ball. Both were Canadians and former members of Canada's Princess Patricia's Regiment. Pilon was French Canadian from Montreal, and Ball was from western Canada. Both men enlisted in the U.S. Army in order to serve in Vietnam. They were two among thousands of Canadians who served honorably and heroically in the U.S. Armed Forces during the war. The names of 103 Canadians, who died while serving with the U.S. Armed Forces, are inscribed on the Vietnam War Memorial in Washington D.C. While our draft-dodgers sought refuge in Canada, these brave Canadians stepped forward to fight and die for our country.

The team was also authorized an assistant senior advisor, an officer's billet, but more often than not each airborne battalion advisory team had only one officer assigned.

I asked each team member to give me their impressions of the battalion, its strengths and weaknesses and so forth. They all agreed that the change in leadership in the battalion was long overdue, and that the new commander was a strong leader who had the loyalty and respect of all the officers and NCOs in the battalion. The primary weaknesses in the battalion were in anti-tank tactics, and the control of helicopter gunships and close air support without the assistance of their U.S. advisors. After our team meeting, Captain Griffin walked me over to the battalion commander's quarters to introduce me to my counterpart.

The Airborne battalion commanders and other officers in the battalion all lived in family housing in each of their battalion areas. The housing was modest even by Vietnamese standards, single-story row-type housing, but it was in a secure area on the base. At least the officers and men were assured in knowing that their families were in a relatively secure situation when they were deployed on operations.

Thieu Ta Manh met us at the door and invited us into his living room. The apartment was modestly furnished. Manh was probably in his early thirties and was solidly built for a Vietnamese. His English was quite understandable, and he seemed to have a perpetual smile on his face as he spoke. He asked me how long I'd been in Vietnam, and where I'd served prior to my assignment with Team 162. His wife served us tea as a couple of young children scurried about the rooms. It was strictly a social call so we didn't stay long.

For the next six weeks I visited the battalion just about every day, even though there wasn't much to do. The battalion was still receiving replacements from the basic combat training and airborne schools. The Vietnamese airborne school based its parachute-training program on the U.S. Fort Benning model. Each class received three weeks of training. The first week was ground training with a heavy emphasis on physical conditioning. The second week was called "tower week," and the trainees were required to perform simulated parachute jumps from 34-foot and higher towers, as well as training on other parachute simulation devices and aircraft mock-ups. The final week was jump week, when each aspiring paratrooper was required to successfully complete five parachute jumps. The airborne school graduated one class per week, and each battalion received a share of newly qualified replacements. I made a couple of jumps with the airborne school trainees during this period, and it was quite an experience.

On each jump we were issued a T-10 parachute, and boarded a VNAF C-123 aircraft. I'd jumped from U.S. Air Force C-123s many times, but I'd never flown with a Vietnamese pilot and jumpmaster. On U.S. jumps, the jumpmaster gets a light signal from the pilot when the aircraft approaches the drop zone. He then gives the paratroopers a series of six jump commands that prepares them to exit the aircraft. When the aircraft is over the drop zone, the pilot gives the jumpmaster a green light signal, and he in turn orders the jumpers to quickly exit the jump doors of the aircraft. The whole procedure is practiced numerous times in aircraft mock-ups during the airborne ground training.

On my first jump with the Vietnamese, I heard only about three jump commands before the jumpmaster started shoving the troopers out the door. We were jumping onto a drop zone near Ap Dong/Hoc Mon only a few minutes by air from Tan Son Nhut. The entire operation took about 15 minutes from take-off to landing on the drop zone. The young Vietnamese troopers who were making their first jump were as wide-eyed and terrified as I was on my first jump at Fort Benning six years earlier. The jump was labeled administrative/nontactical, but I was still a bit apprehensive, since the area around Hoc Mon was considered a VC stronghold during my 1968 tour in Vietnam.

Since the battalion advisors were underemployed while their battalions were in Saigon, we were given special projects to work on by the Division's Senior Advisor's staff. Mine was to prepare a staff-study for the Division G-3 Operations advisor on the possible use of ground sensors during combat operations. The CIA and MACV's Special Operations Group (SOG) had been using ground sensors as early as 1968 to detect enemy troop and supply movements along the Ho Chi Minh Trail and other infiltration routes into Vietnam. Some types of sensors could be air dropped, while others had to be carried in by clandestine teams and emplaced on the ground. Through electronic monitoring of the sensors, it was possible to target enemy vehicular movement and troop concentrations deep inside Laos, Cambodia, and remote areas in Vietnam. Moving targets were then usually engaged with AC-130 Spectre gunships, and stationary targets such as large enemy base camps were targeted for B-52 bomber Arc Light strikes. Unattended seismic, acoustic, and infrared ground sensors were an integral part of the U.S. military's early work in developing an "electronic battlefield."

During my research I visited MACV's Special Operations Group

(SOG), and was shown some of the sensors currently in use. It was real "James Bond" type stuff; sensors made to look like stalks of weeds, rocks, large tree leaves, tree branches, and other natural items that could blend into the jungle and paddies. Other sensors were designed to burrow into the earth after they were dropped by air. Some of the heavier acoustic manned sensors were backpacked in by SOG teams, and monitored from concealed ground locations. It was risky business, but the SOG teams were good at it.

I concluded that unattended ground sensors could be used by ground troops during tactical operations. Sensors emplaced around a night defensive perimeter could detect enemy movement and provide early warning of an attack. Typically, infantry units in Vietnam used two-man listening posts, trip flares, and other field-expedient devices to detect enemy movement around their perimeters at night. However, sensors had their limitations, as the SOG officers reminded me. Like all electronic devices, sensors didn't always work perfectly, especially in bad weather, and false activations were not uncommon. The enemy had also developed countermeasures to neutralize some types of sensors.

A few days later I wrote up my staff study and gave it to the S-3 advisor. He later gave me an "atta boy" for my work and passed it on to the colonel. It was my first introduction to the electronic battlefield of the future.

During the Saigon nights and weekends there was plenty of time to explore the sights, sounds, and smells of the city. During the summer of 1971, Saigon was a fairly safe city if you avoided certain areas. One area that we never entered was only a few blocks from our BOQ. Known as Soul Alley, this back street was the home of what some have estimated as several hundred black AWOLs and deserters from U.S. units in Vietnam. No one knew the exact number, but I doubt if it was that high. Some number of deserters had been living there for years. They made a living through black marketeering and peddling drugs. It was easy enough for the deserters to change their identities by having their Armed Forces ID cards altered by Saigon's expert forgers, giving them access to U.S. military support facilities and bases where they purchased goods at the PXs and sold their drugs.

At first glance, Soul Alley looked like any of the other narrow

back streets in Saigon. It was honeycombed with tiny apartments and
teeming with city life; wiry, aged Vietnamese men pedaling ancient
bicycles and cyclos, mama-sans pushing two-wheel carts peddling
Vietnamese and American cigarettes and other wares, corner food
stalls, and dark-skinned Vietnamese kids playing kick ball in empty
dirt lots. Taking a second look, however, you might notice Army jungle fatigues hanging from balcony railings drying in the sun, and a few
black men lounging on their balconies puffing away at a joint or cigarette, or the occasional Vietnamese girl sauntering down the street
with a baby with distinctive African-American features bouncing on
her hip.

The U.S. Military Police and the South Vietnamese police made
occasional raids on the area, but the AWOLs generally got prior notice
and left the street temporarily, but they soon drifted back after the raid
was over. Life in Saigon went on day by day for the deserters, but their
day of reckoning came with the arrival of the North Vietnamese in
1975. Their fate remains unknown after that.

Despite decades of war and overcrowding by tens of thousands of
refugees, Saigon still managed to retain some of its charm. The cathe-
drals, hotels, and villas built during the French colonial years still
stood, and it was possible to have quiet meals at a number of excellent French restaurants, or enjoy an espresso at one of the numerous
sidewalk cafes. One of our favorite restaurants was La Cave on La Loi
Street. It survived the Communist takeover and is still in business.

A favorite gathering place for Americans from the embassy, the
press corps, and other civilians was the terrace of the Continental
Hotel. We occasionally stopped there for a drink, but it was not one
of our hangouts. Our camouflage fatigues and red berets raised too
many civilian eyebrows, and we sometimes caught a glare from a U.S.
general or colonel from MACV, who was trying to impress a counterpart or girl friends by buying them dinner at the Continental. One
could almost always find a similar crowd hanging out at the nearby
Caravelle Hotel. It was a side of the war that most GIs in Vietnam
never got to see.

From dawn to curfew, the city's streets were teeming with life.
After a while, one got used to the smell of garbage that was stacked
up in piles along the sidewalks. Municipal workers, many of whom

had second jobs with higher salaries on the American bases, rarely picked up the trash.

We usually made at least one trip each week to the Post Exchange (PX) in Cholon. I never understood why the facility was located in Cholon, but it was. Cholon was the Chinese section of Saigon, and it was the scene of heavy fighting during the Tet and May offensives of 1968. Without doubt it was the most crowded and unsavory section of the city. Except for the managers, the PX itself was staffed primarily with Vietnamese employees, and the amount of goods that went out the back gate every day was considerable. The pilferage was limited to small, easily hidden items.

The PX sold just about anything, from expensive jewelry to TV sets to high-quality Japanese stereo amplifiers and speakers, as well as Stateside refrigerators and all brands of liquor. Most Vietnamese, including my counterpart, were particularly fond of French Cognac, and not the cheap variety. Hennessey VS was the most popular brand. Since I only had a couple of months remaining on my tour, I bought or ordered gifts for my family members and girlfriend back home. If you couldn't find what you wanted in the PX you could order it from a catalogue, and they would ship it from Japan directly to the States. I ordered a set of Noritake fine china for my mother, and an expensive watch for my Dad along with a set of stereo speakers for myself.

It wasn't unusual on leaving the PX to see GIs and their Vietnamese girlfriends cramming small refrigerators, air conditioners, or boxes of stereo equipment into one of the blue and yellow Vietnamese taxis ready to set up housekeeping in one of the little $50-a-month apartments that were spread across Cholon and other sections of the city. I have no issues with anyone who served honorably in Vietnam, since everyone's specific assignment was determined by their branch of service, but there were definitely stark contrasts in the tours served by troops assigned to U.S. tactical units, and those who served in support units in Saigon.

* * *

During the first week of July, Captain Marty Tovar, my Ranger friend, visited me in Saigon for the weekend. Marty had regained his health and looked great, having finally put on the weight that he'd lost. He brought me a 4th Ranger Group plaque that was given to all departing officers and NCOs at the end of their tours. He also passed me an invitation from Lieutenant Colonel Witek to a farewell party that the 4th Ranger Group was arranging for me and a couple of other officers who were completing their tours. I thanked Marty and told him that I had no plans to return to Can Tho for a farewell party or any other reason short of a direct order. Besides, my battalion was scheduled to deploy to the Van Kiep National Training Center the following week. The pair of us had a great time that weekend in Saigon.

The 2d Vietnamese Airborne Battalion departed Saigon the following week. We traveled by truck convoy to the Van Kiep Training area near Vung Tau on the South China Sea. It was my first trip to the Vaug Tau area. During my first tour with the 199th Light Infantry Brigade in 1968, I was scheduled to go on R&R to Vung Tau on several occasions, but each time I had to cancel due to one sort of tactical emergency or other.

Vung Tau is a resort town at the very tip of the scenic *Cap Saint Jaques* some 125 kilometers southeast of Saigon. During the war, it was the home of various U.S. support units, and it was an in-country R&R center for U.S. and allied troops. With its world-class white sand beaches and relatively good security, Vung Tau was an ideal in-country R&R center. It was also rumored that the Communists used it as an R&R center for their officers. The Vietnamese Airborne Division's 8th Battalion was home based in the Vung Tau area, and nearby was the Australian Army's Task Force base at Nui Dat.

Although Vung Tau itself was relatively secure, the area surrounding it was not. Phuc Tuy Province encompassed an area of some 2,500 square miles. The terrain ranged from coastal plains with sand dunes along the coast, to the Saigon River Delta (Rung Sat) with its dense mangrove swamps to the west, and three separate jungle-covered mountains. *Nui Dinh* and *Nui Thi Vai* are located between Highways 2 and 15, and the *Long Hai* Hills sit nearer the coast. The Australian Army fought one its largest battles of the Vietnam War at Long Tan near its base at *Nui Dat* in August 1966, and was still conducting combat operations in the Province in the summer of 1971 when we arrived for training.

The Van Kiep training area was on the outskirts of Baria, near the juncture of Highways 15 and 2. The town was the scene of heavy fighting during the Tet Offensive of 1968. Our advisory team was billeted at the Baria District Advisory Team's compound when we were not in the field. I shared a room with an Australian artillery officer who had served as a forward observer with an Australian infantry battalion prior to his assignment to the district advisory team.

The first two weeks of training focused on platoon and company training. The Vietnamese instructors were very good after being trained by their Australian advisors. Much of the small unit training reminded me of what I underwent while attending the British Jungle Warfare School in Malaysia. The training was excellent, but I was disappointed at the limitation on live-fire training. The ARVN was very miserly in expending live ammunition. Also, the battalion commander did not spend much time monitoring the training of his platoons and companies. There was a general tendency among ARVN officers to regard training periods as an opportunity for rest and recuperation.

After visiting the training sites each morning, I usually had my noon meal with the battalion commander and his staff. The meal was served in a mess tent, and was somewhat of a ritual. There was assigned seating for the officers and advisors, and everyone was seated by rank. The commander sat at the head of the table. ARVN orderlies brought large bowls of steaming hot rice and other dishes. I was always amazed at the amount of rice that the average Vietnamese could consume at one sitting. There was much noisy and generally convivial conversation between the officers during the meal. Afterward, the commander and his staff officers retired for their afternoon siestas before returning to work.

Since the Australian base at Nui Dat was close by, I visited it on several occasions and was very impressed by what I saw. Most U.S. Army main base camps were located near villages where the civilian labor force lived. Nui Dat, on the other hand, was fairly isolated, and even the roads that ran through the area were rerouted around the Australian base. Unlike the sprawling U.S. base camps, the land was not cleared of trees and vegetation. The buildings at the base were well camouflaged and concealed in the natural setting. There were also few Vietnamese civilians who had access to the base. Driving through, I also noted that the Australian soldiers carried their rifles with them at all times. This was not a common practice at U.S. bases except during alerts. The aforementioned security measures were prudent and appropriate.

The weekend before my airborne battalion's final week of training, which included a mass tactical parachute jump and tactical training exercise, I had a problem with one of my team members. On Saturday evening, I was relaxing at the Baria officers club with a few Australian officers who had befriended me. About 10 p.m., the Australian Army regimental sergeant major (RSM), a towering giant of a man with hands the size of hams, approached me at the bar and told me that there was a problem with "one of my lads" at the NCO club.

"What sort of trouble?" I asked.

"There's been a bit of a brawl between one of your sergeants and the U.S. First Sergeant, and it seems that the first sergeant got the worst of it," he answered.

"Well, sergeant major, I'm told that sometimes happens among NCOs," I replied.

"Right you are captain, but the bloke who runs the NCO club is a friend of the first sergeant and he's called the MPs. Your sergeant is holed up in the barracks and he's pretty drunk. You'd better see to it if you don't want him to get hurt," the RSM said.

After thanking the RSM I headed for the NCO billets. I knew it was Sergeant Pilon as soon as I heard of the incident. Pilon was a superb NCO, but he didn't hold his liquor as well as most. When I entered the NCO billets, I found the sergeant in full combat gear loading his M-16 rifle.

"Pilon, what in the hell do you think you're doing?" I asked.

"They're coming for me Sir, and I'm getting ready for them," he answered, slurring his words. I could see that he was dead drunk, but completely serious.

"Goddamn it, Pilon, put that rifle down and get all your gear packed now. We're leaving in one minute," I said. I knew I had to get him off the compound and fast.

I loaded Sergeant Pilon and his gear in my Jeep, and we sped out the main gate of the compound just as a Jeep load of MPs from Vung

Tau roared into the compound. I drove Pilon, who was now passed out, to the 8th Airborne Battalion's advisory detachment's billets at the Vung Tau airfield, and turned him over to the detachment's senior NCO.

"Tell Sergeant Pilon, when he sobers up, that he's restricted to your team's billets until Monday morning's jump," I told the sergeant. "If the MPs come looking for him, tell them he's on his way back to Saigon."

"I'll take care of everything, and have him at ramp on Monday morning," the team sergeant replied.

The next morning, I telephoned my Brigade advisor in Saigon and told him about the incident, and that I wanted to keep Sergeant Pilon at Van Kiep for the next week. My boss said he'd have the Team 162 sergeant major give Pilon a good "ass chewing" when we got back to Saigon. As far as I was concerned, that closed the book on the incident, but the senior district advisor, a lieutenant colonel, didn't see it that way. The next day he called me to his office. He wanted Sergeant Pilon's head on a silver platter for "beating up" his first sergeant. I told him that Sergeant Pilon was no longer on the compound, and that he'd be dealt with back at our Detachment headquarters in Saigon. He was really "pissed off," but there wasn't much he could do about it.

Monday morning the 2d Airborne Battalion moved to a marshalling area at the Vung Tau airfield in preparation for its jump into the Van Kiep training area. Sergeant Pilon met us there with his head held sheepishly low. I described the whole incident to him, but he only recalled bits and pieces of his escapade. After a short "ass chewing," I told him to "chute up" for the jump.

I was surprised that we were jumping from C-119 "flying boxcar" aircraft, rather than C-123s or C-130s. I hadn't jumped from the older C-119 aircraft since jump school at Fort Benning several years earlier. There was nothing wrong with the C-119; in fact, its wide paratrooper doors were more accommodating for a fully combat-equipped paratrooper than the C-123 or C-130. We wore T-10 parachutes, reserve chutes, and all other combat equipment that would be carried on an actual combat jump, including our rucksacks, weapons, and a basic load of live ammunition. No drop zone was really secure in Vietnam so we were prepared for the worst.

It was a short flight to the drop zone, and the azure blue sky was soon filled with hundreds of billowing parachute canopies as the aircraft flew over in trail formation. The jump altitude was 800 feet; 400 feet lower than U.S. training jumps. I silently counted the four seconds that it took the static line to jerk my main chute from its pack, waiting for the reassuring opening shock as the canopy suddenly filled with air. Looking around me I followed the flight of the aircraft as they continued to disgorge the paratroopers across the drop zone. There were paratroopers dangling from their chutes above my head and below my feet. I pulled on the chute's risers to avoid colliding with other jumpers.

Getting entangled with another chute often resulted in one or both of the chutes collapsing in mid-air. Also, if you were directly overhead of another parachute's canopy, it could steal the air from your canopy and cause it to collapse. The sky is even more unforgiving than the sea if something goes wrong. A total parachute malfunction can be fatal at 800 feet, since the jumper has only seconds to deploy his reserve chute. I saw a few reserve chutes deployed over the drop zone, but not many. The Airborne Division's parachute riggers did their jobs well, and there were very few malfunctions with the parachutes they packed.

As I approached the ground, I released my rucksack on its lowering line so that it would hit the ground before I did. Then I made a near perfect landing, but I was dragged by the wind for several yards before I could activate the quick releases on the chute's shoulder harness. After collapsing my wind-filled canopy and rolling it up, I placed it along with the harness in my kit bag. Then I double-timed over to a shallow pond where my team sergeant had landed. He was soaking wet and looked "madder than a wet hen." As a master parachutist, Garrison was more than a little embarrassed that he couldn't avoid the pond on landing. Adding insult to injury, I snapped a picture of him with a small camera that I carried. By that time we were both laughing pretty hard as we rolled up his soaking wet chute before double-timing off the drop zone headed for the battalion's assembly area.

The field training exercise went reasonably well, and I was able to observe that my counterpart was a fairly good tactician, maneuvering his companies without much of a problem. The training center's Vietnamese aggressor force could have been a bit more aggressive, but perhaps they were intimidated by the airborne troopers, as most other ARVN soldiers were. The aggressor force didn't "hold a candle" to the Gurkas that the British used at their Jungle Warfare School.

Overall, the training at Van Kiep was beneficial, particularly for the new replacements. However, what the airborne battalions really needed was combined arms training with tanks, armored personnel carriers, and artillery. In addition, the battalion needed training on how to hunt down and kill enemy tanks, employing tank hunter/killer teams. Infantry, tank, and artillery units should have trained together with live fire exercises and command post exercises for the battalion staffs. The airborne operation was good training, but the airborne battalions would, more often than not, be inserted by helicopter than by parachute. In fact, the Airborne Division was to conduct only one more combat jump during the final years of the war. The time spent on airborne training operations should have been spent on airmobile training.

The shortfalls in combined arms training was clearly evident during the high-intensity combat operations in Laos during Operation *Lam Son 719* in February and March, but the Vietnamese Armed Forces moved far too slowly in developing a combined arms doctrine, much less combined arms training programs. The high intensity combat during *Lam Son 719* was a harbinger of things to come, and the South Vietnamese Armed Forces had little time to waste in preparing for the conventional battles to come. I wrote up all my observations on the training in an after-action report, recommending a combined arms approach in all future training.

It wasn't until December of 1971 that the Airborne Division finally got to put the ARVN's new combined arms doctrine to the test during a combat operation in Cambodia's Chup Rubber Plantation. The operation went much smoother than the one in Laos nine months earlier.

After the conclusion of the Van Kiep training, I authorized a three-day R&R for my team in the Vung Tau beach resort. We stayed in the old French Grand Hotel in downtown Vung Tau. They served the best clams I've ever tasted. During the day we went to the beach to watch the Vietnamese girls in their French bikini bathing suits, and drank beer by the case. At night we hit all the local bars and other entertainment venues. I thought the team deserved a break, and knew we'd soon be headed to the jungle on another combat operation. I wasn't wrong.

CHAPTER 13

.CLOSING THE CIRCLE

By the beginning of August 1971, Vietnamization of the war was moving forward at a fast pace. A new campaign, "Consolidation I," was announced on 1 July 1971. During this campaign, the South Vietnamese armed forces were to assume responsibility for the ground war as the remaining U.S. forces withdrew. On 11 August 1971, Secretary of Defense Melvin Laird announced somewhat prematurely that Phase I of Vietnamization was complete, which meant that the ARVN was ready to assume total responsibility for the conduct of the ground war. In reality, U.S. maneuver battalions remaining in Vietnam continued to conduct ground combat operations, but the preponderance of troops in the field were South Vietnamese. The push to put additional ARVN battalions in the field continued as the summer wore on.

Upon our return to Saigon on 1 August, we learned that the 3d Airborne Brigade, including the 2d Airborne Battalion, was scheduled to deploy to an area north of Song Be in the III Corps tactical zone. My rotation date was 29 August and my replacement had arrived, but I was told that I would deploy with the battalion to allow my replacement time to get his feet on the ground. Major Michael Davison, Jr. was assigned as the 2d Airborne Battalion's new senior advisor. Davison was a 1964 West Point graduate who had served a previous tour in Vietnam with the First Air Cavalry Division in 1968, and was to achieve the rank of lieutenant general before his retirement. He was one of several members of Advisory Team 162 to reach the rank of general officer.

The 2d Airborne Battalion departed Saigon by ground convoy on 8 August. We headed north on Highway 13 to Bien Hoa, and then on Route 1A through Phuoc Vinh and Sang. The terrain became progressively hillier as we proceeded north into the central highlands. My experience in Vietnam at this point had been in the mostly flat terrain in III and IV Corps, and the jungle-covered hills and valleys looked foreboding. It also became progressively cooler the further we traveled from the lowlands into the highlands.

We reached our destination, a grass covered hill, late that afternoon. On the dirt trail leading to the hilltop, we passed several *Montagnard* tribesmen carrying crossbows and quivers of arrows. They were hunting birds and small game in the area. The men wore breechcloths and worn, drab olive fatigue shirts, and they grinned and shouted at us in their own language as we passed. It was my first encounter with the indigenous tribesmen of the central highlands.

The artillerymen that accompanied us began to unlimber their new M-102 105mm howitzers and manhandle them into firing positions on the hilltop. Thirty minutes later, the artillery began firing registration missions in the surrounding jungle. Meanwhile, the airborne troopers began to construct bunkers along a perimeter of what would soon be a fully operational fire support base.

The *Montagnards* traded their crossbows with the airborne soldiers for cigarettes and rations along the perimeter wire. By nightfall most of the perimeter bunkers had been dug and covered with PSP and sandbags. We constructed our advisory team bunker in the same manner a few yards away from the battalion commander's command post. As the sun went down the temperature dropped dramatically, and I put on my wool jungle sweater. I doubt if the temperature dropped below 60 degrees that night, but the cool damp air was bone chilling. After a C-ration supper, we organized our radio watch shifts and wrapped ourselves in poncho liners for the night.

The following day Major Davison and I met with the battalion commander, and planned a series of company-size search and clear operations in the areas around the fire support base. Three airborne companies were assigned to search a separate area for the next week and a half, while the battalion headquarters and one company remained at the FSB to provide security for the artillery. I would accompany 21 Company, Staff Sergeant Pilon would go with 22 Company, and SSgt Ball would accompany 23 Company. Major Davison and the new team sergeant would remain at the firebase with the battalion command group. I never anticipated being out in the bush with an ARVN company so close to my rotation date, but I told myself that it was safer than remaining on the fire support base. Chances were good that the base would come under mortar attack over the next few days.

Dai Uy Tri, the 21 Company commander, was as capable a commander as any in the battalion, and he took good care of me. He assigned a very young trooper to carry my radio. The kid looked no more than 15 or 16 years old, which was much younger than my Ranger radio operator in the Delta. He spoke no English whatsoever. I thought he was a bit unhappy about his assignment, and somewhat nervous to be carrying the American's radio. The company had over 100 men in the field, many of whom had yet to experience combat. Only one of the platoon leaders was new to the battalion. He was a recent graduate of the Vietnamese Military Academy at Da Lat. The company's officers were very cordial and had quite a few questions about my background, U.S. tactics, and other general questions about the States. It was a good company, and I felt right at home with them from the start. Their careers and some of their lives, however, would be short-lived.

Our operation kicked off the following morning with an airmobile insertion into the smallest LZ that I'd ever landed on. It was so small that it could only handle one Huey at a time. The LZ was on a hillside overgrown with elephant grass. The Huey pilots would hover a few feet off the ground, and the troops had to jump from the skids. I stood on the skids and leapt off into the grass, losing my balance once I hit the ground. I rolled down the hill a few feet until I grabbed hold of a tree stump. The CP group was about the third or fourth ship in the flight to land, and by the time we hit the LZ, the airborne troopers in the first ships were already scampering up the hill. Fortunately it was a "cold" LZ, and the airborne troopers moved swiftly toward the crest.

I began to climb the steep slope with the company commander. After more than eleven months in Vietnam, I thought myself very fit and hardened, but I was breathing fast and heavy after a few minutes. As the sun rose higher in the pale blue sky, the temperature climbed steeply and I could feel patches of perspiration on the back of my fatigue shirt. We skirted a patch of bamboo and finally made it up to a spiny ridgeline that overlooked a jungle-covered valley.

I recommended to the *Dai Uy* that he send one platoon to search the valley, while another platoon swept down the ridgeline toward a smaller hill at the other end of the ridge. The CP group and reserve platoon would remain in position ready to reinforce the maneuvering platoons if they ran into trouble. This terrain was completely new to me. When I commanded a light infantry company in southern War Zone D in 1968, we typically moved with two platoons forward covering a maximum frontage of about 400 meters. The company headquarters was in the center rear, and the third rifle platoon moved in the rearguard reserve position. Thus, the entire rifle company formation was about 400 meters wide and 400 meters in depth, depending on the terrain and vegetation. This scheme of maneuver worked well in the relatively flat jungle terrain in War Zone D. However, in the mountainous terrain of the highlands, maintaining a 400 meter frontage was impossible. You had to analyze the terrain grid square by grid square, and adapt your formations accordingly.

When the company commander briefed his platoon leaders, he followed my recommendations. Perhaps he'd already decided on a similar scheme of maneuver even before I recommended it. He was pretty savvy, and was no amateur.

While we waited for the two platoons to complete their missions, I had a conversation with the company's newest platoon leader. He was a graduate of the Vietnamese military academy and had also attended the U.S. basic infantry officer course and jump school at Fort Benning. His English was flawless. I was curious about his family background, and he told me that his family had roots in North Vietnam, but his father and one of his uncles had moved their families south after the first Indo-China war. Both had fought for the French, while another brother fought for the Viet Minh and remained in North Vietnam.

According to the lieutenant, his father jumped into Dien Bien Phu with the 5th Vietnamese Parachute Battalion, was wounded and later captured by the Viet Minh. After independence, his father and his uncle, both of whom remained loyal to the French, moved their families south, and later joined the newly formed Republic of Vietnam Armed Forces. Sadly, the lieutenant's father was killed at Hue during the Tet Offensive of 1968, but his uncle was still fighting as a field grade officer in the 21st ARVN Division. I asked about his father's brother who fought for the Viet Minh. I had to pry it out of him, but he finally told me that his estranged uncle was a high-ranking officer in the NVA's 320th Division. "So you see, this war is much like other civil wars, including your own: brother against brother. I believe I also have cousins my age fighting with the North Vietnamese," he added.

The search of the valley and ridgeline turned up no signs of the enemy so the company moved on throughout the afternoon, crossing a logging road and ascending another ridgeline to the north. Soon after crossing the road we came upon a crumbling, deserted house. It was quite old, probably dating back to Vietnam's pre-colonial days. Entering the ruins, the company commander explained that its owners might have been Chinese. The only item remaining in the house was an ancient Chinese water jar. It was in perfect shape, but it was too large for anyone to carry.

As we ascended the ridgeline, the late afternoon sun was beginning to lose its heat, but the valleys below still shimmered in a green haze. There was still no sign of enemy activity. Near sunset, we pushed on down a long finger off the ridgeline and found a suitable night defensive position. The troops began to dig in as the fading light of day gave way to blackness. I strung my hammock between two trees and stretched my poncho over a piece of static line that I'd strung above the hammock to keep the dew off.

Around midnight, a thunderstorm erupted from the blackened sky, and the rain fell in torrents as lightning flashed and thunder reverberated from the surrounding hills. The rain pelted my poncho, but I stayed reasonable dry except for a trickle of rain water that dribbled down my hammock strings. After the storm I had a deep, refreshing sleep until I awoke to the raucous cries of monkeys and jungle fowl greeting the gray light of dawn.

And so it went day after day on our long jungle patrol. We saw no bunkers, human tracks, or other recent signs of life in the area. The beautiful tropical forest was turning out to be a "dry hole." One evening I was approached by two of the company's lieutenants who wanted to know if I could use a bath. They'd located a stream about 100 yards from our perimeter. "What about security?" I asked. They laughed and said, "No VC here, *Dai Uy.*" I was still a bit skittish, but I was feeling pretty ripe, so I accompanied the two officers to the stream.

There was a steep hill on the other side of the mountain stream, and I knew we'd be sitting ducks once we entered the water, but I thought "what the hell," and stripped down to my shorts and had a refreshingly cool bath. Then I pulled my shaving mirror from my rucksack and saw a bearded face burned red by too many months of fierce tropical sunshine. Dutifully, I scraped my face with a razor, removing a week's worth of whiskers. I felt the sharp sting of an insect bite as I shaved, but didn't think much about it. By the time we got back to the perimeter I'd broken out in hives, and I could feel my throat constricting. The company commander took one look at me and told me to lie down before summoning the company medic, *bac si.* I knew the dangers of going into anaphylactic shock, but I'd never experienced it firsthand. The medic gave me a couple of pills to swallow, probably benadryl. There was no way a medevac chopper could have extracted me since there was no LZ nearby, and as darkness fell a dense fog blanketed the entire area.

An hour later I felt lightheaded, but my breathing was less labored. The medic stayed by my side as I slept heavily, waking me on one occasion to give me more benadryl. By morning I still felt dizzy, but the hives had disappeared and I felt pretty good.

The company continued to patrol for another two days, finding nothing. The following day the company commander received a radio message from battalion commander ordering him to move to a rendezvous point where we would link up with the battalion's other companies. The night before we linked up with the other airborne companies, I was monitoring my radio when I recognized Sergeant Pilon's voice calling in to Major Davison. The sergeant sounded in a near panic as he reported hearing animal sounds coming from the jungle near his perimeter. "It sounds like two animals fighting—maybe a tiger and an elephant," he said. "Its terrible!" Sergeant Pilon either has the

DTs or he's really losing it, I concluded. The following morning I asked the company commander if we were in tiger country. "Definitely," he said, "My men reported seeing tracks yesterday." What about elephants, I asked. "It's possible," he answered.

The following day we rendezvoused with the other airborne companies, and the 2d Battalion moved by truck convoy to an area south of Phuoc Vinh. The 3d Airborne Brigade headquarters was set up a few kilometers south of the town. When we arrived I walked over to the advisors' CP tent and spoke to Lieutenant Colonel Ulvenes, the brigade senior advisor. Since my rotation date was only about a week away, I thought that I'd be going back to Saigon to out process. The colonel was under the impression that I had extended my tour of duty with the airborne for another six months, or so he said. I didn't know if he was pulling my leg or not.

"No way, sir," I said. "I thought about it, but I want to get back to the States and I've got orders to Special Forces at Bragg."

The colonel laughed and said, "Just hang in there with Major Davison for another day or two, and we'll get you back to Saigon. You won't miss your flight."

"If I do, I'll just get a surfboard and a compass, and try it on my own," I said.

On 25 August, the 2d Airborne Battalion conducted airmobile assaults into LZs south of the Song Be River. The company I was with landed on a grass-covered area a few kilometers south of the river. There was something familiar about that place.

I plotted the coordinates of our LZ on the map as the airborne troopers began to dig in for the night. A trail led off the LZ to the northeast. I traced the trail on the map with my index finger. There it was, less than a kilometer away from our LZ; it was marked as a "military area." It was the prior site of FSB Nashua, where I had assumed command of Charlie Company, 4/12th Infantry on 1 January 1968, more than three and a half years earlier.

The significance of my final day on a combat operation in Vietnam was not lost on me. The "Warriors" of Charlie Company, who had once swept the battered jungles around me were long gone. It was no longer their war. Only the ghosts of the fallen remained. The South Vietnamese Airborne and Ranger warriors had replaced them.

I had come full circle in my Vietnam experience.

The Rangers and Airborne warriors would fight heroically for four more long years before a conventional North Vietnamese Army rolled southward in the spring of 1975. While many ARVN units broke under pressure during that final offensive, the Airborne and Rangers fought valiantly to stem the tide of defeat. Even after the fall of Saigon, remnants of these elite forces fought on in remote areas for months, becoming the fallen nation's "Forsaken Warriors."

CHAPTER 14

REFLECTIONS

I was fortunate to serve as an advisor with two of the ARVN's most elite units during my second tour in Vietnam. The individual Vietnamese Ranger and Airborne troopers that I had the opportunity to serve with were superb soldiers, as capable as their cousins from the north. They endured incredible hardships and fought heroically. At first glance, their slight build and adolescent features gave the impression that they lacked the requisite strength and endurance required of a good soldier. Nothing could be further from the truth. Most of the men in the ranks came from a peasant background and they were used to backbreaking labor in the rice fields. They could march all day in the tropical heat of the jungles, swamps, and rice paddies without complaint. Most wore a perpetual smile and maintained a good disposition. Even when grievously wounded, the Rangers and Airborne troopers took the pain and accepted their fate stoically. During combat, I observed that these soldiers followed the orders of their superiors, and in many cases performed acts of heroism deserving the highest awards of their army. With the proper leadership at the highest levels of their army and government, they could have won their war. Unfortunately, that leadership did not exist within the Saigon government or the top echelons of the armed forces.

The ARVN officer corps reflected the culture of their country and society. Most of the senior officers had not earned their rank based on battlefield performance. Rather, they were promoted though a system of patronage and control exercised from the highest echelons of the government. Appointments and promotions were based on family connections, friends, and in some cases outright cash payments to the sponsor. Even after taking off his uniform and assuming the office of president, Nguyen Van Thieu exercised tight control over promotions to major and higher ranks. As a result, ARVN officers were loath to "rock the boat," "make waves," or take initiative in the absence of orders. Command was not seen as the surest way to the top. Staff assignments were considered a safer route to promotion and power than command with its inherent risks and responsibilities. When all was said and done, political reliability was the main criteria for achieving high rank in the South Vietnamese military. As a consequence "cream did not always rise to the top"; in fact, it seldom did.

It was my good fortune to advise two battalion commanders who were better than most. Both displayed courage when required, and both had good tactical instincts and common sense. However, even if those commanders escaped death or disabling wounds, it is doubtful if either of the officers would have achieved the rank of colonel, much less general officer, had the Saigon regime survived. Neither of the two men had family wealth or connections within the Saigon regime.

At the company level the leadership was weaker and less experienced than I anticipated. I was surprised at the number of companies that were commanded by first or, in some cases, second lieutenants. Of course, battle losses at the rank of captain and below were particularly high from 1968 through1971 as the ARVN assumed greater responsibility for the ground war. Operation *Lam Son 719* in 1971 decimated the officer and NCO ranks of South Vietnam's strongest units, the Rangers, Airborne, Marines, and the 1st Infantry Division. South Vietnam was never able to replace these losses.

Advising the South Vietnamese Ranger and Airborne battalions were two of the most challenging assignments in my 27 years of military service. My counter-insurgency training experience in Thailand with Special Forces was invaluable in preparation for my advisory assignment. I was used to working with indigenous forces in an alien culture with little to no language training or proficiency. Having had a previous combat tour as a company commander in a U.S. unit also served me well. Most ARVN battalion commanders would accept advice from a U.S. advisor who was junior in rank if that advisor had a reasonable amount of combat experience, proved capable of coordinating U.S. fire support, and could deliver helicopter support for movement, resupply, and medical evacuation. Only after an advisor demonstrated his proficiency in the aforementioned areas was he able to exert his influence in other areas such as tactics, training, and maintenance. Unfortunately, priority was never placed on training ARVN officers in the aforementioned combat skills until it was too late.

Throughout my tour as an advisor, I carried a pocket-sized version of the Army Field Manual 31-73, "Advisor Handbook for Counterinsurgency." The manual was a compendium of information and advice concerning advisor techniques and counterpart relationships. I underlined four that I found particularly relevant and useful: first, the advisor does not command his counterpart's organization; second, the advisor should study his counterpart's personality and background, and exert every effort to establish and maintain friendly relationships; third, after planting ideas, counterparts should be allowed to take the credit if they are accepted and well executed; and fourth, the advisor should keep an account of major events and submit accurate reports to his superiors. In the case of the latter, I always submitted narrative reports to my next higher advisor even when they were not required or requested.

Based on my experience in the MR-4 Ranger Command Advisory Detachment, I concluded that there was a waste of talent and experience within that detachment. The advisory teams at Group and Regional level were fully manned with qualified and experienced personnel. On the other hand, there was always a shortage of experienced, qualified officers and NCOs in the Battalion Combat Assistance Teams, where "rubber met the road."

My final observation on the advisory effort in Vietnam is that the phase-out of the Battalion Combat Assistance Teams was premature. The ARVN combat battalions were not yet ready to "go it alone" when the drawdown of battalion advisors began during the first six months of 1971. This was clearly evident during *Lam Son 719*, when U.S. advisors were not permitted to accompany their units into Laos. Nonetheless, except for Airborne, Marine, and newly raised infantry battalions, all U.S. Battalion Combat Assistance Teams were phased out by 30 June 1971. On the other hand, the Airborne and Marine battalion advisors gave their units a decisive edge during the Easter Offensive of 1972. After the last remaining U.S. combat advisors departed Vietnam in March of 1973, the dye was cast for final defeat. The South Vietnamese armed forces were abandoned, left to fight a final conventional campaign with American doctrine and equipment they could not sustain or maintain.

EPILOGUE

After leaving the 2d Airborne Battalion in War Zone D on 26 September 1971, I returned to Saigon to begin my out-processing in preparation for my return to the United States. The day before my flight, Colonel Vaught, the Airborne Division's Senior Advisor, took me to lunch at the MACV's senior officers mess after an award presentation. It was a nice touch. Throughout his time with the Airborne Division, Colonel Vaught displayed a genuine interest in all of his advisors and their welfare. On 29 September, I boarded a Pan Am flight at Tan Son Nhut Airport for a long flight across the Pacific to San Francisco. I was happy to be going home, and looked forward to my Special Forces assignment at Fort Bragg, North Carolina.

Six months later, on 31 March 1972, the Communists launched an all-out attack on South Vietnam that came to be known as the Easter Offensive. The initial North Vietnamese attacks came directly south across the DMZ into the I Corps area. Less than a week later, the NVA opened a second front in III Corps. Attacking out of Cambodia with two divisions, the NVA surrounded Loc Ninh and An Loc. By the end of April, the enemy had opened a third front in II Corps, invading Kontum Province with two divisions. South Vietnamese Ranger and Airborne units participated in counteroffensives on all three fronts. The fighting was bitter at all points. For the most part, it was all-out conventional warfare involving NVA infantry, armor, heavy artillery, and antiaircraft units.

With the support of U.S. artillery, helicopter gunships, close air support, and B-52 bombers, the outnumbered South Vietnamese were able to defeat and turn back the enemy forces by summer'ss end. The ARVN employed their new combined arms doctrine effectively, and did not repeat the mistakes of *Lam Son 719*. It was also fortuitous that the South Vietnamese Airborne and Marine divisions still had the assistance of their U.S. advisors during the Easter Offensive.

While the NVA offensive was in progress, the withdrawal of U.S. combat forces continued with the last American combat troops departing Vietnam in August 1972. By the end of that month, only about 40,000 U.S. support personnel remained in Vietnam, and by the end of 1972 there were only around 24,000. On 29 March 1973, the U.S. Military Assistance Command (MACV) headquarters was disestablished, and by the end of that year, the size of the U.S. military contingent in Vietnam was limited to 50 personnel, mainly Marines guarding the U.S. Embassy.

The final NVA offensive began in early March of 1975, with attacks in II Corps followed by attacks in III Corps and I Corps. The Airborne and Ranger forces again responded on all fronts. They fought valiantly against overwhelming odds in II Corps, putting up stubborn resistance until they were pushed back to the coast. The survivors had to be evacuated by sea from Nha Trang when organized South Vietnamese resistance in II Corps crumbled.

Meanwhile, other Airborne Division units fighting to hold on to positions in I Corps were ordered south by President Thieu to defend Saigon. Thereafter, the 1st and 2d ARVN Divisions, and the Marine Division were not able to stop the NVA in the north, and Danang, the last remaining enclave in I Corps, fell to the NVA on 30 March 1975.

The NVA then turned their full attention to III Corps and the South Vietnamese capital. The vice began to tighten on Saigon beginning in early March with attacks in Tay Ninh Province on 11 March, followed by multi-pronged attacks all along the Cambodian-Vietnam boundary only a few miles from the city. In mid-March, another NVA force of three divisions attacked Xuan Loc northeast of Saigon. An Airborne brigade launched a counterattack on Xuan Loc from the south, but it came too little and too late. The remnants of the brigade made its way to Ba Ria and ultimately Vung Tau, where some of the paratroopers managed to escape by sea. By that time the Airborne Division was down to about one-third of its original strength, and there were only the remnants of four Ranger groups, less than six understrength battalions, remaining to defend the capital. Slowly but surely, the NVA pushed the last remaining South Vietnamese forces back into the outskirts of Saigon until the country's new President, "Big" Minh, ordered the RVNAF to lay down its arms on 30 April 1975. By that time almost all of the provincial capitals and district towns in the Mekong Delta had also fallen to the Communists. For all intents and purposes the second Vietnam War ended with the surrender of Saigon on 30 April.

There were reports of small groups of Rangers and paratroopers taking to the jungles and swamps to carry on the fight, but they received no support and soon all resistance disappeared.

South Vietnamese Ranger and Airborne officers who did not manage to escape Vietnam during the final weeks of the war were taken into custody and most were sent to "re-education camps," where they spent months, and in some cases years, performing hard labor. While there is no evidence of mass executions of ARVN officers, complete accountability of the fate of all Ranger and Airborne officers was never established. In most cases, men who served in the enlisted ranks of the ARVN were released and returned to their homes, but the former soldiers were required to carry identification cards that barred them from all but the lowest menial jobs in the Communist economy.

During the first week of July 1990, former members of the Vietnamese Airborne Division and their advisors attended a reunion in Arlington, Virginia. The former members of the division were by that time U.S. citizens. Former Vietnamese and U.S. comrades in arms greeted each other warmly and exchanged information on the fate of many others who were not so fortunate. The high point of the reunion was a parade in Washington D.C. presided over by its Grand Marshal, General William Westmoreland, and it was led by former Airborne Division Commander General Le Quang Luong and former Division Senior Advisor Lieutenant General James Vaught.

On that occasion, the famed elite Vietnamese Airborne Division and its U.S. Army advisors marched off together into the annals of military history.

More than five years later, on 12 November 1995, a group of former South Vietnamese Rangers and their U.S. advisors gathered in

Section 47 of Arlington National Cemetery for the dedication of a monument to their fallen comrades. The bronze plaque on the monument displays a Vietnamese Ranger badge and beret badge, along with a U.S. Army Ranger tab. A few short lines on the plaque read as follows: "Dedicated to the honor of the Vietnamese Rangers and their American Ranger advisors, whose dedication, valor, and fidelity in the defense of freedom must never be forgotten." Beneath these lines are the mottos of both the Vietnamese and U.S. Rangers: *"Biet Dong Quan Sat!"* or "Rangers Lead the Way!"

GLOSSARY

ACAV	An armored cavalry assault vehicle: a modified M113 armored personnel carrier
ARVN	Army of the Republic of Vietnam
ASPB	Assault Support Patrol Boat
ATC	Armored Troop Carrier (boat)
B 40	A Communist shaped-charge projectile fired by the RPG2 or RPG7
BCAT	Battalion Combat Assistance Team
Biet Dong Quan	South Vietnamese Ranger
C&C	Command and Control
CIB	Combat Infantry Badge
CIDG	Civilian Irregular Defense Group
CORDS	Civilian Operations and Revolutionary Development Support
Co Van	Advisor
CP	Command post
Dai Ta	Vietnamese Colonel
Dai Uy	Vietnamese Captain

DCAT	Division Combat Assistance Team
DMZ	Demilitarized Zone (boundary between North & South Vietnam
DRAC	Delta Regional Assistance Command
FAC	Forward Air Controller
FSB	Fire Support Base
Gunship	An armed helicopter that provides fire support for ground forces
H&I	Harassment and interdiction fire (artillery or mortar)
KIA	Killed in action
LAW	Light anti-tank weapon
LP	Listening post
LZ	Helicopter landing zone
MACV	Military Assistance Command Vietnam
MARS	Military Affiliate Radio Station
MAT	Mobile Assistance Team
Medevac	Medical evacuation
Monitor	Armored gunboat mounting 20mm, 40mm, .50 caliber guns and 81mm mortar or 105mm howitzer
MR	Military Region
Mu Do	South Vietnamese colonel
NCO	Non Commissioned Officer
NVA	North Vietnamese Army
PBR	Patrol Boat River
PF	Popular Forces (South Vietnamese local militia forces}
PSP	Pierced steel planking (used on aircraft runways in lieu

	of cement on forward airstrips
PX	Post Exchange
RCAT	Regimental Combat Assistance Team
RF	Regional Forces (South Vietnamese)
RPG	Soviet or Chinese-made Rocket Propelled Grenade with a shaped charge
R&R	Rest and Recuperation leave
RVNAF	Republic of Vietnam Armed Forces
SA	Senior Advisor
SF	Special Forces
Swift Boat	Patrol craft fast
Thieu Uy	South Vietnamese 2d lieutenant
Thieu Ta	South Vietnamese major
TOC	Tactical operations center
Trung Ta	South Vietnamese lieutenant colonel
Trung Uy	South Vietnamese 1st lieutenant
VC	Viet Cong
VNAF	South Vietnamese Air Force
WIA	Wounded in action
XO	Executive officer

NOTES

PROLOGUE

The participation of the 199th Light Infantry Brigade in the fighting in and around Saigon during the May Offensive of 1968, is described in detail in my first two books, *Warriors: An Infantryman's Memoir of Vietnam* (A Presidio Press book republished by the Random House Publishing Group in 2004), and *Days of Valor: An Inside Account of the Bloodiest Six Months of the Vietnam War* (Casemate Publishers, 2007).

CHAPTER 1: A FORTUNATE SON

A description of the 46th Special Forces mission in Thailand can be found in Chapter 15: Far East Missions, in Shelby L. Stanton's book *Green Berets at War, U.S. Army Special Forces in Southeast Asia 1956–1975* (Presidio Press, 1985). Another primarily pictorial source is *46th Special Forces Company Thailand: The Professionals May '66– Oct. 67* (Kursisopha Ladrao Press, Bangkok, Thailand, 1967). Limited copies of this yearbook were printed for members of the first cohort of the 46th Special Forces Company. *Time* magazine published a short article on the 46th Special Forces Company titled B-52s & Green Berets in March 31, 1967 edition. This article can be accessed on-line at the *Time Magazine* archive website.

The British Jungle Warfare School at Johore Bahru, Maylasia was established in 1950, during the Malaya Emergency. During the Vietnam War, British, Australian, and New Zealand cadre members trained limited numbers of Thai, South Vietnamese, and Americans in jungle operations at the school. U.S. Army combat tracker teams were also trained at the school. In early 1972, the school was turned over to the Malaysian armed forces.

The drug and racial problems in the U.S. Army in Europe during the early 1970s are documented in Daniel J. Nelson's book, *A History of U.S. Military Forces in Germany* (Westview Press, 1987). In an article by Col. Rogert D. Deinl, Jr. in the *Armed Forces Journal*, 7 June 1971, it was reported that some 46 percent of the roughly 200,000 soldiers in West Germany had used illegal drugs at least once. The article also mentions Augsburg, Krailsheim, and Hohenfels as areas "rife with racial trouble.

George Allen Crocker's military career is covered in some detail in Rick Atkinson's book, *The Long Gray Line* (Houghton Publishing, 1989).

The phase-out of the 5th Special Forces Group in Vietnam and the CIDG Program is described in Shelby Stanton's book, *Green Berets at War, U.S. Army Special Forces in Southeast Asia 1956–1975* (Presidio Press, 1985). A detailed description of the phase out to include closure dates of SF camps by Corps area can be found in the Center for *Military History (CMH) Publication 90-23, U.S. Army Special Forces, 1961–1971*, by Francis John Kelly.

CHAPTER 2: ASSIGNMENT DELTA RANGERS

A brief history of the ARVN Rangers, *Biet Dong Quan*, and their advisors can be found on the 75th Ranger Regiment Association website, http://www.new75rra.com. *Rangers at War* (Ballantine Publishing, 1993), by Shelby Stanton devotes one chapter to the ARVN Rangers and their advisors with various ARVN Ranger battalions including the 44th Battalion.

Two separate newspaper articles describe the exploits of the 44th ARVN Ranger's "Tiger Lady." The first article by UPI correspondent Joseph L. Galloway was printed in the *Billings Gazette* on October 15, 1965. A second article published in the *Albuquerque Journal* on May 6, 1966, reports the conviction of the Tiger Lady's husband for her murder.

CHAPTER 3: MOUNTAINS WERE BROUGHT FORTH
CHAPTER 4: GO TELL IT ON THE MOUNTAIN
CHAPTER 5: DON'T LET THE SUN CATCH YOU CRYING

These three chapters describe the 44th ARVN Ranger Battalions role in the battle for Nui Bai Voi near Kien Luong in the Mekong Delta. The

44th Ranger Battalion participated in this battle from 27 September, 1970 to 21 October 1971. The battalion was under the operational control of 9th ARVN Division during this period. The principal source for these three chapters was the author's unpublished manuscript, *The Battle for Nui Bai Voi*, completed in September 1971. Headquarters, United States Military Assistance Command, Vietnam, General Orders Number 7921, dated 11 December 1970, Award of the Bronze Star Medal for Valor to Captain Robert L Tonsetic citation describes the action on the first day of the battle. A broader description of the battle can be found in *Rangers at War* (Ballantine Publishing, 1993), by Shelby Stanton. The Kien Luong Biodiversity Study published in August 2002, provides an excellent description of the geological formations, flora, and fauna in the area.

CHAPTER 7: INTO THE FOREST PRIMEVAL

Unlike the Nui Bai Voi operation, the 21st ARVN Division and Ranger Operation in the U Minh forest area received considerably more attention in the news media. This was due in part to the interest taken by President Thieu in the operation. Thieu was running for reelection in 1971, and wanted to showcase the U Minh campaign as an example of the success of the Vietnamization and Pacification programs. Also, a personality "cult" was growing around the 21st ARVN Division Commander, General Nghi, one of the ARVNs best commanders. The *New York Times* ran articles on the U Minh operation on 5, 7, and 9 December 1970, and *Pacific Stars and Stripes* reported on the operation on 4, 6, 11, 13, and 31 December 1970. Other smaller newspapers such as the *Daily Capital News* in Jefferson City Missouri, and the *Albuquerque Journal* also ran stories on the operation.

An excellent article on the U.S. 9th Infantry Division's operation in the U Minh in July 1968, appeared in the Division's 1968 *Octofoil* magazine. First Lieutenant Howe McCarty reported on the operation.

For readers interested in the story of James "Nick" Rowe's experience as a POW in the U Minh, his book *Five Years to Freedom* (Little, Brown and Company, 1971) is a must read. The book is based Rowe's own Vietnam diaries and includes vivid details of his captivity, and the U Minh forest where he spent five years as a POW.

There have been various studies conducted documenting the ecological damage done to the forest during the Vietnam War particularly the damage done by the use of defoliants. In recent years, the U Minh forest has become a popular destination for tourists interested in the ecology and biodiversity values of the forest.

Martin Tovar, who was senior advisor to the 42d Ranger Battalion, was also an excellent source of information on the U Minh operation along with my own recollections and notes.

CHAPTER 8: THE LONG AND WINDING ROAD

The phase out of the 5th Special Forces Group in Vietnam and the CIDG Program is described in Shelby Stanton's book, *Green Berets at War, U.S. Army Special Forces in Southeast Asia 1956–1975* (Presidio Press, 1985). A detailed description of the phase out to include closure dates of SF camps by Corps area can be found in the Center for *Military History (CMH) Publication 90-23, U.S. Army Special Forces, 1961–1971*, by Francis John Kelly.

Army Regulation 600-8-22 (Military Awards), paragraph 2-6 specifies criteria for the award of the Combat Infantryman's Badge for personnel assigned as advisors to Vietnamese units. Basically, the regulation establishes two criteria. First the individual must be assigned as an advisor to a regimental or smaller size Vietnamese unit. Second, the individual must be personally present and under fire while serving in an assigned primary duty as a member of a tactical advisory team while the unit participated in ground combat.

Colonel David H. Hackworth, along with John Paul Vann, were two of the most controversial figures to emerge from the Vietnam War, and both had unique insights into the way it was conducted that attracted wide national attention. Both spent considerable time in the Mekong Delta. Readers interested in the careers and Vietnam experiences of these two men should read Hackworth's book, *About Face* (Simon and Shuster, 1989), and Neil Sheehan's book, *A Bright Shining Lie: John Paul Vann and America in Vietnam* (Vintage Books, 1988).

The South Vietnamese Operation *Cuu Long 44/02* in Cambodia is discussed in the Department of the Army's 1989 publication, *Mounted Combat in Vietnam* by General Donn A. Starry. The operation is also summarized in the Headquarters MACV Command History 1971, Volume 1.

The *Albuquerque Tribune* published an article, January 15, 1971, "Cambodia Struggles to Live," that describes the January 1971 Cambodian operation. *Time* magazine also reported on the operation in an article, Cambodia: Triumph and Terror in its February 1, 1971 edition of the magazine. The presence of an Army major on the ground near Route 4 in Cambodia is mentioned in the story, along with a photograph of same. The article ignited a firestorm among Congressional "Doves" who viewed this incident as a violation of the Cooper-Church Amendment.

CHAPTER 9: ANCHORS AWAY

John Grider Miller's book, *The Co-Vans: US Marine Advisors in Vietnam* (Naval Institute Press, 2000) provides relevant information on some of the problems experienced by the Navy at the Solid Anchor Base in 1971, prior to the arrival of the 44th Ranger Battalion. As advisors, we were given no background or history of the operations and security problems at and around the base prior to our arrival.

A summary of U.S. Navy operations in the area around the Solid Anchor Base can be found in the Headquarters MACV Command History 1971, Volume 1. More detailed information on these operations and the problems experienced at the base can be found in the U.S. Naval Forces, Vietnam Monthly Historical Summaries for January and February 1971. A *Pacific Stars and Stripes* article published on April 12, 1971, reports on the transition of the base from U.S. Navy control to South Vietnamese control.

CHAPTER 10: JEREMIAH WAS A BULLFROG

The plans for restructuring of Combat Assistance Teams is are explained in Section VIII, of the Headquarters MACV Command History 1971, Volume 1, along with a reappraisal of the advisory effort, advisory accomplishments, utilization of advisors, and future advisory reductions. The withdrawal of the Ranger battalion advisors was in the opinion of the author premature. In May 1971, two months after *Lam Son 719*, a review was conducted to determine the impact of removing battalion tactical advisors. Based on the review, it was decided that the phase down in battalion advisors would continue as planned except for the Airborne Division and selected units in Military Region 1. General Bruce Palmer Jr. in his book, *The 25-Year War: America's Military Role in Vietnam* (Simon and Shuster, Inc. 1984), commented that "Serious weaknesses in ARVN's ability to command and control their forces were apparent, and the degradation of effectiveness caused by the absence of American advisers was also quite noticeable."

CHAPTER 11: INTO THE MIDST OF BATTLE

Operation *Lam Son 719* is one of the best-documented ARVN operations of the Vietnam War. The following principal sources were used: 17th Military History Detachment Interviews with COL James B. Vaught, Senior Advisor, ARVN Abn Div, COL A. W. Pence Jr., Senior Airborne Advisory Detachment Commander, Vietnam & MAJ Kenneth C. Fogelquist, G3 ADV., ARVN Abn Div. Interview with *Lam Son 719*, by Maj. Gen. Nguyen Duy Hinh published by the U.S. Army Center of Military History, 1981, Vietnam Interview Tape (VNIT)–918 ARVN COMVAT, Center for Military History, Washington, D.C., Operation Lam Son 719 in 1971 by Colonel Hoang Thich Thong published by the U.S. Army Center of Military History, the Theodore Mataxis Jr. interview (The Vietnam Center and Archive, Texas Tech University, 31 March 2000). The following documents were used to prepare this chapter: U.S. Military Assistance Command Vietnam–Combat After Action Report LAM SON 719, Headquarters XXIV Corps, Combat After Action Report, Operation Lam Son 719, Headquarters 101st Airborne Division (Airmobile), Airmobile Operations in Support of Operation Lam Son 719, and Advisory Team 162, After Action Report: Lam Son 719.

The following general sources were used in preparing this chapter: *The Blood Road: The Ho Chi Minh Trail and the Vietnam War* by John Prados (John Wiley & Sons, Inc. 1999, *The 25-Year War: America's Military Role in Vietnam* (Simon and Shuster, Inc. 1984) by General Bruce Palmer, *Angels in Red Hats* by Command Sergeant Major Michael Martin (Harmony House Publishers, 1995), and *South Vietnam on Trial,* by David Fulghum and Terrence Maitland (Boston Publishing Co., 1984).

In addition the following secondary sources were used: *Time* Magazine, "Pinching the Arteries," January 25, 1971, "Indochina: The Soft-Sell Invasion," February 22, 1971, "But Who Hath Measured the Ground?" March 15, 1971, "Was It Worth It?" March 29, 1971, and "The Invasion Ends," April 5, 1971, and *Pacific Stars and Stripes* articles, "Bolstered Viets Control Hill 31," March 4, 1971, "Reds Charge Base in Laos," March 23, 1971, and "NVA Trying to Disrupt Viet Pullback," March 23, 1971.

CHAPTER 12: "FIGHTING SOLDIERS FROM THE SKY"

An excellent account of the Royal Australian Regiment's 1966 battle near Nui Dat is the book, *The Battle of Long Tan–As Told by the*

Commanders to Bob Grandin (Allen & Unwin, 2004).

A principal source for documenting the development of unit training and combined arms training in the ARVN, is the 1991 Department of the Army publication, *Development and Training of the South Vietnamese Army 1950–1972*, by Brigadier General James L. Collins, Jr. Robert K. Brigham's book, *ARVN: Life And Death in the South Vietnamese Army* (University Press of Kansas, 2006) also reports on deficiencies in ARVN training.

BIBLIOGRAPHY

BOOKS

Atkinson, Rick. *The Long Gray Line*. Boston: Houghton Mifflin, 1989.

Brigham, Robert K. *ARVN: Life And Death in the South Vietnamese Army*. Lawrence, KS: University Press of Kansas, 2006.

Claussewitz, Carl Von. *On War*. Pinceton NJ: Princeton University Press, 1976.

Collins, James L. *The Development and Training of the South Vietnamese Army, 1950-1972*. Washington, DC: Department of the Army, 1991.

Davidson, Phillip B. *Vietnam at War: The History: 1946-1975*. Novato, CA: Presidio Press, 1990.

Fall, Bernard B. *Hell in a Very Small Place: The Siege of Dien Bien Phu*. Philadelphia & New York: J.B. Lippincott Company, 1966.

Fulghum, David & Maitland, Terrence. *South Vietnam on Trial: Mid-1970 to 1972*. Boston: Boston Publishing Company, 1984.

Grandin, Bob. *The Battle of Long Tan*. Crows Nest, NSW, Australia: Allen & Unwin, 2004.

Hackworth, David H. & Sherman, Julie. *About Face*. New York: Simon and Schuster, 1989.

Karnow, Stanley. *Vietnam A History*. New York: Viking, 1983.

Kelley, Francis J. *The Green Berets in Vietnam, 1961-71*. Washington DC: Brassey's, 1991.

Krepinevich, Andrew F. Jr. *The Army and Vietnam*. Baltimore: John Hopkins Press, 1986

Martin, Michael. *Angels in Red Hats*. Louisville: Harmony House, 1995.

Miller, John Grider. *The Co-Vans: U.S. Marine Advisors in Vietnam*. Annapolis: Naval Institute Press, 2000.

Nelson, Daniel J. *A History of U.S. Military Force in Germany*. Boulder CO: Westview, 1986.

Nolan, Keith W. *Into Laos: The Story of Dewey Canyon II/Lam Son 719 Vietnam 1971*. Novato, CA: Presidio Press, 1986.

Palmer, Bruce Jr. *The 25-Year War: America's Military Role in Vietnam*. New York: Simon & Schuster, 1984.

Prados, John. *The Blood Road: The Ho Chi Minh Trail and the Vietnam War*. New York: John Wiley & Sons, Inc., 1999.

Rowe, James N. *Five Years to Freedom*. Boston: Little, Brown and Company, 1971.

Sheehan, Neil. *A Bright Shining Lie: John Paul Vann and America in Vietnam*. New York: Vintage Books, 1989.

Stanton, Shelby L. *Green Berets at War: U.S. Army Special Forces in Southeast Asia 1956–1975*. Novato, CA: Presidio Press, 1985.

Stanton, Shelby L. *The Rise and Fall of an American Army: U.S. Ground Forces in   Vietnam, 1965–1975*. Presidio Press, 1985.

Stanton, Shelby L. *Rangers at War: LRRPS in Vietnam*. New York: Ballantine Books, 1995.

Starry, Donn A. *Mounted Combat in Vietnam*. Washington: Department of the Army, 1989.

Stewart, Richard W. *American Military History-Volume II*. Washington: Center of Military History United States Army, 2005.

Summers, Harry G. Jr. *The Vietnam War Almanac*. Novato, CA: Presidio Press, 1985.

Tonsetic, Robert. *Warriors: An Infantryman's Memoir of Vietnam*. New York: The Random House Publishing Group, 2004.

Tonsetic, Robert L. *Days of Valor: An Insider's Account of the Bloodiest Months of the Vietnam War*. Philadelphia: Casemate, 2007.

Westmoreland, William C. *A Soldier Reports*. New York: Dell Publishing Group Inc. 1976.

Wiest, Andrew, Webb, Jim. *Vietnam's Forgotten Army: Heroism and Betrayal in the ARVN*, New York: New York University Press, 2008.

Zaffiri, Samuel. *Westmoreland: A Biography of General William C. Westmoreland*. New York: William Morrow & Company Inc. 1994.

PERIODICALS

"B-52s and Green Berets." *Time Magazine*, March 31, 1967.

"Between Two Truces." *International Herald Tribune*, January 6, 1967.

"Bolstered Viets Control Hill 31." *Pacific Stars & Stripes*, March 4, 1971.

"Bombing in Cambodia Reported." *The New York Times*, December 7, 1970.

"But Who Hath Measured the Ground?" *Time Magazine*, March 15, 1971.

"Cambodia Struggles to Live." *Albuquerque Tribune*, January 15, 1971.

"Cambodia: Triumph and Terror." *Time Magazine*, February 1, 1971.

Durham, John. "NVA Trying to Disrupt Viet Pullback." *Pacific Stars & Stripes*, March 23, 1971.

"Eighty-three Eneny Killed in Clashes with Viet GIs, Militia." *Pacific Stars & Stripes*, December 6, 1970.

"Enemy Toll Put at 59 in Forest." *New York Times*, December 5, 1970.

"Enemy Killed in Clash with GIs." *Albuquerque Journal*, December 21, 1970.

Galloway, Joseph L. "Tiger Lady Marches, Nurses, and Fights." *The Billings Gazette*, October 15, 1965.

Heinl, Robert D. "The Collapse of the Armed Forces." *Armed Forces Journal*, 7 June 1971.

"Indochina: Tough Days on the Trail." *Time Magazine*, March 8, 1971.

"Indochina: The Soft-Sell Invasion." *Time Magazine*, March 29, 1971.

"Killing of 144 Viet Cong Reported in First 8 Days of Drive in Forest." *The New York Times*, December 9, 1970.

"Life with the Communists." *Time Magazine*, May 5, 1975.

Lipsky, Seth. "U Minh Gains Bring ARVN Smiles." *Pacific Stars & Stripes*, October 6, 1970.

McCarty, Howe. "U Minh Forest–No Longer a VC Sanctuary." *Octofoil*, 1968.

"Pinching the Arteries," *Time Magazine*, January 25, 1971.

Ramsey, Robert D. "Advising Indigenous Forces: American Advisors in Korea, Vietnam and El Salvador." *Occasional Paper 18, Combat Studies Institute.*

"Reds Charge Base in Laos; Viets Kill 314." *Pacific Stars & Stripes*, March 23, 1971.

"Reds Shell Cities, 3 Air Bases." *Pacific Stars & Stripes*, December 4, 1970.

"Saigon: A Week Under Communism." *Time Magazine*, May 10, 1975.

"Shrinking Sanctuary." *International Herald Tribune*, April 26, 1968.

"Stalking Reds in U Minh." *Pacific Stars & Stripes*, December 13, 1970.
"The Invasion Ends." *Time Magazine*, April 5, 1971.
"The End of a Thirty Years War." *Time Magazine*, May 12, 1975.
"The War: New Alarm, New Debate." *Time Magazine*, February 8, 1971.
"U Minh Woods." *Pacific Stars & Stripes*, December 11, 1970.
"Viets Given Riverine Operations." *Pacific Stars & Stripes*, April 12, 1971.
"Was It Worth It?" *Time Magazine*, March 29, 1971.

DOCUMENTS

Department of the Army Pamphlet, No. 550-40, U.S. Army Area Handbook for Vietnam, September 1962.
Department of the Amy Field Manual, FM 31-73, Advisor Handbook for Counterinsurgency, April 1965
Department of the Army Regulation 600-8-22, Military Awards.
Headquarters U.S. Military Assistance Command Vietnam General Orders 7921, 11 December 1970.
Headquarters U.S. Military Assistance Command Vietnam – 1971 Command History, Volume 1.
Headquarters, United States Army Vietnam, 17th Military History Detachment – Interview with MAJ Kenneth C. Fogelquist, G3 ADV., ARVN Abn Div, 19 May 1971.
Headquarters, United States Army Vietnam, 17th Military History Detachment – Interview with COL A. W. Pence Jr., Senior Airborne Advisory Detachment Commander, Vietnam, 17 May 1971.
Headquarters, United States Army Vietnam, 17th Military History Detachment – Interview with COL James B. Vaught, Senior Advisor, ARVN Abn Div, 20 May   1971.
Headquarters XXIV Corps, Combat After Action Report, Operation Lam Son 719 (MACJ-3-32).
Headquarters 101st Airborne Division (Airmobile), Airmobile Operations in Support of Operation Lam Son 719, 8 February – 6 April 1971.
Headquarters, U.S. Army Advisory Group, 1st Ranger Group – Combat After Action Report LAM SON 719.
Ranger Handbook, SH 21-78, United States Army, Ranger Training Brigade, US Army Infantry School, Fort Benning, Georgia, July 2008

Senior Officer Debriefing Report of Major General John H. Cushman, RCS CSFOR-74

Unpublished manuscript, The Battle for Nui Bai Voi, Tonsetic, Robert L. September, 1971.

U.S. Military Assistance Command Vietnam – Combat After Action Report LAM SON 719, 1971.

U.S. Military Assistance Command, Advisory Team 162 – After Action Report: Lam Son 719, 1971.

U.S. Naval Forces, Vietnam Monthly Historical Summary for January 1971.

U.S. Naval Forces, Vietnam Monthly Historical Summary for February 1971.